Southern Literary Studies
Louis D. Rubin, Jr., Editor

Ellen Glasgow's Reasonable Doubts

Ellen Glasgow in 1909

# Ellen Glasgow's Reasonable Doubts

A Collection of Her Writings

Edited by Julius Rowan Raper

Louisiana State University Press
Baton Rouge and London

10 9 8 7 6 5 4 3 2 1

Designer: Sylvia Loftin
Typeface: Garamond Book
Typesetter: Focus Graphics
Printer: Thomson-Shore, Inc.
Binder: John H. Dekker & Sons, Inc.

Library of Congress Cataloging-in-Publication Data
Glasgow, Ellen Anderson Gholson, 1873–1945.
    Ellen Glasgow's reasonable doubts : a collection of her writings /
edited by Julius Rowan Raper.
        p. cm. — (Southern literary studies)
    Includes index.
    ISBN 0-8071-1412-X (alk. paper)
    I. Raper, Julius Rowan, 1938– . II. Title. III. Title:
Reasonable doubts. IV. Series.
PS3513.L34A6 1988
813' .52—dc 19   87-32491
                                                                            CIP

The editor gratefully acknowledges the following publishers and institutions for per-
mission to reprint certain pieces: Alderman Library, University of Virginia, for "'My
Fellow Virginians,'" "Opening Speech of the Southern Writers Conference," "Liter-
ary Realism or Nominalism," and "An Inadequate Comment on 'Primary Literature
and Coterie-Literature,'" in Ellen Glasgow Papers (#5060), Manuscripts Department,
University of Virginia Library; Harcourt Brace Jovanovich, Inc., for "Some Literary
Woman Myths," which appears, somewhat reworded, in *They Stooped to Folly* and
A Certain Measure, "The Novel in the South," which appears, in an altered form, in
The Miller of Old Church and *A Certain Measure*, and "One Way to Write Novels,"
which appears, somewhat altered, in *The Sheltered Life* and *A Certain Measure* (ex-
cerpts from the novels of Ellen Glasgow are reprinted by permission of Harcourt
Brace Jovanovich, Inc., copyright © 1929, 1932, 1935, 1941 by Ellen Glasgow,
copyright © 1954, 1957, 1960, 1969 by First and Merchants Bank of Richmond,
copyright © 1926 by Doubleday Page & Co.); Harper & Row, Publishers, Inc., for
"'Evasive Idealism' in Literature," from *Literature in the Making: By Some of Its
Makers*, presented by Joyce Kilmer, copyright © 1917 by Harper & Row, Publishers,
Inc., renewed 1945 by Kenton Kilmer and Christopher Kilmer; the *Nation*, for
"What I Believe," in the April 12, 1933, number; and the Richmond Society for the
Prevention of Cruelty to Animals, beneficiary of the Estate of Ellen Glasgow, for ma-
terials belonging to the estate.

Frontispiece courtesy of University of Virginia Library (from Papers of Ellen Glasgow
[#5060], Manuscripts Department)

The assistance of the University Research Council of the University of North Carolina, Chapel Hill, is gratefully acknowledged by Louisiana State University Press.

To Fern and Keith
Who Face the Hard Facts

Contents

Preface

Ellen Glasgow's Reasonable Doubts brings together in a convenient form the shorter works of Ellen Glasgow—essays, interviews, reviews, even a story and a poem—that heretofore either remained scattered through the pages of newspapers and magazines, many of them now difficult to obtain, or lay in manuscript in the Glasgow Collection of the University of Virginia. With the present collection, the reader should be better equipped to evaluate the mind of this remarkable woman who, according to Van Wyck Brooks's *An Autobiography* (1965), "was the turning-point in the literary history of the South," yet who, in the section titled "The Ideas" of *Ellen Glasgow: Centennial Essays*, stands represented by only two pieces, one on her "Civilized Men" and another on her role as feminist.

The reader of the present collection should come away convinced of what he certainly already suspects if he has read any of her novels: that the author had ideas, often very pronounced ones, on far more than those two subjects. Unlike the novels, however, which generally strive for dramatic irony rather than to stake out a position, the essays show what the author, not her characters, thought on a wide range of topics. Even the story and the poem republished here are less dramatic than polemical and thus deserve inclusion in this profile of Glasgow's mind, especially since they, like the interviews, belong to a phase of the author's life about which so little is known.

Few modern authors have fared as ill as Glasgow from efforts to edit out of the record the spontaneous and rebellious acts of youth. For Glasgow was not always the grand lady of southern literature she appeared to be after the late 1920s, when the Southern Renaissance began to take note of her influence. In her own twenties, she was a forthright rebel on the sexual, intellectual, and literary fronts. In her thirties she was a leader of the feminist cause. But the record she left is full of gaps. She herself tried to blot out the pain of her early, apparently illicit romance by destroying letters and other reminders of her exuberance. And she was joined in this all-too-successful effort by relatives seemingly more concerned about preserving reputations than expunging pain.

What remains are the early documents—a poem, a story, interviews, essays—that, because they became part of the public record, escaped destruction. These pieces are uneven, in some cases stylistically crude. But they are nonetheless valuable for readers interested in the times and in the author, because so little else remains. Where, for example, Glasgow's contemporary Theodore Dreiser preserved his records down to matchbook covers and purchase receipts, in the *Letters of Ellen Glasgow* the sections covering four decades (1891–1930) take up fewer than eighty pages. Of the thirty-three items collected and annotated in *Ellen Glasgow's Reasonable Doubts*, however, over half come from the four decades from which little of the record, other than the seventeen novels, remains. Here are raw statements of Glasgow's views on feminist issues, the South, politics, science, her literary friends and competitors. Neither admirers nor detractors will be totally pleased by the things she says. They will, however, very likely be surprised.

Each reader of *Ellen Glasgow's Reasonable Doubts* will no doubt come away with a different estimate of the mind that produced these short works, but there are several themes worth noting from the start. The earliest pieces, especially Glasgow's first published fiction, the long-neglected "A Woman of To-Morrow," raise the strong possibility that a good deal of the critical intelligence that informs her earliest fiction arose from tensions generated by her youthful commitment to a concept of the free woman, the woman who is neither economically nor romantically dependent upon men; for the heroine of this story, which appeared two years before Glasgow's first novel, declares her independence in a manner that anticipates Dorinda Oakley, thirty years later, in *Barren Ground*. At the opposite end of Glasgow's career, the reader can, through this collection, trace the development of the author's jaundiced view of what she considered the despairing and sadistic qualities of American fiction in the 1920s and 1930s; the reader may thereby determine for himself to what degree her embittered estimate of several of the more esteemed novelists of the twentieth century may have been part of her counterattack, after 1932, against such politically committed arbiters of taste as Clifton Fadiman who, in the *New Re-*

public, glibly dismissed one of her most subtle works, *The Sheltered Life*, with the announcement, in effect, that no one any longer
cared to read about southern aristocrats. Readers who sense that
many of her remarks on brutality in literature were directed at
Faulkner will be struck by parallels between the endings of her two
credos and the Nobel Prize acceptance speech he gave over a decade later.

The reader may perceive the role Glasgow played in the middle
phase of her career, not only by example but also as publicist, in the
development of what has since been called the Southern Renaissance: although her novels show that she was as aware as any southern writer of the value the "concrete universal" holds in literature,
her essays reveal that she was more alert than many to the dangers
of picturesque local detail; for she thought that southern writers
should aspire, as many have, to become world writers. Of all southern writers, James Branch Cabell was most her confidant; these essays contain a partial record of the way Glasgow came to terms with,
and profited from the friendship of, her once very notorious Richmond neighbor. Her comments on the novel outside the South are
multifaceted and, at various points in her career, attack everything
from evasive idealism to nominalism and brutality; critics may find
her opinion of modernism's "complete plunge into consciousness"
useful in evaluating the work she herself did during her final three
decades. Even her reviews, which were obviously written to publi-
cize rather than criticize the work of people she either admired (Virginia Woolf and George Santayana) or valued as friends (Cabell, Stark
Young, and others), are generally, in truth, occasions for essays on
larger subjects, including American Puritanism, the stereotyped roles
of black characters in American fiction, and the glorified empty violence of some modern literature. Finally, the two credos that conclude this collection provide the most concise and thoughtful statements available of her positions on society, economics, religion, and
science, views which taken together shine with the light of Thomas
Jefferson's South more than with the fire of fundamentalism, the Ku
Klux Klan, and the one party that filled the South in which they were
written. For at the forefront of her mind stood the simple ideal: "that
skepticism remains the only permanent basis of tolerance"—"that a
reasonable doubt is the safety-valve of civilization."

Most of the pieces in this collection have been reprinted from newspapers and journals, which appear to have been carefully proofread, or have been taken from reasonably clean typed manuscripts. The chief exception is Glasgow's "Opening Speech of the Southern Writers Conference," which exists in two very different drafts or parts marked "Very Rough"; the aim with this piece has been to recover all that remains legible of both drafts, including the author's eccentric but expressive punctuation (obvious mistakes have been silently corrected) and several comments that, though she marked through them, nevertheless reveal what she felt about that important occasion, in October, 1931, when, at her suggestion, many of those who had created the Southern Renaissance gathered in Charlottesville to acknowledge publicly that, in one field at least, the South had returned to a position of national leadership, and to congratulate themselves for their various contributions to that re-emergence. If Van Wyck Brooks is correct about Glasgow's role, then much of that congratulation was, no doubt, due this woman whose skepticism had created an umbrella of tolerance for the plural forms modern southern writing had taken and has continued to assume.

Acknowledgments

In making this collection, the original intent was to keep the editorial apparatus at a minimum with the thought that individual scholars and critics, who at the time seemed to compose the majority of readers interested in Glasgow, would prefer to bring their own expertise and interpretations to the texts. During the past several years, however, with a number of Glasgow's very best novels again available in editions suitable for classroom use, a new generation of younger readers has discovered this very accessible and brilliant novelist. Because their use of the works assembled here is likely to differ significantly from that of professional scholars, it now appears appropriate to provide the editorial assistance essential to illuminate passages in the texts rendered somewhat opaque by the decades that separate contemporary readers from the milieu in which Glasgow wrote.

An editor who sets out to annotate a collection ranging over subjects as diverse as this one must begin by invoking the muses to illuminate what is dark in himself and the texts. When the muses refuse to appear, he discovers that omniscience, however convenient it might be, is neither possible nor, finally, essential. In the present case, the vacuum left by the muses has been filled by the familiar array of resource materials, the various encyclopedias, dictionaries, companion volumes, and more specialized books available to the contemporary editor. The majority of the annotations to the texts that follow echo one or more of the standard reference works in the fields Glasgow's essays draw upon.

But consulting such varied sources would have remained a forbidding task had it not been for the assistance of several young scholars at the University of North Carolina. While meeting their responsibilities as students, Anthony Wallace Lee and Allen Rubinoff have also found time to research and compose many of the annotations that clarify Glasgow's texts. At an earlier stage, Nathan Antila, Elizabeth Dunn, and Beth Lynne Lueck helped assemble and transcribe the materials of the collection. More recently, Jimmy Cantrell and Lance Cole have given the collection their careful attention. Were this book the product of a scientific laboratory, the names of all seven would properly appear as coeditors. I wish both to acknowledge their contributions and to thank them for their assistance.

In addition, I wish to thank the Research Council of the University of North Carolina for financial assistance; the University of North Carolina English Department for help in preparing the manuscript; and Joyce Bradshaw, Tonya Carter, and Tobi Schwartzman of the University of North Carolina English Department for typing the manuscript under sometimes difficult circumstances.

To locate several of the quotations Glasgow uses in her essays, I have had to consult colleagues scattered across the American academic landscape. I wish to thank each of the following for responding generously with their time and interest to my pleas for assistance with writers on whom they are recognized authorities: Professors Irving Singer, Herman J. Saatkamp, Jr., Richard Lyon, and John McCormick for help with Santayana; Professors Thomas P. Saine and Christoph Schweitzer for assistance with Goethe; and Professor Dorothy Kish for suggestions about Glasgow.

Biographical Note

Ellen Glasgow (1873–1945)

Although modern southern literature grew out of ground cleared and for the most part tended by Ellen Glasgow, traditional attitudes about women have left important episodes of her life distorted by rumor and speculation. No official record exists to show whether she was born April 21, 1874, or April 22, 1873. In either case, she was the eighth of ten children (eight lived to maturity) of Francis Thomas Glasgow, who managed Tredegar Iron Works in Richmond and whose roots ran back to the Scotch Presbyterians of the Shenandoah Valley. Her mother was the orphaned daughter of an orphaned mother, although her ties were to many of the oldest families of Tidewater Virginia. Ellen Glasgow received almost no formal education, but relatives and tutors taught her to read and write.

In her late teens she started a novel and shortly thereafter fell under the guidance of Walter McCormack of Charleston, her sister Cary's husband-to-be, who directed her attention to Charles Darwin and the other thinkers who shaped her views of man and society. Her interest in critical realism hardened to pessimism when within the period of a few years she experienced difficulty hearing, rebelled against her father's inflexible religion, watched her mother die (1893), failed to conclude either of two novels satisfactorily, and, finally in 1894, learned that McCormack, for whom she had developed a deep respect, had committed suicide under sordid circumstances.

To work out her bitterness she finished the second of the novels she had begun, a Darwinian study of New York's Bohemia called *The Descendant* (1897), which she followed with a second Bohemian study before choosing her native state as the scene of *The Voice of the People* (1900), the first of the novels eventually to compose her social history of Virginia. By 1905 this series included a Civil War novel and a powerful exploration of tensions that beset agrarian classes after the war.

During this fruitful period (1899–1905), she found herself involved in the most devastating of her three important affairs, a sometimes ecstatic romance with a married man she later called "Gerald B." "Gerald B." has been variously identified as a figment of her imagination, as another woman, as a middle-aged New York aurist, H. Holbrook Curtis (1856–1920), as an important New York neurologist, Pearce Bailey (1865–1922), and as the fiction editor of Bobbs-Merrill, Hewitt Hanson Howland (1863–1944). Although some of these possibilities need not exclude one another, recent evidence points toward Howland, whose wife of fifteen years sued for divorce in 1903 on grounds that he had failed to provide. Glasgow was later engaged twice: between 1906 and 1909 to Frank Ilsley Paradise, a roving Episcopal minister and author, and from 1917, off and on, to Henry Watkins Anderson, a prominent Richmond lawyer, adventurer, and experimental politician, who remained her frequent visitor long after their engagement wore itself out.

Each of the latter two romances spanned a fallow phase in the career of Glasgow, who reached her full power with *Virginia* (1913), the best of her books before 1925. After her closest brother committed suicide in 1909 and Cary her sister died in 1911, Glasgow, now a feminist, took an apartment in New York, where she lived for the most part until 1915, the year before her father, from whom she still felt estranged, died; thereafter she lived in the family home in Richmond, with a nurse-secretary. Her poorest work fell around 1918, when Howland remarried, Walter Hines Page, her early publisher, died, and rumors of Anderson's wartime flirtation with Queen Marie of Romania caused the author to attempt suicide. After these troubles forced her to confront deeper levels of herself, she exceeded her former powers in the lacerating *Barren Ground* (1925) and the two scintillant comedies of manners that preceded her finest book, *The Sheltered Life* (1932). During this period many writers formed friendships with her, but her special confidant was James Branch Cabell. As woman of letters she reached her height in 1931, when she presided in spirit and flesh at the first modern Southern Writers Conference, held at the University of Virginia.

With *Vein of Iron* (1935) the intensity of her characterization began to fail, and *In This Our Life* (1941), written despite two heart attacks, revealed a weakening of stylistic control, although it brought her the Pulitzer Prize (1942). Her exceptional contribution to regional and national letters had previously earned special recognition from four universities, the National Institute of Arts and Letters (1932), the American Academy of Arts and Letters (1938 and 1940), and the *Saturday Review of Literature* (1941). Her collected prefaces (1943) presented Ellen Glasgow as master of the novel, the mask she wore for her public. When she died, November 21, 1945, she left in manuscript a sequel to *In This Our Life*, plus her autobiography in which she exposed the victim's mask she wore for her intimates and, it seems, for herself.

WORKS: *The Descendant* (1897); *Phases of an Inferior Planet* (1898); *The Voice of the People* (1900); *The Battle-Ground* (1902); *The Freeman and Other Poems* (1902); *The Deliverance* (1904); *The Wheel of Life* (1906); *The Ancient Law* (1908); *The Romance of a Plain Man* (1909); *The Miller of Old Church* (1911); *Virginia* (1913); *Life and Gabriella* (1916); *The Builders* (1919); *One Man in His Time* (1922); *The Shadowy Third and Other Stories* (1923); *Barren Ground* (1925); *The Romantic Comedians* (1926); *They Stooped to Folly* (1929); *The Sheltered Life* (1932); *Vein of Iron* (1935); *In This Our Life* (1941); *A Certain Measure* (1943); *The Woman Within* (1954); *Letters of Ellen Glasgow*, ed. Blair Rouse (1958); *The Collected Stories of Ellen Glasgow*, ed. Richard K. Meeker (1963); *Beyond Defeat*, ed. Luther Y. Gore (1966).

I *Woman to Woman*

A Woman of To-Morrow

atricia paused.

Sharply defined she stood against the sodden sky, a strong, straight figure with superb head erect.

Beyond her the neutral sweep of a chain of hills broke the gray horizon with jagged lines as though penciled by a child's uncertain hand. And, here and there, where a hollow rose and fell, faint azure peaks were visible, standing but half revealed in the hazy distance like dim ghosts of dimmer realities.

Over gray landscape and gray sky evening was falling. The prospect was sombre and remote. Hill and plain showed bare and unlovely as a chill study in crayon; all the warm tones of day were blotted out.

Occasionally, with an all but futile effort, a single ray of sunshine burst the woof of cloud, stretching across the gloom like a luminous search-light thrown from a lantern above—stretching across ragged hill and ragged meadow until, reaching the creek below the road, it lost itself in the sluggish water.

On either side, wide unplowed fields swept far into the distance. Long ago the land had gone to waste. Good Virginia soil it had been once—some years before the war—yielding many a crop of sun-dried tobacco and fine red wheat; but its returns had gradually diminished, and, at last, it had been left to run wild in golden-rod and sassafras bushes, its productions consisting in some bushels of sour blackberries, which bloomed, ripened and rotted without the aid of man.

The fields were skirted by rail fences upon which the wind and rain of many years had beaten with merciless force. In some places the rails had rotted and fallen to the ground, leaving wide spaces through which a stray cow or so roamed at her will.

Upon the rotten rails trumpet-vines fed with rank luxuriance, fes-

---

The first of Glasgow's fictions published, this story appeared in *Short Stories*, XIX (1895), 415–27. She was twenty-two.

tooning themselves along the broken fence in great gorgeous clusters of scarlet bloom.

Patricia listened.

Across the tangled meadow, over broom-sedge and brush, came the faint low note of a catbird, and fainter still, like the breathless minor-tone of an unspoken thought, the music of a cow-bell rose softly from the glade below, sometimes losing itself against the hillside and again swelling clearly upon the rising air. Nearer still, in the turnpike just beyond, fell the heavy tread of oxen and the roll of a covered wagon as it lurched from side to side.

She heard the crack of the long whip and the slow drawl of the driver. Then the wagon passed and all was still.

Patricia leaned upon the low rail-fence, her strong white fingers interlaced, her troubled gaze just touching the landscape and then branching off into a futurity of space. Some long brown grasses growing beside the fence brushed her dress lightly and then, with a sensitive movement, swayed aside, their slender spirals silhouetted against the gradual distance. In the path in which she stood a yellow lovevine grew in a delicate web.

Patricia had trampled it under foot until it was bruised and broken.

Still sharply defined, she stood against the sodden sky, her superb head erect.

Upon an adjacent hill a group of hayricks stood out forlornly in the landscape. A pale ray of sunshine shifted uneasily over them, casting violet-toned shadows at their feet and touching their yellow crests with the promise of a benediction that could never be fulfilled. Among the dried stubble a tender growth of white clover showed in emerald patches—a healing balm after the blade of the reaper.

Without, all was rest and age. It was the peaceful repose of a land that had yielded much and been of much service.

It seemed to Patricia, standing there, that she herself, with her young strength and troubled eyes, belonged to another scene, another age. Upon the fence beside her a whippoorwill alighted, watching her with shrewd, suspicious eyes. Yes, she belonged elsewhere—she, a woman of the twentieth century. Even nature seemed distrustful of her here—here where she was encircled by phantoms of the past.

In a tumultuous wave thought swept over her, brushing aside all sense of the present.

The quiet, restful air grew restless. Across the tangled field the note of the catbird still sounded. The cow-bells grew clearer as the cattle were driven home along the winding path.

Patricia thought.

Up to to-day life had all seemed a straight road to her—so straight, her strong young eyes had seen no stumbling-stones in her way. A year ago she had cast her first vote, and from that day she had been free—capable and free.[1]

All the lingering remnants of nineteenth century prejudices she had defied. They had ceased to exist for her. She had begun to believe that they had ceased to exist for every one until, drifting by chance into this out-of-the-way corner of Virginia, they had arisen and stared her in the face. Here, for the first time, her fresh young force, her splendid development had met with no approbation; here, where the women shrank from contact with her rude health and unbroken spirit; where the men could not be taught that she needed no protecting hand, no arm to lean upon. Half scornfully to herself she acknowledged that it touched her—that it aroused in her something besides the old cynical amusement. She remembered so well the indignation that had tinged that amusement when Aunt Jane had said to her once:

"Yes, you'd best not work that buttonhole. You're not smart about such things yet, but you'll learn in time, I reckon." Learn in time! Patricia fancied Aunt Jane asking a man who had carried off the honors at Yale to work a buttonhole!

Well, she had been a success at college, if not with her needle. Six weeks ago, with many honors, more flowers and most congratulations, she had received her degree with becoming indifference.

1. By 1895, women could vote in sixteen states in school elections and in four states on tax bills. The first state to grant total equality in politics was Wyoming (1890). Three other states, all western, would match Wyoming before 1900. Growing sentiment to enfranchise women would eventually lead to the Nineteenth Amendment, ratified in 1920. Glasgow's story is futuristic in this sense, though very much a part of the local color movement in its treatment of setting.

Six weeks more, minus the honors, flowers and congratulations, she would face an inquiring public as—

"Patricia Yorke,

Attorney-at-Law."

It had a beautiful sound. She had written it at least a thousand times during her two years' study. It was so suggestive in its simplicity. It spoke of hard work and ambition and a public.

Yes, a public! There were many scores to be settled between Patricia and that public, and she had little doubt as to which would be the victor.

She was always victorious. She had met with no force yet capable of defying her strong young spirit.

Resistance only stimulated her. She was not afraid. The public might resist, but she, Patricia Yorke, she, the embodiment of freedom and the twentieth century, would carve her name, an indelible mark, upon its constitutional history.

Yes, she was to become a power in the nation. She would grasp with firm hands at control, and the country should feel the strength of her hold. She would look with firm eyes into the public institutions, tear the dirty bandages from their cankerous sores and heal them with the surgeon's knife.

Standing there with the sombre sky about her and the sombre mere around her, she threw back her young head with a swift, courageous gesture. A great responsibility seemed to have fallen upon her. It was as though she carried the fate of womankind upon her broad shoulders.

"It is a mission!" she had once said to Uncle John.

"It is hypertrophy of the conscience!" said Uncle John to her.

Uncle John was simple—distinctly a product of the nineteenth century. Patricia knew it. Patricia was not simple, but sometimes simple people tell the truth when wise ones don't. Wise ones know better. But Patricia was honest, even though she wasn't a fool. "It isn't unselfishness, after all," she had said to herself. "It is ambition," and, she added, "Why shouldn't it be ambition?"

Why, indeed!

Her gaze passed lightly over the meadow and rested upon a clump of trees beyond. Above the trees the gabled roof of a house was visible, and from one of the blackened chimneys a thin line of smoke arose, creeping in slow, serpent-like circles against the sodden sky, and, at last, melting like a gray cloud upon the mountain height.

The house was Fairfax Place. Patricia knew it well. Too well, she had almost said. She had taken tea there the night before. She had taken tea there very often within the last four weeks. She knew the dining-room by heart—with its worn leather chairs, its faded portraits and its silver tea-urn, whose battered sides still bore the Fairfax crest.

Behind the tea-urn Patricia seemed to see the gentle hostess, looking as faded and dainty as the thread lace above her smooth white hair. She knew the cracked china cups with their washed-out pattern of blue willow. It was genteel poverty; but Patricia hated poverty—gentility but made it the more irksome. Another sham! She hated shams! She was at the age when one wants truth—truth only.

Most of us have known that age. It is a brief one, praise God, for as we grow older and have tasted truth and have found it bitter, we prefer lies—lies are pleasanter.[2]

Idly Patricia watched the thin line of smoke curling lazily along the gray mountain height.

She knew whose hands had lighted that fire, had drawn the water and had placed the bread to bake within the oven. Gentle, ladylike hands they were—white and ringless, with delicate wrinkles where the dimples had been once.

They were young hands, too. Hannah Fairfax was not more than thirty; but her youth and dimples had waned long ago. There had been much work and few servants, so the gentle, ladylike hands had been put to the tiller. True, there had been a liberal application of mutton suet, and gloves had been drawn on—but the work was none the lighter because it was done in gloves; perhaps the heavier.

There was something about Hannah Fairfax that repelled Patricia. Something, she knew not what. Perhaps the coquettish timidity of her manner, perhaps the weakness and whiteness of her hands, that seemed half ashamed of their honest labor.

---

2. Here Glasgow sounds one of her major themes, evasive idealism, a state of self-deception in which the mind protects itself with willed illusions from unpleasant realities.

She was a pretty, sensitive creature with tired brown eyes and a fringe of carefully curled hair above her forehead.

Patricia wondered why she took the time to curl it—why she didn't brush it back and forget to put the frilling of lace in her collar. If she would only forget it once Patricia might forgive her. But the hopeless air of dressiness, the coquetry, baffled the younger woman. She could not ignore it, and it was always there.

Once, indeed, she had met her by chance coming from the well with a water-bucket in her hand. Then she had worn a faded cotton wrapper and her hands were in gloves, but the curls were there, and a dainty covering of rice powder protected her skin from the sun.

At sight of Patricia she had started and fallen back, a deep flush showing beneath the powder on her face, her tired eyes growing hurt and appealing.

"Our servant was sick to-day," she had said, deprecatingly, and Patricia had been stung by the polite lie. In one moment she had loved and hated the woman before her—loved her for her strength to labor and her beautiful pride—hated her for the appealing blush and the shamefaced little lie.

Why should she be ashamed of the truth—she, living in the twentieth century—when honest labor is more than luxury and strong hands above white ones?

Then, from thinking of the sister, Patricia passed to thinking of the brother.

Yes; there was a brother.

The thin line of smoke still curled against the sky.

Patricia could fancy him returning from the fields, his broad shoulders erect, his eyes glowing beneath the brim of his harvest hat. She could see him pause beside the water-bucket in the hall and lift the gourd in one strong hand.

She knew his story as every one about her knew it—as Mrs. Simonds, the postmistress, knew it. He had gone through a college course and was starting out into the world, when his mother had called him home.[3] In response to a selfish whim of the gentle old

---

3. Such demanding mothers recur in novels from all phases of Glasgow's career, including *The Deliverance* (1904), *Virginia* (1913), and *In This Our Life* (1941). In *Barren Ground* (1925), Jason Greylock's father plays a parallel role.

lady he had come. "You must stay by me," she had said, "and by the old place."

And he had stayed.

"Ah!" cried Patricia, bitterly. She flung out her hands with a gesture almost of despair, a hot red mantling her face. "It is not just! It is not just! He might have done so much—so much—and now——"

Suddenly she straightened herself and stood up, her black skirt clinging closely about her, her arms hanging loosely at her sides. From the open collar of her dress her white throat showed its sensitive lines. She wore no hat, and the heavy coil of hair had slipped low on her splendid head. She was thrilled with life—a superb specimen of health and strength, capable of passion and of action. She turned and followed the winding path, treading ruthlessly upon lovevine and clover.

At the end of the path, just where it passed into the turnpike, a small, sluggish stream crept along. A rotten log was stretched across it. Patricia paused upon the log, her face showing white in the gray dusk. The croaking of frogs from their bed among the rushes fell mournfully upon her ears. The heavy odor of white thunder-blossom half oppressed her.

She leaned over the stream, seeing in its shallow water a faint caricature of her sensitive face.

Then she drew back.

"Patricia!"

Some one came from out of the dusty turnpike and faced her, standing upon the further end of the rotten log. With a sudden tremor she recognized him. His eyes glowed beneath the brim of his straw hat, his strong hand was outstretched. There was a sudden stirring in her pulses—a vague sense of exaltation.

She gave him her hand. Then, with a sudden breathless gesture, she threw back her head and looked into his eyes.

"I was thinking of you," she said.

"Patricia!"

"Hush! I was thinking of the shame of it—of the pity of it! Have you no ambition? Are you utterly without manhood that you are content to waste your life like this? That you let the world go by without a care, preferring to spend your youth upon a wornout plantation, tilling a wornout soil? Ah, the shame of it!"

7

Her hot, reproachful eyes flashed over him. Beneath the fire of her words he wavered and trembled. The glow died from his face. It looked white and set through the gray gloom.

"Don't you see?" he said appealingly. "It is a question of duty. My post is here. I cannot desert it. I owe it to my family—to my mother. Don't you see?"

But she turned away with a little hopeless gesture.

"I don't see," she said coldly. "I could never see. It is absurd. It is a remnant of that old chivalry—so called—of which the world is well rid."

Then her mood melted. She turned to him with sweet, prayerful eyes, stretching out appealing hands.

"Oh, go away!" she cried. "Go out into the world. You owe it to yourself. Success is so dear—so dear. Why shouldn't you know it?"

He took her hands, his warm, rapt gaze still bent upon her. "I love you!" he said. "You know that I love you—love you well enough to sacrifice everything for you—everything. Love you so that the hardest life with you would be heaven."

The girl did not tremble, did not turn away. She looked at him steadily, her proud lips slightly apart.

"Well enough to leave this place for me—to come away and work and earn success for me—well enough for that?" Her voice was almost mocking in its earnestness.

"Can't you understand?" he cried. "Can you never understand? My mother needs me. I am her only son. It is duty, plain, practical duty. Will you yield nothing to that?" Then he grew yearningly tender.

"Ah, my love! my love!" he said. "Am I nothing to you? Is your love so weak? Can you not sacrifice something for me? Come to me here—here for a while—perhaps ten, perhaps twenty years. I am bound, hand and foot, but you—you are free. Be a woman, Patricia; give yourself to me. It will not be hard, and there is love. What is the world, what is anything to love?"

Then Patricia wavered.

"Not hard!" she cried passionately. "Not hard! Ah, it is a hard, hard thing to be a woman!"

With a sudden desperate movement she broke from him and fled along the dusky turnpike.

Once in her room the sense of oppression became unbearable. She went over to the window and, kneeling beside it, laid her hot cheek against the sill. All was dark and quiet, save for a faint stir in the room below and a faint stream of light cast from an open window upon the graveled path. Far away the mountains stood like phantom sentinels guarding futurity. "I cannot bear it!" cried Patricia; "I cannot bear it!" Then the question rose and faced her blankly. It was a moment of supreme indecision. On one side all the womanhood within her quivered with desire; on the other, a man's ambitions struggled to survive. It was the new woman warring against the old—the twentieth century rebelling against the nineteenth.

Love or ambition? With love went the inheritance of ten thousand centuries, the heart that had beaten out the brain, the passion that had strangled reason to thrive in rank luxuriance. With ambition warred the strong young intellect, fresh from its swaddling bands—the intellect that had quickened and been born with bitter pangs.

Love is not for you, said reason. But reason was checkmated. Passion, like a loosened tiger, pinned it down.

"I want him! I want him!" she cried, "and I must have him! Yes, I must have him!"

Yes, she would have him, she would come to him, as he had said. She would become a woman for his sake, suffer as other women suffer, be patient as other women were patient. She would merge her identity into his and, letting the world go by, think only of him and his child, as it lay upon her breast. She would give up her profession. She would let ambition go. She would—yes, she would clean the house in gloves, like Hannah Fairfax, and churn the butter. She saw herself growing old and wrinkled, saw the faded calico wrapper and the rice powder.

"Ah!" cried she, suddenly, "What a life! What a life!" She rested her head upon her arm, still kneeling beside the window. A luxuriant wisteria vine that grew without peeped shyly in at her, its purple blossoms just brushing her cheek. She looked across hill and plain far into the grayish distance. The freshness of twilight came stealing in upon her, mingling with the faint odor of purple wisteria.

In the turnpike a strong, straight figure was moving along. Patricia raised her head and leaned far out, straining her eyes to catch the

9

last outlines of the straight figure as it vanished beyond the sombre stile.

"Ah!" said Patricia again, and left the window.

That night Patricia wrote a letter.

"You have asked me to decide," it said, "but I cannot. Love is stronger than I, but is love as strong as ambition? I do not know. Time must decide. I am going away. Do not follow me, do not seek to find me. You say you love me; then you must bear with me. Love will last. If I want you I will come back to you; if not—my life must be lived, and as yet my life means my work.

"You may not understand, for the women of to-day are different from the women you know—the women you have read of. In the nineteenth century a woman would have stayed; in the twentieth she must go."

And the next morning at daybreak she was driven to the depot. As she passed Fairfax Place her eyes sought eagerly for some trace of life. The house was dark and still. The shutters were tightly closed. A bony hound, lying upon a shuck mat in the hall, howled dismally.

Behind the gabled roof of the house a glorious herald of dawn was rising. Over the meadows a heavy morning fog lay damp and chill. As the glimmer of day touched it, it glistened and deepened with a thousand iridescent rays. How chill it seemed and how desolate!

Then, as Patricia looked, a figure appeared in the narrow path leading from the pasture—a figure in a faded cotton gown with a milk-pail in her small hand. Patricia could see the frothy whiteness of the new milk.

A pathetic figure it was, all alone in the desolate, chilly morning, with the fog creeping damp and heavy to her feet and the first rays of sunlight revealing the old wrinkles in the young face.

"Ah, what a life!" cried Patricia breathlessly.

Then the cart jogged along and the figure was lost in the foggy distance.

Ten years later a woman sat alone in her office—a tall woman with a beautiful dark head.

She was sitting before a small square desk, upon which some loose papers were scattered. Upon the paper under her hand was written "Brown *vs.* Battle," followed by a summing up of evidence.

The woman leaned her head upon her hand and looked thoughtfully through the open window.

Along the street people were passing hurriedly.

A square or so away a hand-organ was grinding out a discordant air, the tune of an old-fashioned polka. She breathed quickly, pushing the hair from her brow as she did so with a firm, white hand. A letter lay upon the floor at her feet. Suddenly her eyes lowered meeting the written lines.

"Your name has been suggested," it said, "in connection with the office of——"

She frowned and placed her foot upon it with a half displeased gesture.

"So I may become an Associate Justice of the Supreme Court," she said. "And—I am tired."[4]

For a moment she was silent. People still passed hurriedly in the street. The hand-organ was moving farther away; its air grew fainter. Suddenly a baby's cry sounded fitfully without. Her gaze reached the window. A beggar woman had stopped upon the sidewalk, her shawl blown in the wind and upon her breast a child.

The woman on the inside leaned forward. A little cry escaped her; all the wonderful instinct of motherhood, which is strong in proportion to the weakness of women, swelled within her.[5] There was a passionate leaping of her pulse. She longed to tear the child from the other woman's breast—to feel its soft lips against her own. The letter lay trampled underfoot. Suddenly she spoke.

"My God!" she said. "What have I missed?"

The firm, flexible mouth softened.

"Oh, to know what it means," she cried. "To have one word, ever so little, only to know what his life had been—his life and mine—and mine. I would not change it," she cried. "I would not change it. And yet—and yet——"

4. The first female associate justice would be Sandra Day O'Connor, who made a rapid rise in Arizona politics, serving as assistant attorney general, state senator, and superior court judge, before becoming associate justice of the Supreme Court in 1981.

5. This emotion contrasts remarkably with Glasgow's own claims that she had never "felt the faintest wish to have babies" and that the maternal instinct had been left out of her by nature.

She rose suddenly, some loose sheets of paper fluttering to the floor. She stretched out her arms with a wide, free movement.

"I will go to Virginia to-day," she said.

As the sun was setting she stepped from the train at the little station and walked rapidly across the fields. She felt strangely restless. Now that the journey was ended, the vague impulse that had prompted her to undertake it seemed to fail her. By the act she seemed to have put the ten long years aside—to have come back to her girlhood and undisciplined passion—to nature in its free, primitive state.

Once again she paused upon the hillside, resting her arms upon the rotten fence, her gaze sweeping the tangled fields and resting upon the gabled roof of a house in the hollow below. A warm color had risen to her cheeks and her eyes had dimmed and softened. She felt a sudden timidity—the sweet impulsive shyness of ten years ago. In the turnpike below she almost thought to see the strong, straight figure passing along.

For a moment she wavered upon the hillside, then, with a firm step, she followed the winding path.

The house was quiet. From the kitchen chimney smoke was rising. It was near the supper hour. There was a sound of clinking plates and a faint odor of steaming coffee.

About the grounds the old sense of desolation asserted itself. The paint upon the shutters which had been fresh ten years ago was almost worn away; some of the front steps had rotted and were gradually sinking in; and the gate had fallen from its hinges and lay overgrown with weeds at a little distance.

Patricia leaned against a post that had once supported the gate. She was filled with sudden yearning for the neglected old place. The ten years which had wrought in her young life such buoyant changes seemed to have touched so lightly this quiet spot in its broken age. With her, time had meant action and advancement; here it meant merely the passivity of decay. Had she thrown in her destiny with that of the old place, what would it have brought her? The old words awoke from somewhere, ringing upon her ears: "Come to me here—perhaps for ten—perhaps for twenty years!" Twenty years! Why, in twenty years decay would feed upon the rafters.

Then a man came quickly from the garden and stood in the graveled path. In one moment all the latent passion within her took fire and flamed hotly forth. At first she saw only the aggressive manliness—all the straight length of him. The womanhood of her being had asserted itself after ten years of sexless suppression.

She went toward him—a beautiful, advancing presence—one capable hand outstretched, a hint of awakened passion tingeing her cheeks.

Then, as she neared him, her eyes cleared. Looking upon him, she saw that the years had passed him as they had passed the old place. She saw that his bronzed face had reddened and roughened, that the glow had left his eyes—saw that they were dull and content as he was content. The direction in which she had progressed he did not know; he had taken no step forward for ten long years.

With a little gasp she met his outstretched hand, looking with passionate, groping eyes into his face—looking for something which she had not found, and could not find—something which was not and had never been.

"Patricia!" There was a pathetic awkwardness in his speech. "Patricia—I—never thought that you would come back."

Then suddenly their hands fell apart and they stood silent, for a woman had come from behind the house and neared them—a small, tired woman in a soiled gown, with a child upon her shrunken breast—a woman who had borne many burdens and whose strength had not been sufficient unto her need.

The man wavered.

"I—I never thought that you would come back," he repeated, "and—and this is my wife."

A while later and Patricia walked rapidly away. She no longer felt the restless stirring of her pulses. The warm red had faded from her face. It looked white and set.

At the fence on the hill she halted and looked about her, drawing a long, quiet breath. She saw with clear eyes the landscape. She saw the ragged, rolling plains. She saw the distant mountains. She saw the sun, a fiery ball, setting beyond their summits, flooding the hollow below with a roseate glow. The gray fog had not risen, softening the prospect. She saw it as it was, ragged and barren. And looking inward, she saw her own life with its strong, bold lines unaltered. The old romance had fallen from her like a shadow, melting from her feet and passing to take its place among the many shadows that stood flanked within the past.[6]

The woman held her head erect; not a muscle quivered. She stretched out her arms with a gesture of thankfulness.

"Oh, thank God!" she said, "thank God!"

Then the great head fell upon her arms and she burst into tears. And the sun went down.

6. The story thus sets a pattern many Glasgow novels will follow: it moves from romantic self-deception to the disenchantment of reality. This, of course, is a common structure for realistic fiction, including major works by Mark Twain and Henry James.

Woman Suffrage in Virginia: Ellen Glasgow Interviewed

With regard to the [suffragist] movement in Virginia . . . it has been the privilege of the writer to interview Miss Ellen Glasgow, the authoress, who very recently returned to America from England. The views of Miss Glasgow on the subject of woman suffrage, while pronounced, are not radical.[1] . . . Upon returning last from England, where she was thrown in contact with many of the leaders of the suffragist movement in that kingdom, Miss Glasgow visited the State of Colorado, where women enjoy the full privilege of the franchise.[2]

Apart from a thorough appreciation of the absolute justice of representation where there is taxation, Miss Glasgow . . . remarked this singular circumstance in Colorado, that in the large majority of instances the more militant or active and enthusiastic advocates of the movement were to be found among men, and not women. Which singular condition may arise from the fact of a comparative unfamil-

These excerpts from an interview by Carter W. Wormeley appeared in *Jewish Record*, I (November 28, 1909), 5, 16. Wormeley's introduction touches on the suffragist campaign in England and America; his editorializing throughout has been eliminated where possible, but his summaries of Glasgow's statements have been retained.

1. The Equal Suffrage League of Virginia, formed during the month this interview appeared, grew out of a meeting held in Ellen Glasgow's home.

2. Ellen Glasgow spent the spring of 1909 in England. *The Romance of a Plain Man* appeared in January. During August and September, she vacationed in Colorado Springs, Colorado.

iarity with public affairs on the part of the average American woman, which fact will be far more accentuated in the South.

Miss Glasgow . . . said: "While in England I was impressed with the fact that the most ardent and enthusiastic advocates of woman's suffrage were to be found among the most exclusive, retiring, brilliant and intellectual literary circles and among the most representative classes of society. I may mention Miss Beatrice Harraden, authoress of 'Ships That Pass in the Night,' or Miss May Sinclair, who wrote that impressive and powerful song, 'The Divine Fire,' in illustration of this point.[3]

"I may add, that I know of no woman more timid or retiring than Miss Harraden, which observation holds equally true of Miss Sinclair. And so it is throughout England, the leaders in the very forefront of the present campaign are earnest, modest and refined. I met with Mrs. Pankhurst while last in England.[4] She is a woman of great executive capacity and of a wonderful ability for organization. She is, moreover, a woman of high ideals, and one who will perform unflinchingly her duty as she sees it." In commenting upon the great earnestness of those enlisted in the success of the cause in England, Miss Glasgow mentioned the conduct of Lady Constance Lytton.[5] Lady Lytton is said to have voluntarily had herself placed under arrest and imprisoned that she might demonstrate to the English people class distinction, even in the boasted English law, as illustrated in the difference of treatment accorded her ladyship and the wife of a common laborer by the name of Lee, who had just been incarcerated.

In the estimation of Miss Glasgow, the radical distinction be-

3. The English novelist Beatrice Harraden (1864–1936) marched with women writers and thirteen thousand other suffragists in a procession by the National Union of Women's Suffrage Societies on June 13, 1908. The march led from the Embankment to Albert Hall. May Sinclair (1865–1946) was a British novelist known for her psychoanalytical novels as well as her feminist stance. She would participate in several British suffrage movements, including the protests and imprisonments in Kensington in 1910. *The Divine Fire* (1904) was her first important success; *Mary Olivier* (1919) would be an early contribution to stream-of-consciousness fiction.

4. Emmeline Pankhurst (1858–1928) came from Manchester to London in 1905 and led the militant Women's Social and Political Union before World War I. She was originally a member of the Independent Labour party but resigned in 1903 to form the Women's Social and Political Union, with her daughter Christabel.

5. Lady Lytton (1869–1923), daughter of the Earl of Lytton, viceroy of India, became involved with the suffragette movement in 1906, when she joined the Women's Social and Political Union. She was imprisoned several times and went on several hunger strikes, eventually becoming so ill that she remained partially paralyzed.

15

tween the movement for woman's suffrage in America and in England lay in the fact that the fight had been waged in the British Kingdom for a considerable number of years. Municipal franchise has for some time been enjoyed by English women, while, with the exception of some four or five States in the far Northwest, the American woman is unfamiliar with the ballot. Miss Glasgow saw enough in England, however, to convince her of the ultimate success of the present movement. Her faith in its final triumph was based not alone in what she conceived to be its unquestionable right, but in the personnel of those leaders enlisted in its behalf, not only in England, but also in this country. This was with Miss Glasgow an evident source of gratification and of pride. And while she spoke of herself as no great motive force in the active advancement of the cause, she gave evidence that her every sympathy was engaged in its furtherance, and spoke of the participation in the local movement by the women of Richmond with nothing short of enthusiasm.[6] As bearing on this phase of the question, Miss Glasgow said: "I must confess myself as agreeably surprised at the apparent earnestness and wide scope assumed by the woman suffrage movement at Richmond. Yet I am proud of the women who are bravely coming to the front in this cause of right. Such names as those mentioned as the leaders of the movement here might well invest with dignity and lend strength and mighty impetus to any movement," and, she added, "it is just such sympathy that we stand most in need of at this time. At Richmond the movement has appealed to the domestic and to the more quiet type of womanhood. There is nothing superficial in the character of women such as have announced their co-operation with the cause in this city. As for myself, I regret to say that I am not one fitted to head any organization (I leave that to my more gifted friend, Mrs. B. B. Valentine). But, while sadly lacking in executive ability, I am none the less heartily in sympathy with the movement, which I look upon as an inevitable reform." Miss Glasgow continued by saying that she considered the movement in point not as a question of sex, but as one of justice, of right, and of truth. That she contemplated the issue as an inevitable se-

6. Lila Meade Valentine, Mary Johnston, and Ellen Glasgow were active in the formation of the Equal Suffrage League of Virginia.

quence in the evolution of the political economy of the times, and one which, as such, was predestined and foreordained to success.

As regarded her more personal opinion of the primal just principles of the cause, Miss Glasgow expressed it as her conviction that the question, taken as an abstract proposition, was grounded on irrefutable, incontrovertible logic. Applying this proposition in the abstract to existing conditions, Miss Glasgow was unable to understand how the privilege of political and personal liberty could militate against the dignity of woman, although she considered the question not from a standpoint of mere dignity, but in the double light of equity and truth. She said: "Take the woman of the poorer class, for instance, and see the unjust and unutterable hardship implied by the widely recognized fact that such a woman is hopelessly debarred from commanding or compelling any proper remuneration for business by reason of the circumstance that she is disfranchised and absolutely without voice in political or governmental affairs. The American heiress also occupies an anomalous position. And if I mention the well known name of Miss Helen Gould, I would say that that is a singular state of society which will withhold from such a woman a voice in matters vital to her interests, and at the same time grant to foreign immigrants naturalization papers and the privilege of the franchise."[7]

That Miss Glasgow was out of sympathy with the militant attitude of the suffragettes of England was taken for granted before she herself touched on the subject.[8] Her own criticism of this violence in agitation, however, was certainly severe, although she looked upon it as savoring strongly of English custom. She said, referring to the conduct of the London suffragettes: "It is related to the first great principle of woman's rights, which is the essential cause, much as the throwing of tea into Boston harbor is related to the first war between this country and England. It is the first effervescence of a

7. Helen Miller Gould Shepard (1868–1938) was an American philanthropist especially known for her gifts to U.S. Army hospitals in the Spanish-American War. She was the eldest daughter of railroad magnate Jay Gould.
8. Because the general election was to take place in 1910, women doubled their efforts to force suffrage into the political arena in 1909. Pankhurst's followers began using hunger strikes (eventually leading to force-feeding) as a means of escaping prison sentences. In June of 1909, the first meeting of the Council of the Women's National Anti-Suffrage League took place. The dissident followers of Pankhurst formed the Women's Franchise League.

great cause yet to be consummated. It is but a sign of the times, indicating a spirit of disquiet and unrest. It is absolutely without significance, as regards America, and is the outcome of environment and local cause.''

Miss Glasgow concluded her remarks by professing herself to be, in no sense of the term, a political economist, but one who, viewing the question of woman's suffrage without undue feeling or dogmatism, was convinced of its absolute and high righteousness. She was of the firm belief that the right, in this instance, would win. She mentioned the fact that Mark Twain was a staunch advocate of the movement, adding that nearly all among the eminent literary men and women of America were in hearty accord with his views.[9]

9. Mark Twain (1835–1910) in a public address in 1901 said: "I should like to see the time come when women shall help make the laws. I should like to see the whiplash, the ballot, in the hands of women. . . . If all the women in this town had a vote today . . . they would rise in their might and change the awful state of things now existing here.'' Twain's speech, "Votes for Women," was given to the Hebrew Technical School for Girls, New York, January 20, 1901.

The Call

Woman called to woman at the daybreak![1]
  When the bosom of the deep was stirred,
In the gold of dawn and in the silence,
  Woman called to woman and was heard!

Steadfast as the dawning of the polestar,
  Secret as the fading of the breath;
At the gate of Birth we stood together,
  Still together at the gate of Death.

Queen or slave or bond or free, we battled,
  Bartered not our faith for love or gold;

This poem appeared in *Current Literature*, LIII (November, 1912), 596. It was also printed in *Collier's Magazine*, XLIX (July 27, 1912), 21; and in *Current Opinion*, LIV (January, 1913), 68.
1. In 1910 the Equal Suffrage League of Virginia (of which Glasgow was a founding member) had presented a petition to the Virginia legislature for a federal amendment. After 1911 the league began holding annual meetings. In 1912, however, the first resolution proposing an amendment to the Virginia state constitution enfranchising women failed by a vote of 84 to 12. In 1911 and 1912 the national woman suffrage movement was focusing its campaign on California and Illinois.

Man we served, but in the hour of anguish
    Woman called to woman as of old.

Hidden at the heart of earth we waited,
    Watchful, patient, silent, secret, true;
All the terrors of the chains that bound us
    Man has seen, but only woman knew!

Woman knew! Yea, still, and woman knoweth!—
    Thick the shadows of our prison lay—
Yet that knowledge in our hearts we treasure
    Till the dawning of the perfect day.

Onward now as in the long, dim ages,
    Onward to the light where Freedom lies;
Woman calls to woman to awaken!
    Woman calls to woman to arise!

No Valid Reason Against Giving Votes to Women: An Interview

"Any social movement which has vitality and hardihood will have enlisted the services of many kinds of women before it is grown as old as the present agitation for equal suffrage, and it seems to me that the general surprise at the London militants is therefore disproportionate."[1]

Thus did Ellen Glasgow, with characteristic sagacity, answer a TIMES reporter, who sought her out and begged her to speak her mind on the subject of the English suffragists; for although a further investigation of her opinion discovered her personally averse to extreme measures, she would not be lured into a direct condemnation of them, nor would she hazard a guess that they might have "injured the cause" in the eyes of the unthinking.[2]

This interview appeared in the New York *Times*, March 23, 1913, Sec. 6, p. 11.

1. Under the banner of various women's organizations (*e.g.*, Women's Social and Political Union), several prominent agitators demonstrated in Parliament Square, held hunger strikes, and organized protests among the workers. Among the notable agitators were Mrs. Pankhurst and her daughters, along with Annie Kenney, Teresa Billington, and Vida Goldstein.

2. The Equal Suffrage League of Virginia would hold its first outdoor demonstration in Richmond the following year (1914), and in 1915 would demonstrate at the office of the governor of Virginia for an amendment to the state constitution.

"I am too far away from the conditions and emotions of the English suffragists to be able to speak of them with authority," continued Miss Glasgow. "I grant you that I myself do not incline to violence. I have never seen it prove anything. The spirit which prompts violence seems to me to go back to the days of dueling, when two men with a mental or spiritual difference undertook to establish a mental or spiritual supremacy by dexterity with their swords.

"Again, there are still many people in the world who think that arguments are settled, and causes are proved, by means of war. My own convictions are against these.

"In the first place, women will never in the history of creation come to equal men physically, and the sooner they learn that, and eliminate that, the better for us all. And so I do not quite see why the Englishwomen should want to begin their fight, or continue it, on a basis of physical conflict.

"But, as I have said, my opinions are no more than the voice of one individual, and I know that any just and righteous cause will recruit many individuals, with many voices, and that just as to accomplish anything else in the world one requires half one's force to think and half one's force to act, so to achieve the ballot here and in England we need women who will go into the open and battle for their convictions, as well as those who remain behind to think.

"Again I am inspired to a considerable leniency toward the militancy of England by the women I have known who were in it and of it. I cannot do less than respect any activity which produces such a woman as, for example, Miss Harraden, whom I admire with extravagance.[3] And I argue to myself that these women, with brilliant, farseeing minds and perceptions heightened by the stress of their position, will surely be able to judge of militancy better than I, who am so far away.

"Then," added Miss Glasgow, with the flash of a smile, "I do not like fighting myself, and I am not so impartial a judge as otherwise I might be. All told, I think we had better leave the subject of London's militancy till we are more sure of it. I half suspect that there is not so much of it anyway, as we have been led to believe. Of course I have only seen the cable dispatches in the newspapers, and they may or may not be accurate.

3. Beatrice Harraden, English novelist and suffragist

"But from them I have gathered that the suffragists are not yet in an organized state of armed revolution. The violence seems to be sporadic and unrelated—a flash in the pan here, there, and the other place, with no great significance to any of it.

"One feature of the suffrage movement here and elsewhere that strikes me as being deplorable is the tendency it has to foster sex antagonism. I do not like to see men and women ranged against each other on any question whatever. I do not see why it should be necessary, for one thing. I am convinced that when women have once made it plain to men that they all want the ballot and that suffrage is not merely the hysterical and agitated ambition of a handful of overwrought women the men will promptly let them vote. Of course, there will always be a sprinkling of reactionaries who will die in the belief that women at the polls will mean ruination to the country: but they are in a minority.

"Opposition to suffrage, in this country at least, is all emotional. It does not exist—certainly not in the average run of cases—where its judges have troubled themselves to think.

"In fact, there is not a single valid reason that I have ever heard against giving votes to women."

Miss Glasgow sank comfortably into the woods-green cushions behind her, content that she had landed a broadside. It is well worth while, even at this somewhat critical juncture of her argument, to stop and look at her as she speaks. She is both pretty and young—an extraordinarily unexpected combination in an author of more than National renown.

She has chosen for her surroundings in the apartment on Eighty-fifth Street, which overlooks Central Park, a color scheme of soft dull greens and browns. Into these she blends with a very perfection of art. Her gown is a tone deeper than her brown cushions and catches a sheen from the Japanese gold wall behind her. More brilliant still is her burnished nimbus of red-brown hair. Her eyes are kind, responsive, and a little watchful. And she just has told you in a clear, warm-toned Southern voice, which carries a striking accent, that there is no valid reason why women should not vote.

"Isn't there anything in the contention that the majority of women would be unfit voters, Miss Glasgow?" she was asked.

"Oh, yes," she said. "Probably the majority of them would be, but, for that matter, so now are the majority of men unfit to vote. Any argument which really impairs the claims of women for suffrage applies equally to men's rights to it, and therefore to the very form of government itself. As long as we are living under a representative form of government, in which the final word is supposed to come from the whole people, we must accept that word when it comes and abide by it. We dare not set aside this or that portion of the plebiscite and say, 'You are unfit to vote because you know nothing.' That assails the very essence of democracy. And I am essentially a Democrat.

"A friend and myself were discussing, the other day, this problem of women's fitness to vote, and I maintained then, as I have just done to you, that such discrimination struck directly at democracy.

"'But, after all, democracy is only an experiment,' said my friend. 'That is true enough,' I said, 'but monarchy is a failure, and I certainly prefer an experiment to a failure.'

"I am still convinced that a democratic form of government is the finest, most constructive, and most beneficial to the whole people. No government is going to be perfect. They will all have faults, and serious ones, as long as our only possible practice is to strain our theories through imperfect humanity to get our final results. But I am an evolutionist, once and for all, and I believe that we are constantly and inevitably growing into better conditions, better states of mind, better possibilities."

"What of suffrage in the South, Miss Glasgow? Is it really the stronghold of the anti-suffragists, or is the new movement there considerable?"

"It is, indeed, a considerable movement, though it is not numerically strong, I believe. You know the South is pre-eminently conservative—more so, I think, than any other part of this country. But the thinking women of the South are all in favor of enfranchisement. It is their quality rather than their quantity, as yet, which entitles them to be called 'considerable.'

"As a matter of fact, the women of the South are probably more fitted for the ballot than any other American women, though you would not think so, at the first blush. The women of the ante-bellum days, and of the Reconstruction period, although they were remarkably sheltered from contact with the outside world, had really an enormous responsibility in the management of their own households.[4] They had to direct an amount of labor which to-day would appal the great majority of women. They had this complete and bustling world of their own, behind their own walls, and they had absolutely to govern it. This sense of responsibility the Southern woman still has, and she is, to-day, less appalled at the gravity of being allowed to vote, and of helping to govern, than the women of any other portion of the country.

"Then, superimposed upon this sense of responsibility, born of governing their extensive households, is the self-reliance which came with the post-bellum conditions. It is difficult to describe to you how unprepared were the Southern women for the struggle of making their own way. Their ideas on the subject were absolutely naive and would have been comical if they had not been pathetic.

"I remember, when I was a little girl, being told by an old lady whose daughters had grown up since the war and during the Reconstruction time, that So-and-So, her daughter, was ignorant of everything that women should know—she could not sew, and she could not cook, and she could not conduct a house—so there was nothing left for her to do but teach! And teach she did. And I have often heard since that teaching was the sole occupation of the Southern women, because 'they did not know anything by which to earn a living.'[5]

"Well, naturally, this condition could not last, and the Southern woman has been learning her lesson, earnestly, ever since. Although she is still conservative and prone to suspend her judgments, she belongs to the finest type of suffragist in this country.

"Now here we have been talking of suffrage for dear knows how long, when the really important thing to talk about is the feminist movement as a whole. I think that the ballot itself is a very small and unimportant factor in the whole movement to emancipate women, and I imagine that many, many women agree with me. It is the splendid growth of the whole world in its attitude toward women that is the beauty and the glory of our century.

4. Glasgow had presented this view of antebellum southern women in her 1902 Civil War novel, *The Battle-Ground*, especially in the characterization of Betty Ambler.

5. *Cf.* Glasgow's character Miss Priscilla Batte in *Virginia* (1913).

"Of course, it was all inevitable—had to come—it is an integral part of evolution itself—an obedience to the laws of growth. I, for one, rejoice that I am here to see the dawning of it. I would rather be a part of this creative, constructive country, agitated and unrestful as it is, than to have come prosily along after the battle had been fought and won.

"I have never understood why the world should seem so unwilling to release women. Their development and their increasing facility in self-expression can only be beneficial. But it has taken us a mighty long time to establish this. Everything else in the world has traveled forward, and even inanimate things have undergone an enormous change for the better, every hundred years or so, but women—they were supposed to remain static and undeveloped, and it has been the inspirational fact of centuries that finally they should refuse to stagnate any longer. The foes of the feminist movement have been fairly staggered—astounded. I do not see what else they could have expected.

"The most important thing for women to learn is co-operation," continued Miss Glasgow, adjusting a pillow and turning her gaze out into the sunlit park.[6]

"Their lives have been absolutely aimless, and, for that matter, actually cruel, and they have endured and endured simply because they never stood shoulder to shoulder about anything. Each woman has been a host unto herself, as far as she could go, but she was pitifully limited. She needed the help of her sisters, and she could not get it.

"When I realize the lives of the women of the South, of the generation before me, I am fairly horror-stricken at the loneliness and depression they must have endured. Even those who married were only occupied for a limited time—say for twenty years of their lives, in bringing up children and preserving their homes. Then what? Their children grown, and off to make homes of their own; their

6. In 1913, Alice Paul (1885–1977) formed a national organization rivaling the older National American Woman Suffrage Association (NAWSA). First called the Congressional Union and soon the National Woman's party, Paul's group replaced the state-by-state strategy of NAWSA with a national campaign that included outdoor rallies and parades and a sex boycott, in 1914 and 1916, against the Democratic party. Paul had close ties to English suffragettes.

habits already formed; the better part of their lives spent—oh, to me, they are inexpressibly tragic.[7]

"And if their lives were aimless, and unoccupied, just picture to yourself the existence led by the woman who did not choose to marry.[8] Her mind lay fallow for awhile, of course, but soon it lost its elasticity, and its urges to activity, and there was nothing for her but to settle into half-developed apathy and wait until she died.

"Multiply that case by the number of women in this country fifty years ago and you have a condition which shrieks loudly enough, surely, for redress and remedy. Even to this day we are not wholly out of the woods, though we have made an incredibly vast stride. The point of value is that we have realized our plight and have set ourselves to abolish it, and that we have stumbled on the important truth that co-operation is strength. That will lead us out of the wilderness.

"We should have divined long ago that what we needed most was the spirit of organization. Men have always taunted us on our refusal to do likewise. You realize how often men comment, kindly or caustically, as the case may be, on woman's lack of loyalty to woman.

"It has been true. We have deserved it. But that is all changing now, and we are losing not only many old personal prejudices, but, more important still, by means of the feminist movement and the effort for equal suffrage we are wiping out class distinctions and class prejudices. Nowadays it is refreshingly common to see women of the highest social training at work in social settlements.[9] They have an acute interest in other women—particularly women who are doing things, who have established their economic value.

"From one end of the social scale to the other the beneficences of the feminist growth and unfolding are making themselves felt. To me it is as inspiring as a battle cry.

"By the way, do not misunderstand me when I call for equality of

7. The fate of the married woman in the South is movingly revealed in *Virginia* (1913).
8. Such independent women are exemplified by Susan Treadwell in *Virginia* and Gabriella Carr in *Life and Gabriella* (1916).
9. When she was about seventeen, Glasgow joined the Richmond City Mission and, a year later, switched her concern to a private charity hospital called the Sheltering Arms.

opportunity. I do not want women to become like men, even granting the possibility that they ever could. I do not think there would ever be anything more than a sheer surface similarity in any event, and I should not even value that. I rejoice that at least we are shaking off our chains—many of them our own welding—and that we are receiving our just and honest privileges.

"And I rejoice, too, that the world is to have the benefit of the freedom of women, as much, if not more, than the women themselves. It will require a shrewd social observer to sum up, in the histories of the future, the incalculable good to the world and to progress that will come out of this feminist movement.

"Women are near to the vital issues of life. They stand always at the portals of birth and death, and all the sacred, solemn things between. They will carry out into the world with them, when they go for their education and to do their work, a depth and intensity of feeling that few men ever attain to.

"There are some certain things, for example, that will simply never be attended to, till women go out and attend to them. White slave traffic is among these, and many of the economic wrongs of women. They sense the vast importance of them more than men, and they are less casual in their attitude toward evil. You have known men who said, in regard to evil, that deplorable though it was, it seemed inevitable. Yes, but no common woman would let it go at that. She would fight it out, and win, on the basis that anything which is really evil is not necessary—cannot be—and that anything that is really necessary cannot, and is not, evil."

And Miss Glasgow, smiling prophet of the new social conscience, leaned from her brown and green cushions to say good-bye.

Feminism

When the most popular of men's heroines, after being blighted by love, went to the undertaker's to select her coffin, ordered that a broken lily should be engraved on the lid, and had it sent home to be used as a writing table during her decline, an admir-

This essay appeared in the *New York Times Book Review*, November 30, 1913, pp. 656–57.

ing eighteenth century public exclaimed that this touching episode had immortalized the womanly woman.[1] No other heroine in fiction has been so passionately eulogized or so widely mourned, and even to-day she remains the most convincing of the feminine prigs with which the imagination of man has enriched the pages of literature. For Clarissa belongs not only to the evolving novel, but to the evolving masculine ideal of woman.

And since the hardest conditions to shake are those relating to women, since even a realist is apt to romance about women in English fiction, and so great a writer as Thackeray went to life for his heroes and to the Victorian pattern of femininity for his heroines, it is, perhaps, asking too much to expect an avowed sentimentalist to create a natural Clarissa. When woman herself has shown much eagerness to conform to man's ideal of her that she has cheerfully defied nature and reshaped both her soul and body after the model he put before her, one can hardly demand of a man novelist that he should write of her as she is and not as he desires that she should be. Ages of false thinking about her on the part of others have bred in woman the dangerous habit of false thinking about herself, and she has denied her own humanity so long and so earnestly that she has come at last almost to believe in the truth of her denial.

So it is not surprising that, until the day of George Meredith, English novelists, though they often wrote of men and things as they were, invariably treated woman as if she were the solitary exception to natural law, and particularly to the law of development.[2] Fielding, Thackeray, Dickens, and a host of others prepared their womanly woman after the same recipe—modesty, goodness, self-sacrifice, an inordinate capacity for forgiveness, "about as much religion as my William likes," and, now and then, a little vivacity—all sufficiently diluted to make the mixture palatable to the opposite sex. And in time, after the manner of mankind, this formula received the sanction of custom.

1. Clarissa Harlowe, the heroine of Samuel Richardson's (1689–1761) *Clarissa, or The History of a Young Lady* (1747–48)
2. George Meredith (1828–1909) is said to have been influenced by his father-in-law, Thomas Love Peacock (1785–1866), in his affirmation of the intellectual equality of women with men. In a secular framework, he gave women an importance similar to that George Eliot (1819–80) had given them in a philosophical one. In 1859, he published *The Ordeal of Richard Feverel* and, in 1879, *The Egoist.*

From Richardson to George Meredith there was little change in man's ideal of the womanly woman. In fiction man might wear his cloak of many colors, but woman appeared changelessly white except on the occasions when, for purposes of plot, she was depicted as changelessly black. Never by design or accident could the colors run together—never could Amelia become Becky for an hour or Becky become Amelia.[3] The womanly woman of the earlier novelists was wholly contented with her immemorial position as the spectator of man: and when she wasn't womanly, and wasn't contented, she was inevitably, as in the case of poor Beatrix, hunted to her destruction.[4] Because it has pleased man to imagine that woman is passive and hates change, no English writer of fiction before George Meredith—or, I may say, instead, before Mr. Hardy—ever dared to recognize that she is, and has always been, in her heart at least, the adventurous sex. Even Fielding, who feared nothing else on earth, lived in terror of offending against the popular legend of the womanly woman, and was oppressed by the curious delusion that woman is made of different clay from man—that, while he progresses, she, corresponding to some fixed ideal of her, remains static. To be sure, the period in which he lived was one in which, to quote from Mrs. James, "No woman could be genteel, who was not entirely flat before," and for this reason, perhaps, his vision of the eternal feminine is as sentimental as Thackeray's.[5] And yet, in spite of the fact that the world, or a part of it at least, has outgrown the belief that the worship of a dissolute husband is an exalted occupation for an immortal soul, it is impossible to resist the charm of Fielding's Amelia. Never before or since has man's womanly woman been made so lovable; and if she no longer commands our un-

3. Becky Sharp is the central character in William Makepeace Thackeray's (1811–63) *Vanity Fair* (1847–48). A friendless girl whose object is to rise in the world, she is agreeable, cool, selfish, and entirely amoral. Amelia Sedley, her friend from school days, is pretty, gentle, unintelligent, and totally devoted to the memory of her worthless husband, George Osborne. Amelia, of course, is also Henry Fielding's (1707–54) idealized heroine, a long-suffering, virtuous wife, whose purity and high sense of conscience cause her to refuse overtures made to her while her husband is imprisoned. *Amelia* appeared in 1751.
4. Beatrix was one of Thackeray's characters who appears both in *Henry Esmond* (1852) and *The Virginians* (1857–59). In *Henry Esmond*, she is caught in a love triangle between Esmond and another suitor.
5. Mrs. James is a character in Fielding's *Amelia* (1751).

questioning esteem, she still continues to enchant and delight us. For, passive as she is in every quality, except that of sex, she is drawn by the hand of a lover and there is good, red blood, not printer's ink, in her veins.

As for the two greatest novelists of the nineteenth century, they never forgot for a minute, like the kind-hearted gentlemen they were,[6] that the souls of their heroines were encased in crinoline. The Victorian ideals of femininity lay as an incubus upon the earlier fiction of the period—for it is, after all, an imperfect transcript of life that paints man as a human being and woman as a piece of faintly colored waxwork. It was a cherished tradition of the century, and in the beginning was probably construed into a delicate compliment to the young Queen, that the womanly woman had been created by the hand of God wholly passive and perfect, without the faults or even the ordinary impulses of human nature. It is true that when she became old and ugly she was permitted to be funny; and it is entirely to the saving fiction of the womanly woman's imperishable outward loveliness that we owe some of the most entrancing characters in Dickens's novels. His heroines belong in a gallery of waxwork figures; but his old women, his ugly women, and his wicked women are wholly delightful. For the old, the ugly, and the wicked, growing cramped in their positions or dissatisfied with their entertainment as the audience of man, become miraculously alive. When they cease to be valued as witnesses of the achievements of others, they display an amazing activity.

But with Meredith and Hardy woman, for the first time in men's novels, drops her cloak of sentimentality and appears no less human and vital than does the source of her being. And yet even here the ancient tradition is not completely discarded, and these great writers, unlike in so much else, are alike at least in this—that they both appear, in many of their books, if not in all, to regard caprice as the ruling principle of woman's nature. That a real Diana would have sold her lover's secret is exceedingly doubtful; that a real Sue would have deserted the suffering Jude is almost unbelieveable— but caprice is probably the last quality that the masculine imagination will relinquish in its conception of woman; and certainly to

6. Probably Thackeray and Charles Dickens (1812–70), as mentioned above

make the womanly woman capricious is a pleasant change from the earlier fashion of making her insipid.[7]

For before Meredith's splendid heroines appeared, when English novelists portrayed woman in heroic dimensions, it was invariably in dimensions of sex. She lived for man, and failing this, she died for man, and at long intervals she even disguised her sex and wore man's clothes for man—but the beginning, middle, and end of her existence was simply man. Without the prop of man she was as helplessly ineffectual as the "tender parasite" to which Thackeray compared her. And with the sacred inconsistency possible only to tradition, she was represented as passive even in the single activity to which her energies were directed—for in love, as in all else, she was supposed to sit with smiling patience and wait on the convenience of man. When she grew restless it proved merely that she was not the womanly woman—since to grow restless in the opinion of most novelists is the exclusive prerogative of man. And so deeply rooted in the masculine mind is this inherited belief in the right of the male to want to rove, if not to actually pack up and go, that we find so essentially modern a writer as Mr. Galsworthy speaking of the aching for the "wild," the passionate, the new, that never "quite dies in a man's heart,"—implying, one gathers from the context, that this aching has either never been born in the heart of a woman or has died there in its infancy. Yet Mr. Galsworthy possesses an understanding of woman's nature—of her strength, her weakness, her blindness to the virtue of expediency, her tragic wastefulness in love—that is not equaled—that is not even approached by any other of our younger novelists. In his perfect novel, "The Dark Flower"—for it is impossible for one who is by temperament a novelist, not a reviewer, to speak in measured terms of praise of work so rare, so delicately wrought as this—he has painted the portraits of four women that stand out as softly glowing, as mysteriously lovely, as the figures in Titian's Sacred and Pro-

---

7. Diana is from Meredith's novel *Diana of the Crossways* (1885), one of his most overtly feminist novels. Diana dreams of "accepting martyrdom, becoming the first martyr of the modern woman's cause—a grand position." Sue Bridehead appears in Hardy's *Jude the Obscure* (1895). Her insistence on sexual independence breaks Jude's heart; yet she herself admits, "It was damnably selfish to torture you as I did."

fane Love.[8] About them one and all, ardently as they are imagined, there is a certain wistfulness—a pathos that seems inherent in sex— as if Mr. Galsworthy were oppressed by the feeling that woman could never really be happy—that Nature had, from the beginning, ordained her for suffering. These four women are but exquisite variations from the indestructible type of man's womanly woman—the woman who lives by love alone—the woman for whom Goldsmith wrote his famous advice on the simplest and most satisfactory way of wringing her lover's bosom.[9] These women exist only in their relation to man; and, despite a feverish energy that love gives them, one feels that they could never become free women, that they are doomed to remain the slaves of passion or of memory. Only in self-sacrifice have they power, and it is not often that the beauty of self-sacrifice in woman is denied by one of the opposite sex. But it is Mr. Galsworthy's peculiar distinction that in his masculine insistence upon the beauty of self-sacrifice in women, he should understand the full cost of it to women themselves, the tragic waste of useless renunciation, the bitter loss to the world of that joy which is the crown and heritage of fulfillment, never of crucifixion.

Now, it is only by perfectly realizing this tradition of the womanly woman, it is only by completely understanding how deeply it has colored almost all that man has written about women from the wisdom of Solomon to the folly of Sir Almroth Wright, that we shall begin to grasp the profound significance of the woman's movement.[10] For what we call the woman's movement is a revolt from a pretense of being—it is at its best and worst a struggle for the libera-

8. John Galsworthy (1867–1933), known for his portrayals of British upper classes and his social satire. His early works attacked the smug conventionality and self-righteous hypocrisy of the middle class and championed the artist, rebel, and underdog. *The Dark Flower* (1913) is a novel of three loosely connected episodes whose only link is the male hero, Mark Lennan; the episodes describe his romantic attachments to four separate women.

9. From Oliver Goldsmith's (1730–74) *Vicar of Wakefield*, Chap. 24, comes the song, "When lonely woman stoops to folly"; her only recourse is to wring her lover's bosom and to die. Although Glasgow's heroines generally refuse to follow this advice, her minor characters may withdraw into their houses to become invalids. Goldsmith's song will provide the title and theme of Glasgow's 1929 novel, *They Stooped to Folly*.

10. "Wisdom of Solomon" probably refers to the "Judgment of Solomon" according to which Solomon distinguished the true mother of an infant when two harlots came before him, each claiming the baby was her own; he threatened to slice the baby in half, and the true mother begged to save its life. Sir Almroth Wright

tion of personality. After centuries of silence or of idle chatter on the part of women about their own natures, there has come, within the present decade, a rather startling burst of world confidences. Women novelists are still content, with some honorable exceptions, to copy the models as well as the methods of men, but in the brilliant and fearless books of Ellen Kay, of Rosa Mayreder, of Olive Schreiner, of C. Gasquoine Hartley (Mrs. Walter Gallichan), woman has become at last not only human, but articulate.[11] Mrs. Gallichan's "The Truth About Woman" is an honest and courageous attempt to view woman, not through man's colored spectacles of tradition and sentiment, but by the clear, searching light of reality. It is not a book for babes, nor, for the matter of that, is it a book for octogenarians, unless they have abandoned most of the opinions held by the octogenarians of my acquaintance. She destroys much that the world has long valued, and particularly does she destroy the image worship of the womanly woman of fiction. One may not always agree with her conclusions, but she has admirably succeeded in freeing herself from sex prejudices and superstitions, and she brings to the familiar facts of biology and history an entirely fresh point of view and a remarkable keenness of insight in preaching the gospel of freedom to women; however, it is well to remember—and it is not fair to imply that Mrs. Gallichan wholly forgets this—that the best use man has made of his liberty in the past has been to place re-

---

(1861–1947) was an English pathologist who discovered a method of inoculation for typhoid used during World War I. He was vigorously antifeminist and wrote letters to the press and a book, *The Unexpurgated Case Against Woman Suffrage* (1913), to show that women were biologically and psychologically inferior, a work that brought forth a devastating response from George Bernard Shaw (1856–1950). Shaw nonetheless admired Wright and his writings and modeled the leading character of *The Doctor's Dilemma* (1906) upon him.

11.   Rosa (Obermayer) Mayreder (b. 1858), an Austrian painter, wrote *Survey of the Woman Problem*, a shocking argument, at the time, against the force of custom in hindering the development of independence and personality in women. The book originally appeared in German as *Zur Kritik der Weillichkirt* (1907). Olive Schreiner (1855–1920), from Cape Colony, came to England in 1881, and, under the pseudonym "Ralph Iron," published *The Story of an African Farm* (1883) and *Women and Labour* (1911). C. Gasquoine Hartley (also Mrs. Arthur D. Lewis [b. 1866]) wrote many travel books and books on issues of concern to women. *The Truth About Woman* appeared in 1913. Her husband, Walter M. Gallichan (1861–1946), wrote books on travel, sports, conduct, psychology, diet, and hygiene. Ellen Kay has not been identified, but Ellen Key (1849–1926) was a Swedish feminist, called "the Pallas of Sweden"; she was the author of sociological, literary, and historical works on the feminist movement, child welfare, and related topics.

strictions upon it. For love, which would be so easy a solution of life's problems if it existed as a pure essence, may become sometimes, through its strange interminglings, as morally destructive as hatred.[12]

But Mrs. Gallichan writes with conviction, fairness, and sincerity, and she appears splendidly above that feminine priggishness, the irritating assumption of woman's moral superiority to man, which to the present writer at least sounds out of place, though not without humor, on a woman's lips. For virtue, after all, is not biological, but spiritual, and is of an infinite complexity—yet there are modern crusaders who seem to have forgotten that the Wisdom that forgave the thief and the Magdalen had only scorn for the Pharisee and drove the money changers out of the temple.[13] So it is a pleasant change to find that Mrs. Gallichan rejects the popular doctrine of man's natural grossness as fearlessly as she denies the other sanctified fallacy of "woman's consecration to suffering." Of the one, she says wisely: "We women are so easily deceived by the outside appearances of things. The man who calls a spade a spade is not really inferior to him who calls it 'an agricultural implement for the tilling of the soil,'" and of the other: "The female half of life has not been pre-ordained to suffer any more than the male half; this belief has done more to destroy the conscience of woman than any other single error. You have only to repeat any lie long enough to convince even yourself of its truth. But assuredly free woman will have to yield up her martyr's crown."

And it is just here, in this yielding up of the crown of the martyr and the manner of the Pharisee, that Mrs. Gallichan seems to make her greatest contribution to her subject. There is a song of joy in her pages—a song so different from the many mournful hymns with which men have celebrated the fact of sex, that one is tempted to ask if, after all, the sorrows of woman have existed chiefly in the imagination of men. She rejoices in womanhood, but it is a woman-

12. This would be the theme of Glasgow's *Barren Ground* (1925), in which abused love fuels Dorinda Oakley's lifelong project of revenge.
13. "Wisdom" refers to the merciful actions of Christ when he forgave the thief who begged forgiveness from his cross at Calvary, and when he accepted and welcomed Mary Magdalene, the prostitute, into his community of followers. He chastised the Pharisees, who allowed the temple to become a marketplace rather than a solemn house of instruction and worship.

hood so free, so active, so conquering, that the word takes a new meaning from her interpretation, and she strikes her deepest note when she adds: "that from which woman must be freed is herself—the unsocial self that has been created by a restricted environment. * * * Woman is what she is because she has lived as she has. And no estimate of her character, no effort to fix the limit of her activities, can carry weight that ignores the totally different relations toward society that have artificially grown up, dividing so sharply the life of woman from that of man."

In the three main divisions of her book—the Biological Section, the Historical Section, and the Modern Section—Mrs. Gallichan discusses at length, and with a personal enthusiasm that makes it very interesting reading, the evolution of the woman's part in nature as the guardian of the life force, and therefore as "the predominant and responsible partner in the relations of the sexes." The ancient social dominance of woman in the mother-age, the transition from this to the inferiority and dependence of the mother during the father-age, and the present unstable efforts of the sexes toward a balance of power—all these periods of bondage or of liberty she regards merely as nature's provisions for the better care of the race. In contrast with much that man has written about woman—in contrast with the intolerant bitterness of Weininger, of Nietzsche, of Schopenhauer—there is a large, calm justice in her criticism of this man's world in which we are living.[14] To her clear vision man appears, not as a conscious tyrant, but, equally with woman, as a victim to the conditions of social evolution. Beneath the historic fact of man's dominance, she discerns the invincible purpose of nature without which man's efforts to dominate would have been as useless as a child's cries for the moon. If the balance of power passed from the matriarch to the patriarch, this was possible only because the growing race needed to cradle itself in the father-age before it could gather its strength. Not male tyranny, but the selective agency of life decided the issue. While the race needed woman's subjection, she was condemned to remain subject; when it needs her freedom, she

14. Called the "sex philosopher," Otto Weininger (1880–1903) argued that sex is a fundamental attribute of living things, even protoplasm. Friedrich Wilhelm Nietzsche (1844–1900) and Arthur Schopenhauer (1788–1860) were revolutionary German thinkers who helped create the modern sensibility.

is inevitably ordained to become free. It is as useless for men to fight progress as it is for women to fight men—"For to go on with man, not to get from man, this is the goal of woman's freedom. Just in measure as the sexes fall away from love and understanding of each other do they fall away from life into the futility of personal ends." In the harmonious adjustment of the future she sees:

"Neither mother-right alone, nor father-right alone, can satisfy the new ideals of the true relationship of the sexes. The spiritual force, slowly unfolding, that has uplifted, and is still uplifting, womanhood, is the foundation of woman's claim that the further progress of humanity is bound up with her restoration to a position of freedom and human equality. But this position she must not take from man—that, indeed, would be a step backward. No, she is to share it with him, and this, for her own sake and for his, and more than all, for the sake of their children and all the children of the race. This replacement of the mother side by side with the father in the home and in the larger home of the State is the true work of the Woman's Movement."

But where this very modern interpretation diverges most widely from the traditional ideal of the sexes is in the writer's rejection of the belief in woman's natural passivity, and by this single point, small as it may appear to some thinkers, will probably be decided the future success or failure of the movement we know as Feminism. If, as man has so confidently asserted in the past, woman exists, not as an active agent of life, but merely as the passive guardian of the life force, then, indeed, is her revolt doomed to fail and her struggle to bear fruit in her sorrow. If her fight is a fight against law, if it is nature's purpose that woman shall sit and watch, then, as surely as night follows day, she will continue to sit and watch until the end of time. To Mrs. Gallichan, of course, as to all feminists, this apparent passivity is not inherent, but acquired, and is obliged, therefore, to disappear in the higher development of the race. By an appeal to history, indeed, she shows how often it has vanished in the past when it ceased to be one of the necessary conditions of woman's relation to man. "Woman," she repeats, "is what she is because she has lived as she has." It is foolish to talk of a revolt against nature as if, by taking thought, one could change the principle of one's being; and it is not without deep significance that woman's long endeavor to exist artificially, instead of naturally, should result in the violent reaction of the present. For this hunger for freedom that is driving women to-day into strange countries, as it drove the pioneers of old across oceans to the wilderness of new continents, is bound up with the imperative striving of life.

Some Literary Woman Myths

It is the peculiar distinction of all woman myths that they were not only sanctioned but invented by man. Into their creation has entered many of the major prejudices and a few of the minor prerogatives of the male sex. For these genial myths inherit the strange masculine aversion from calling the facts of life by their right names, as well as the opposite, but by no means conflicting, preference for the indecent anecdote over the romantic adventure which makes the Colonel and Pat O'Grady blood brothers under their skins.[1]

From the slow dawn of history, women have been too much occupied with the serious business of life, with planning, contriving, scheming to outwit an adverse fortune and tilling the fertile soil of man's vanity to bother about the primitive science of mythology. But even amid the distractions of an arboreal social order, man found an opportunity, between the seasons of hunting and mating, to evolve a cosmogony that flattered his self-esteem and to moralize, with increased assurance but diminished flattery, upon the enigma of woman. The results of his cosmogony have been public property from the beginning. At an early date they secured permanent habitation in that sheltered area of the mind where superstitions reside and they have been long embodied in innumerable rubrics and rituals. Though his conclusions about women are less renowned, they have been appropriately commemorated in those fixed opinions which we persist in calling masculine ideals and fem-

This essay appeared in New York *Herald-Tribune Books*, May 27, 1928, pp. 1, 5–6. Parts were reworked and included in the preface to *They Stooped to Folly* in the Virginia Edition of her novels and in *A Certain Measure*.

1. In Rudyard Kipling's (1865–1936) poem "The Ladies," we are told that "the Colonel's Lady an' Judy O'Grady / Are sisters under their skins!" The poem appears in *The Seven Seas* (1896).

inine instincts. These also, though subject to decay from within, are equally invulnerable to time and chance, enlightenment and the Darwinian hypothesis.

In some green April dawn, soon after man first aspired to stand upright, no doubt he peered into a silver stream and decided that his appearance justified the belief that he had been created in a divine image. On the same occasion, or within a reasonable space of time, he concluded, with even better authority, that the pattern of His Maker was not so closely followed in the design of his companion. Since that memorable decision, among all the vivid fluctuations of faith and fact, masculine intelligence has clung firmly to the primal commandment, "He for God only, she for God in him."[2] Owing to the curious mind of woman, who is able to believe anything that is useful and to think anything useful that she believes, an idea, however uncomplimentary, becomes sacred to her as soon as the tentacles of her faith have fastened upon it. Much practice, indeed, has perfected her in the fine art of dissembling. For the *double entendre* is older than Mr. James Branch Cabell.[3] It is older, probably, than the famous conflict of the sexes which has been found so profitable in modern prose fiction. And woman, informed by some secret wisdom that there are four dimensions to sex but only three to sex relations, has judiciously embodied her discovery in a pragmatic philosophy. When she addressed man as "my author and disposer," it was with an air of knowing more than she told, which, by pricking the instinct of curiosity, first established her as an influence and later exalted her as a literary inspiration. As this final apotheosis is the only one that concerns us, I shall leave the ancient legends asleep in their flowery soil and hasten to approach the two superior woman myths which have exerted a benign and sinister influence over the English novel. The myth of woman as an inspiration occupied an immovable pedestal from Richardson to Mr. John Galsworthy. Not until it encountered all the sad young men and the Freudian perils of the postwar years was it overthrown and replaced by the bold modern myth of woman as an impediment. Between these two major legends a whole flock of minor myths has

2. Milton, *Paradise Lost*, IV, ll. 297–99.
3. James Branch Cabell (1879–1958), Glasgow's confidant in Richmond, became infamous for the *double entendres* in *Jurgen* (1919).

flitted as airily as the doves of Venus over the passive female principle in literature. From Richardson, who constructs a world of two solids and one ideal, to Mr. Cabell, who weaves a fabulous territory of two illusions and one impediment, masculine inclination has varied, according to the quality of mind or the habit of body, between these extreme and dominant creeds.[4]

We shall not examine deeply before we discover that the myth of woman as an inspiration has many advantages, especially for the myth maker, over the opposite myth of woman as an impediment. The cult of an inspiration has been always a remote worship. Even a feminine inspiration does not persist in getting in the way of adventure after the unfortunate habit of a feminine impediment. For an inspiration is scarcely more solid than an ideal; and an ideal, conforming to the law of atmospheric refraction, appears not only higher than it is in reality, but looms still larger and brighter in situations of danger. This popular worship has never lost, therefore, its safe and honored position in all masculine adventures, particularly when they have led into the Arctic Circle or the jungles of Africa. Moreover, it has never failed to provide a respectable and often highly chivalrous excuse for the most exciting and violent warfare. But an impediment, being on the spot, demands immediate lip-homage; and it is in the faculty of lip-homage that men have so frequently proved themselves to be inadequate as lovers. In love as in literature, they have, with the exception of a few impotent poets, preferred deeds to words. And even the poets, who are obliged to devote the greater part of their time to the exigencies of verse, have found that while an inaccessible ideal quiets the mind and assists composition, an accessible impediment is disposed to breed far too many bitter realities. After this reminder it is not difficult to understand why the myth of feminine inspiration has been the favorite influence in literature since that celebrated moment when "Beatrice upward gazed—and I on her."[5]

4. In *Jurgen*, the wife functions as an impediment to Jurgen's adventures, especially with other women. Glasgow's combination of "two illusions and one impediment" may be her own *double entendre* inasmuch as Freud identifies three as the masculine number.

5. Dante, *Paradiso*, Canto I, ll. 64–66, reads: "Beatrice stared at the eternal spheres / entranced, unmoving; and I looked away / from the sun's height to fix my eyes on hers" (John Ciardi's translation). These lines occur as Dante rises toward Heaven.

The earliest, and still the longest, commemoration of man's ideal woman in English prose fiction is the immortal "Clarissa, or the History of a Young Lady."[6] Many seasons have passed since I read these six (or were there eight?) fascinating volumes; and if life is sufficiently long I hope in some spacious latter year to repeat that thrilling adventure. No abridgment, I feel sure, can do justice to this substantial, vivid and now slightly ridiculous novel. Though Clarissa was, of course, not the first completely living woman in English fiction, she was the first completely embodied feminine influence. "Moll Flanders" and "Roxana" were both instinct with vitality; but they could scarcely be called inspiring examples.[7] For they were very far from genteel; they were not even respectable. They belonged, in fact, to that generous persuasion which men have invented with more courage than economy, in the lighter interludes of moral idealism. But the divine Clarissa, who clung as firmly to virtue as the modest Virginie to her clothes, remains, in spite of changing fashions, an extraordinary creation for any novelist.[8] Even if we admit that the picture is more remarkable as a reflection of man's sentiment than as an analysis of woman's mind, this does not impair its inestimable value as the portrait of an ideal. Only the fecund imagination of man could have created the moving scene in which Clarissa orders her coffin. After designing for the lid a broken lily, "just falling from the stalk," on a plate of white metal, she has her "palace," as she touchingly calls it, placed "near the window, like a harpsichord, and reads or writes upon it as others would upon a desk or table." This pathetic episode, which dissolved the impressionable eighteenth century into tears, is the crowning achievement

6. In Samuel Richardson's novel (1747–48), Clarissa, the ever-virtuous heroine, suffers isolation and scorn from her family, persistent harassment and imprisonment by her would-be lover, Robert Lovelace, and the ultimate destruction of her honor and purity from rape by Lovelace. She wants to die to rid herself of a life unfairly abused and misunderstood.

7. *Moll Flanders* (1722) by Daniel Defoe (1660-1731) describes the career of a woman whose desires to become a "gentlewoman" lead her to a life of whoredom, thievery, incest, adultery, imprisonment, and so on. As an old lady, she "repents" and retires to a farm in Maryland. *Roxana* (1724), also by Defoe, was often called *The Fortunate Mistress*. Like Moll, Roxana was loose in morals.

8. In *Paul et Virginie* (1787), a romance by Jacques-Henri Bernardin de St. Pierre (1737–1814), a shipwrecked Virginie refuses to remove her clothes to save her life—and so perishes.

of the most influential woman myth in the whole range of English fiction.

After so auspicious a dawn, it is needless to pursue the glorious cult which dominated the English novel until Mr. Arnold Bennett and his contemporaries introduced the drab style which we are pleased to call modernism.[9] Fielding, the greatest of the English novelists, was too robust to amuse himself with the flimsy practice of myth-making; but he was also of too warm a nature and too fond a husband not to wish to pay all possible honor to the wife of his youth. Though he still cherished the sentimental tradition, he was fortunately as rich in humor as he was in humanity. "No woman," remarks a character in "Amelia," "can be truly genteel who is not entirely flat before"; but Amelia herself is as round, as ample, as smooth in texture and as radiant in color as the "Flora" of Titian. She remains, in spite of the web of sentimentality that enmeshes her, one of the most adorable women in English fiction. Compared to her the Amelia of Thackeray is as flat and stale as a pressed flower. Indeed, the literary myth of woman as inspiration attains its apotheosis in Thackeray and Dickens. Amelia praying for George and Agnes Wickfield with "her solemn hand upraised toward Heaven," these are the eternal symbols of a triumph of faith over fact in the masculine mind.[10] Fallen from its high estate, damaged by time and chance, and debased by ignoble adversity, this once supreme cult lingered on as a popular superstition until, at the end of the World War, the inferior myth of woman as an impediment was born of an irregular union between democracy and disenchantment.

Many masculine ideals have flourished and faded in the novel since Clarissa, hopeless of inspiring Lovelace to better things, se-

9. Arnold Bennett (1867–1931) wrote naturalistic novels of characters who were the creatures of their environment. His best work is distinguished by his rendering of the passage of time, his accurate descriptions of ordinary, apparently quite dull and unromantic lives, and his sympathetic portrayal of women. His "naturalistic" contemporaries Glasgow refers to are probably H. G. Wells (1866–1946) and John Galsworthy (1867–1933). Glasgow visited Bennett during her 1914 English tour, which included friendly meetings with Thomas Hardy, John Galsworthy, Joseph Conrad, and Henry James.

10. Thackeray's Amelia is probably modeled after the virtuous Amelia of Fielding. Thackeray considered Fielding's Amelia "the most charming character in English fiction." George and Agnes Wickfield are from Dickens' *David Copperfield*.

lected a broken lily as the emblem of her moral career.[11] Unhappily the world is not what it once was; nor is the novel of manners; nor, for that matter, is an ennobling influence. If women are less devoted than they used to be, it is true, also, that they die less easily, even in fiction. Masculine fervor and feminine inspiration have both declined since the hero of "Children of the Abbey" exclaimed with rapture: "Estimable Amanda! I esteem, I venerate your virtue!"[12] After Jane Austen, that delicate iconoclast, the romantic tradition was slowly blighted by drought and the literary portrayal of sex was no longer restricted to the conventional pose of man the inspired, and woman the inspiration. More and more the years since the war are becoming the dark of the moon for a number of exalted illusions. Many feminine students and admirers of the male sex must have noticed with concern an increasing reluctance on the part of heroes to dispose their limbs in the classic posture of chivalry. It is at least open to question if woman would ever have grown stiff in her confining attitude had she not observed a diminishing humility in the novels written by men. But, after the war, masculine disillusionment with romance, which had been thickening like dust for a number of years, invaded the whole flattened territory of modern prose fiction. By some obstinate "reversals of the situation," woman, for so long the ideal of man, became in a literary sense the impediment to all his higher activities. In most modern American novels, since it is easier to employ the philosophy than the art of Mr. Cabell, woman, the impediment, stands between almost every male character and some bright particular moon for which he is crying. The credulous American public, fondly imagining that the sad young men, especially if they had lived in Paris and tasted absinthe, have discovered all there is to learn about vice, swallow the newest honey-coated complex as meekly as the serried rows of blameless ladies in woman's clubs submit to the disrespectful berating of Mr. Louis Bromfield.[13] For science, which has chained the lightning and

11. After her honor has been destroyed by Lovelace
12. In *Children of the Abbey* (1798) by Regina Maria Roche (1764?–1845), the heroine, Amanda Fitzalan, is another virtuous eighteenth-century woman in the mold of Richardson's Clarissa; the speaker of the quote is her lover, Lord Mortimer.
13. Louis Bromfield (1896–1956), an American novelist, spent much of his life in Paris. He is most famous for his series of four novels, *A Good Woman*, *The Green Bay Tree*, *Possession*, and *Early Autumn*, all dealing with American life.

demolished the superwoman, has made little impression upon our simple faith in authority from afar. The only difference appears to be that while in the past we revered authority because it was hoary with age, to-day we respect only that wisdom which is downy with juvenescence.

To return to the most distinguished, if not the most youthful, of our myth makers, Mr. James Branch Cabell is fond of repeating in his agreeable style that the desire for unattainable perfection is a masculine prerogative. When we read his books, and especially his latest one, which tells us something about Eve but more about Adam, we are almost persuaded that to pursue the infinite and attain the finite has been the disillusioning career of man alone.[14] From Mr. Cabell's deceptive allegory (in which he proves with wit and learning that he knows but one kind of woman and knows that one kind of woman wrong) there emerges man, the poet and the dreamer, in perpetual flight from woman, the devourer of dreams and poets. And it is not Mr. Cabell alone who resigns his heroes to this romantic predicament. For these masculine authorities all unite upon the modest axiom that while man desires more than woman, woman desires only more of man. This is a theory so well established in contemporary fiction that, as far as I am aware, no man and few women have ever felt inclined to dispute it. Yet, like some other firmly established beliefs, it is, perhaps, more vulnerable to attack than a casual observation would lead one to suppose. For the capacity to pine for what is not is a weakness or a privilege that is independent of sex and not, as Mr. Cabell would delude us into believing, an inalienable faculty of the masculine mind. If man has dreamed of Helen and embraced Penelope, woman, condemned to an even more prosaic lot, has sighed for fleet-footed Achilles while she was embraced by Odysseus.

But Gerald Musgrave is not the first Southern gentleman who, having stayed to answer a woman according to her folly, in the end fled to regret it. Though, as Mr. Cabell sagely remarks, no lady is ever a gentleman, it must be admitted that the Southern gentleman,

14. In Cabell's *Something About Eve* (1927), Gerald Musgrave finds his way to the fabulous city of Antan impeded by the state known as domestic bliss. *Something About Eve* bears the dedication "To ELLEN GLASGOW—very naturally—this book which commemorates the intelligence of women."

in "Something About Eve," is not infrequently a lady. Nevertheless, like other aspiring males in similar embarrassing situations, he applies to his stinging vanity that natural panacea of masculine disappointment, a general maxim, and reflects consolingly that women do vary in their given names. Probably it is human to cherish a deep-rooted distaste for the feeling that we have missed the best which our unfavorable planet can bestow. The abyss between the ideal and the actual has swallowed up too many of our rainbow bridges to the stars and left floating in the void merely a fragment of our shattered illusions. To solace one's self with the reflection that men are different, but that women are all made after a single pattern, is less arduous, no doubt, than pursuing the end of the rainbow, or even than weaving withered fig leaves into a garland. For what Mr. Cabell actually proves is that Gerald Musgrave, in common with all his ancestors and his descendants of the same sex, inherited the lion's share of that "insane and magnificent" code invented by the chivalrous gentry of Lichfield.[15] Even God and the prayer book of the Protestant Episcopal Church were ways of escape for him.

But woman as an impediment to the higher life has not confined her activities, as far as the English novel is concerned, to the destruction of masculine dreams. Nowhere has she exerted a more fatal influence than in the practical business of getting on in the world and making a living. Never, at least in fiction, has she impeded so successfully as in her latest literary aspect of nymphomaniac. Since Mr. Michael Arlen introduced Iris Storm into the best social circles, almost every novel by a very young and very serious man novelist has been enlivened or depressed, according to the point of view, by one or more of these unfortunates.[16] It is true that this malady was not entirely unknown to English fiction before Mr. Arlen arrived, but I cannot recall that any of these earlier victims of repression had ever moved in so glittering a world. Though Mr. Lawrence had dealt with nymphomaniacs in detail, he had filled so

15. Where Gerald Musgrave lives in *Something About Eve*; it is the setting of various works by Cabell.
16. Michael Arlen (1895–1956), American-born English author, is best known for his popular novel *The Green Hat* (1924), whose heroine, Iris Storm, lived in a fast, glittering world but ultimately committed suicide.

many of his books with them that, while exciting enough in the beginning, they had ceased before he finished to be to us exactly a treat.[17] Miss May Sinclair, too, had turned her piercing glance in that direction, but in her restrained novels the inevitable end of the nymphomaniac was the asylum, where she did dreadful things, such as taking her clothes off in public or plucking the feathers from canary birds.[18] Miss Sinclair's pictures were horrible, but it was the horror of tragedy; and sex in her world was innocent of the sardonic spirit which animates Mr. Cabell's symbol of the devouring female principle in nature. Until Mr. Arlen's Iris Storm and Mr. Hemingway's Lady Ashley,[19] who is merely Iris Storm with a title for decoration, I can recall no nymphomaniac in fiction who moves freely about the world and impedes to her heart's desire man's exclusive right to the pursuit of liberty and happiness. Amusing as many of these intemperate ladies are in recent novels, one begins to realize presently that most of them are merely inquisitive little boys trying to be outrageous in their elder sister's clothes. They know how to strut, but they have never learned to walk or to think as a woman. When they grow up and have had, perhaps, a thorough course, not a superficial dash, of psychology with their authors and Havelock Ellis, they may, one and all, discover that they still have something to learn about women.[20] In the mean time Mr. Hemingway, who writes more neatly than Mr. Arlen and leaves less silver polish to rub off, continues to pare down human nature to two pronouns and one instinct. Even when he writes about men without women, his art has too little flesh on its sex.

And so it appears that, if the myth of woman as an inspiration has already vanished, there is abundant vitality for several literary

---

17.   D. H. Lawrence (1885–1930) dealt frankly with sex in many of his novels, including *Sons and Lovers* (1913), *The Rainbow* (1915), and *Women in Love* (1921), as well as *Lady Chatterley's Lover* (1928).

18.   May Sinclair (1865–1946) wrote her best books as technical experiments based on the new Freudian psychology. The nymphomaniac referred to may be Maggie in *The Allinghams* (1927), who, feeling that "love is a lust like that of a starving animal," eventually goes violently insane.

19.   Major female character in *The Sun Also Rises* (1926) by Ernest Hemingway (1899–1961)

20.   Havelock Ellis (1859–1939), English psychologist, essayist, and art critic, is best known for his pioneering and, at the time, scandalous *Studies in the Psychology of Sex* (7 vols., 1897–1928).

movements left in the companion myth of woman as an impediment. Until yet another reversal occurs in the oldest and most interesting of situations, we may cheerfully assume that an obstacle rather than an ideal will be the arresting feature of our novels.

II. *Southern Arts and Politics*

The Dynamic Past

ecause I am a Virginian in every drop of my blood and pulse of my heart, I may speak the truth as I understand it—realizing, as Thoreau has said in what Stevenson calls the noblest passage in any modern author, that, "It takes two to speak truth—one to speak and another to hear."[1] At least the faults I deplore are my own faults, just as I hope the peculiar virtues of Virginians are my own also. To know thyself, said the Greeks, is the beginning of wisdom.

Since so much has been said and sung in praise of the cavalier, I should like to speak a few modest words in favour of the frugal virtues of the Pilgrim Fathers. I have the very highest regard for the Fathers. I respect and admire them for much that they did, and for much also that they did not do. I wish to detract from none of their industrious efforts to compose the kind of past that they would like to have had; and I realize with proper humility that, since "nothing," as someone shrewdly observed, "succeeds like excess," they have accomplished far more than our comparatively indolent ancestors. When the thrifty Pilgrims needed a past, they not only applied themselves to improving their own; they peacefully assimilated the heritage of their neighbors. While we allow our own relics to crumble about us, we have taught our children that the beginning of American history was at Plymouth Rock, and that the earlier settlers at Jamestown were merely a band of adventurous pleasure-seekers, animated not by godly disputes in theology, but by a profane love of travel.[2]

No, our cavalier may be an ornament to romantic fiction and the Episcopal Church, but when it comes to the simple business of re-

This essay was an address Glasgow first gave in Richmond and then published in *Reviewer*, I (March 15, 1921), 73–80.

1. Quote from "Wednesday" in Henry David Thoreau's (1817–62) *A Week on the Concord and Merrimack Rivers* (1849); Robert Louis Stevenson (1850–94), Scottish author

2. Jamestown in Virginia was settled in 1607, Plymouth in Massachusetts in 1620. Jamestown's first representative government, the House of Burgesses, was created in 1619. Oscar Wilde is credited with the quip about excess succeeding.

forming truth, he is no match for the Puritan in the plain pine pulpit. If there had been a single Pilgrim in that gallant band of adventurers who were deluded enough to believe that the sword was mightier than the sermon, what an enviable place we might occupy in the nation today! For in spite of Mr. Drinkwater's observation that "Religious quarrels cut no ice tomorrow morning," the record of the Pilgrim Fathers proves, I think, that, even though religious quarrels "cut no ice," they sometimes swell into a veritable Niagara of history.[3] With our past attached to the indomitable determination of the Puritan theology, we might dare to assert, in spite of the bulky literature of New England, that this country was founded, and representative government established, before there was any spot on the American continent known to eulogy and piety as Plymouth Rock.

But I am here to speak of the future, not of the past. I am here to speak of a future that must be glorious indeed if it is to prove worthy of the soil from which it springs. No Virginian can love and revere the past more than I do. No Virginian can find greater inspiration in the lesson that it teaches. To me Virginia's past is like a hall hung with rare and wonderful tapestries, or perhaps it would be truer to say that it is like a cathedral illumined by the gold and wine-colour of stained glass windows. It is a place to which we should go for inspiration and worship; it is a place from which we should come with renewed strength and courage; but it is not a place in which we should live and brood until we become like that ancient people whose "strength was to sit still."

This thought came to me again last April, when I stood at Jamestown, and looked out over the beautiful grave river, and felt the mystery and the darkness that surrounded those dauntless pioneers. The Old World, the unfriendly seas, the work of yesterday, lay behind them. Straight ahead was the virgin wilderness, the promise of things to come, the Great Perhaps of tomorrow. That was a sublime moment in history, and like all sublime moments, either in history or in the personal lives of men and women, it is immortal not because it repeated or reflected an act of the past, but be-

---

3. John Drinkwater (1882–1937), English dramatist, poet, and biographer. His historical plays (*e.g., Abraham Lincoln,* 1918; *Robert E. Lee,* 1923) contributed to the revival of drama in England after World War I.

cause it expressed the supreme purpose of the future. For the glory of men as of nations is measured not by the strength with which they cling to the past, but by the courage with which they adventure into the future. Genius is more than the patience that Goethe once called it—for the soul of it is courage. It means a departure from tribal forms and images. It means a creation of new standards and new ideals of beauty and new rules of conduct. It means a fresh vision of familiar things. It speaks a strange language. It is always a wanderer, and very often an outcast from the caves or the tents of the tribe. The first man who said to himself, "I will no longer carry on the torch of the tribe. I will make fire when I need light and heat"—was the first genius on earth. For it is well to remind ourselves that in movement alone is there life—that the only permanent law of our nature is the law of change. The way to new worlds lies beneath alien stars over uncharted seas. The past, however splendid, must be the fruitful soil in which the seeds of the future are planted; it must not be the grave in which the hope of the race lies buried. It is tomorrow, not yesterday, that needs us most.

If we stop and look back a moment we shall see that the heroic figures in our own race are the figures of men who, one and all, broke away from tradition when tradition endangered natural development, who, one and all, spoke in terms of the future, who, one and all, recognized the law of progress as superior to the rules of precedent. Of all the men whom we revere most, there is not one whom we revere simply because he held fast by the old habit, the old form, the old custom. There is not one whom we revere because his "strength was to sit still." There is not one who did not when the choice came to him step boldly forward into the undiscovered continent of the future. "They were behind us then," Macaulay said of the English Reformers, "but the question is not where they were, but which way they were going."[4] And of each of the great Virginians it may be said that he was going onward, not backward.

If Washington had placed tradition above freedom there would have been no Revolution. A Tory once wrote to him, enumerating the sacrifices he was making for what seemed then a forlorn hope.

4. Thomas Babington Macaulay (1800–59) in his essay "Sir James Mackintosh" (1835)

He was breaking with almost all that he had once held in veneration—with the secure and established order of society, with his country, his King, his traditions, and, as some thought, with even his plighted word of honour. "You are the Revolution," said this writer, "and if you stop the Revolution will be ended." Yet Washington did not stop, did not turn, did not look back. He went onward, the great Revolutionist, into the future.

And with Jefferson? Today we hear much in Virginia of the Jeffersonian principles—and those who tell us that we are forsaking them appear to forget that the two fundamental principles of Jefferson were first freedom of conscience, and secondly freedom of speech. Yet there are those among us today—there have been such among us for generations—who would suppress freedom of thought and speech in the name of the greatest progressive statesman of his age. The Jefferson who gave us religious freedom, who supported the French Revolution when that Revolution was condemned in America, who sought to embody in the Declaration of Independence a flaming attack on the slave trade—this Jefferson, who in 1784, almost one hundred years ahead of his time, proclaimed the principle upon which Abraham Lincoln was elected to the Presidency—the name of this very Jefferson has been used as an anchor to keep us moored for generations in the backwaters of history.[5]

And the last and greatest of our Revolutionists—the beloved leader. If Lee had clung to tradition, to crumbling theories of right, would he have left the old army and the old standards, and have passed on into the new army to fight under the new flag?[6] Like Columbus, like Washington, like all the great leaders of history, he spoke the language of the future—he marched onward, not backward.

What I am trying to make clear to you is simply this—that we can make a great future—a future worthy of Virginia's history, not by copying the past, but by lighting again and again our fresh torches by the flame of the old. The gestures of our great men were gestures

5. Jefferson's attack on the role of the Crown in the slave trade was unacceptable to the southern delegates at the Continental Congress and was stricken from the document. His Ordinance of 1784 would have admitted the western territories into the Union on terms equal to those of the older states.

6. Robert E. Lee (1807–70) was originally a commander for the Union army. Although Lincoln offered him the field command, his love for his native state caused him to resign his commission in April, 1861, and to assume command of the military and naval forces of Virginia.

that led onward, never that beckoned backward. The inspiration of the past should be an active, not a passive force—the motive power of new dreams and new hopes. "For each age," wrote a great and almost forgotten poet, "is a dream that is dying, or one that is coming to birth."[7]

When Virginia was noblest, she was freest. She was creating, not copying. The supreme acts of her history are not acts of surrender to tradition, but of defiance of tradition. For Truth, which is the greatest of hunters, was ever a poor quarry. Not in caves and in hidden places, not in withered husks of political theories, but in the clear sunlight of courage and wisdom, lie our vision, our hope, and our prophecy. The world moves and we must move with it, either with spontaneous energy or as dust flying after the wheels of its chariot.

Of one thing we may be sure. We can take our right place in the present and the future—a place worthy of our past—only by making some fresh, some ever-green contribution to the periods in which we live. When we hitch our wagon to a star we must choose a living star, not a dead one. We must have something to give besides proverbs. Our strength must be the strength for marching, not for sitting still.

I have spoken of the onward spirit, but I wish, before I finish, to emphasize our need of correct standards of art and life—standards of our own—not those we have copied from others. As a nation, we have lived for centuries under borrowed standards. We speak proudly of our past, and yet do we really appreciate it until some stranger—it matters not how ignorant he may be—pays it a passing compliment? We write in our papers that Patrick Henry has been honoured by the admission to some Hall of Fame—as if any Hall of Fame could contribute the shadow of an honour to Patrick Henry! We fret and pine because the name of Lee is excluded from some record or some building—as if the fame of Lee were not as far as the sun above any candle that Congress could light! The only Hall of Fame that could contain the memory of Lee is the imperishable collective soul of the world.

Yet in great ways and small is this not true of us? If we have an art-

---

7. Quote from *Ode* by Arthur O'Shaughnessy (1844–81)

ist among us, do we not pass him by in silence until some wayfaring man or woman stops and points and asks a question? Do we ever dare to praise our own until some foreign country has first acclaimed him? Are we really afraid of own glory until we catch it in reflected light?

There are few places in the world richer in color and inspiration than our own South—yet because of the stagnant air, the absence of critical values, the flaunting of borrowed flags, the facile cult of the cheap and showy, art has languished among us. The native artist has been smothered for want of freedom and space and light. Original creative genius is a delicate blossom; it is like one of the early wild-flowers which we plough under in order to clear the ground for something big and showy that we can recognize at a distance.

True greatness either in life or in art is serenely confident of itself; yet we are capable of working ourselves into a nervous flutter before the lowest average of European or especially of British culture. We are never so complacent as when some foreign critic pats us on the back and stoops to assure us that we may become something some day if we will only imitate successfully the gestures of the Old World.

Over and over again they have come to lecture and stayed to laugh; but this would not matter if we paid homage only to true greatness and authentic genius. It is worth while to be ridiculed by a Dickens—especially worth while when the point of offense in his ridicule is its truth. The complaint I make is not that they laugh at us—I can forgive anybody for possessing a sense of humor—what I cannot forgive is that we allow ourselves to be lectured, instructed, harangued, and admonished by the sham and the inferior. Anybody may patronize us, provided only that his name is shouted first through a megaphone and that he comes from a distance.[8]

Beneath it all, of course, beneath this national attitude of childlike credulity, is the fundamental lack of critical values, of a true sense of proportion in matters of art. Before we can erect standards of our own we must first clear away the rubbish heap of old patterns, of empty moulds, and ink-spattered copybooks. Whether or not we

8. As H. L. Mencken (1880–1956) had ridiculed southern culture in his important article "The Sahara of the Bozart" (1917)

shall ever succeed in democratizing our industries, we have certainly achieved the most perfect democratization of our art. When we build a memorial our first step is to appoint a committee of politicians—in order that we may offend against no political prejudices and against all artistic standards. We have applied for fifty years or so the convenient American theory that anybody with two eyes in his head can tell whether a statue looks like a man—or a horse. Then, after we have enjoyed for a generation the amiable habit of sublimating the second best and turning every politician into an Elijah Pogram, some casual visitor remarks that much of our architecture and some of our statues are inferior—and we gasp and look again, and wonder if he can be right.[9] We are, all of us, very much like the man in one of Miss Repplier's delightful essays, who left the Unitarian Church because "somebody told him it wasn't true."[10]

Perhaps we must have patience a little longer. Perhaps it is too soon to hope that we have really attained self-consciousness as a nation, that we have at last become articulate. It may be that the national impulses must germinate in deeper soil before they put forth and blossom into permanent forms of art and beauty. Of one thing only am I confident—and this is that we cannot separate the part from the whole, and say "this must go onward, but the rest must sit still in a tomb of the past." We cannot separate our art from our culture or our politics or our daily living. They are linked each to each, and one cannot move forward while it is dragged back by the dead weight of the other. As long as we are slaves in thought we shall be slaves in deed. As long as we are cowards in conduct, in speech, in politics, we shall be cowards in literature. We shall never write great books or paint great pictures or make great statues until we are free—for the soul of genius, as I said a little while ago, is courage—and freedom is the air that it breathes. It is all one—in art, in statesmanship, in science, in life, in thought, in speech—there can be no supreme achievement, no permanent contribution, that has not sprung from courage and developed in freedom—that has not *"dared again, and dared again, and always dared."* Here in Vir-

9. The Hon. Elijah Pogram, a bombastic politician in Dickens' *Martin Chuzzlewit* (1843)
10. Agnes Repplier (1858–1950), American essayist born in Philadelphia

ginia we need liberation not from the past, but from the old moorings which have held the past and ourselves anchored in stagnant waters. The spirit of the past, I repeat, is not a dead, but a living spirit. It is not static, but dynamic. It is the spirit that led onward over the empty husks of discarded theories to a new day. That spirit, when it speaks to us demands of us freedom, courage and an open mind. It demands of us freedom to search for the truth; courage to speak the truth when it is found, and the open mind that receives truth when it is spoken.

This was Virginia's priceless heritage, and this will be Virginia's salvation in that day of small things which is now upon us. We can be as great as we were in the past only when we open the floodgates of thought, and the river of the past flows through us and from us onward into the future. For the past and the present and the future are the same endless stream, and with all our efforts we can merely change the course a little—we can never break the eternal continuity of the race.

And, therefore, we preserve the past more perfectly when its rhythm in our hearts and minds inspires us to action, not when we stand and gaze backward. We are most like Washington, not when we droop in chains of tradition, but when we stride fearlessly toward the future. We are most like Jefferson, not when we repeat parrot-like the principles he enunciated, but when we apply these great principles to ever changing conditions. We are most like Lee, not when we hesitate and hold back, but when we leave the haven of the past, and go onward with that courage which

> Neither shape of danger can dismay,
> Nor thought of tender happiness betray.[11]

11. William Wordsworth (1770–1850), "Character of the Happy Warrior," ll. 72–73

"My Fellow Virginians"

Love of Virginia is the special privilege of no group or party. It is the inalienable right of every Virginian; and since I am a

The manuscript of this speech bears a note by William W. Kelly and another by Jonathan Hildreth suggesting it was written between August and November, 1921. Kelly's

Virginian in every drop of my blood and pulse of my heart, I shall speak to you, not as the exponent of any doctrine, but as one who places loyalty to Virginia above the loyalty to any political creed.

My people have always been Virginians—conventional Virginians in as much as my grandfathers were all good Democrats and my grandmothers were all good housekeepers. I have felt in the past, and I am still able to sympathize with in the present, all the sentimental associations that gather in childhood around cherished familiar names. I also have been bound in ties of habit to the Democratic Party long after it had ceased to be more than the empty husk which once contained the vital Jeffersonian idea of freedom. As a little child I believed that the "publicans and sinners" of the Bible meant Virginia Republicans, and my Father used to say that one of the first sensible questions I ever asked him was, "Are there only angels and Democrats in Heaven?"

It is the confirmed habit of politicians, I am aware, to attempt to confuse the Democratic Party with the State of Virginia——an optical illusion which would probably afflict no vision except the political one![1] But, since this appears to have become the general custom of the dominant faction, I wish to say with perfect frankness in the beginning that, when I speak of public conditions in Virginia, I mean conditions for which a single political group is responsible, and I do not intend to criticize the history, habits, manners, soil, climate, or drinking-water of Virginia. I have for Virginia a deep and romantic devotion. Nothing could prove this more incontestably than the fact that, after I had lived away for a number of years, when I had the whole world before me in which to choose a home, I came back to make my home in Richmond because I preferred Virginia and the Virginia people to any place and people on the earth.[2]

---

note adds that it was never given. It exists only in manuscript. The eccentric punctuation indicates the length of the pauses Glasgow intended to make when she delivered the speech.

1. Henry W. Anderson (1870–1954), a prominent Richmond attorney, was the Republican nominee for governor in 1921. The Republicans attempted to persuade Virginians "to break the Democratic monopoly of the state government." Since July, 1917, Anderson had intermittently been Glasgow's fiancé.

2. After her dearest sister, Cary McCormack, died in 1911, Glasgow took an apartment in New York, near Central Park, and lived there, for the most part, until 1915.

I believe that much could be done by a more efficient and progressive government of the State; I believe that an active and vigorous party of the opposition would be extremely beneficial to Virginia; and I believe that, in the coming election, the Republican platform is far more constructive in its purpose than anything that the Democrats have advanced.[3] I believe these things; but I am not fighting for freedom in Virginia in order to deny to any one else the right of free thought and free speech. The last thing I would take from any one is the right to hold an opposite opinion. We have politics enough for all; we have patriotism enough for all——though it is difficult to recognize it in some of its disguises. Not having the party mind, I find it difficult to understand why politics, which has the reputation for picking strange company, should be unable to preserve even a bowing acquaintance with either facts or good manners. The ignoble practice of obscuring fundamental issues by personal abuse and drowning reasonable argument in loud shoutings of "disloyalty" has been the favorite method of arrogant majorities ever since the earliest of the demagogues of Ancient Athens——and it speaks poorly for the political imagination that it has not, in all the centuries of sound and fury, been able to invent and use a more effective weapon. I have always wondered, and I am wondering tonight if such methods do not in the end recoil on the faction that uses them. "We will grow strong by calmness and moderation," said one of the greatest of Americans. "We will grow strong by the violence and the injustice of our adversaries."

After this introduction it is not necessary for me to explain that, since I am not a candidate for any office (for which I may thank my stars!) I am in the enviable position where I may confine my remarks entirely to the promises, pledges and performances of other persons. Many speakers of both parties have bound you in chains of words—or even wisdom. The facts of the situations have been put before you so often that I shall try to leave politics to the politician and statistics to the statistician (for which you may thank *your*

3. The Republican platform for the 1921 election called for "an exclusively white Republican party in Virginia." This "lily-white" emphasis was designed to get away from the earlier association of the Republicans with bought black votes and Reconstruction. The platform also called for poll-tax repeal, election-law reform, right of labor to organize and bargain collectively, better schools and roads, and a business administration.

stars!) and speak to you about the subject that is closest to the hearts of all of us—the best interests of Virginia. I wish to talk to you frankly and earnestly about the difference between the Virginia of the past and the Virginia of the present; and I hope that from your hearts and mine (for as a great writer once remarked, "it takes two to speak truth, one to speak it and another to hear"——I hope that from your hearts and mine there may come an understanding of the way in which we can make Virginia all that she was in the past—— the richest in resources, the first in light and learning among the States, the Mother not only of Presidents but of great thinkers and of free spirits.

I do not wish to attack or belittle any political faith——least of all do I wish to attack any political faith which was that of my Father——and of his fathers before him. I am not one of those who believe that there is any intrinsic virtue in a name——or that human nature when it is labelled Republican differs even in flavour from human nature when it is labelled Democrat. There is no sanctity in a political party, no infallibility in any political doctrine. No party is always right, and few parties are always wrong——for a party is merely an instrument to express more effectively the united will of the people. The only vitality in any instrument of government must be breathed into it by the will of the people to work together for a definite end. It is only in the mind of man, so indissolubly wedded to forms and phrases, that names become sometimes mistaken for things——or even for acts—and whenever this happens widely in any country, it is inevitably followed by the gradual decay of the national life—by the deterioration of political fibre, and the desiccation of political thought. In such periods, as history shows unmistakably, an arid formalism replaces the native spontaneous impulses of the national spirit, and the Government ceases to be a republic and becomes [an] oligarchy or a bureaucracy. Then political machines, such as we have with us now, act automatically as a nominal expression of the free will of the people——but of free will and the free expression of that will there is really as little as there is under the outward form of a monarchy.

If we need an immediate illustration of this truth, we have only to turn to the political history of Virginia during the last twenty years. If the record of that period has been barren of great statesmen——it is not because there were no statesmen in Virginia, but because there has been no field in which they might grow and develop; it is because the political soil has become so impoverished and the political air so stagnant that names have passed for ideas and personalities have been mistaken for principles. In the recent campaign for the nomination of Governor neither of the two candidates—both estimable and able men, I do not doubt——were permitted to come within speaking distance of a principle——for fear, I suppose, lest they should recognize one if they saw it.[4]

But there could be no better example than this of the evil which I have tried to describe. In this lifeless atmosphere——this political cave——Virginia has been held back and dragged down by a management which has bound her in the dry moss of ancient prejudices and superstitions.[5] She, who once led, has been made to follow. She, who once held the feast for the nation, has been compelled to beg for crumbs from the national table. She, who was once the living mother of Presidents, is content that her younger sons shall become doorkeepers in the house of the Government! The Democratic party has treated her with the contempt bred of familiarity, the Republican party has treated her with the indifference of ignorance——and from both parties she has had to sue for favours instead of demanding her just rights and rewards. With her marvellous resources almost untouched——with one of the greatest harbors in the world neglected, with the largest open territory east of the Mississippi River without a railroad,——she has surrendered her prosperity to a superstition and her independence to a habit of thought——or of voting. To the Democratic Party we may charge these deplorable conditions——not because it is the Democratic Party, but because it is a party that has been too long in control. The fault lies not with the party, but with the people who have delivered the State and the management of the State into the absolute power of one group of men——or politicians. If the Republican Party had been in power for thirty years, the results could not have

---

4. Glasgow may be referring to the Democratic contest between E. Lee Trinkle and Henry St. George Tucker. The real issue of this race was between the Democratic organization's appointed candidate (Trinkle) and an independent Democrat (Tucker).

5. Glasgow probably refers to party prejudice—to blind allegiance to the Democrats; Virginia's "habit of thought——or of voting" she mentions later.

been different,——in the presence of the shrewdest "wire-puller" of the Democratic machine, it [is] well to remind ourselves, with the humility of the great English dissentor that, "there, but for the Grace of God, goes a Republican." It is human nature, and it is particularly man's nature——this is what every woman knows——not to make an effort when one can get all that one wants without making an effort. For almost thirty years the Democratic Party has had everything that it wanted, without an effort, by sitting still and simply pulling a wire——and the consequences of these effortless thirty years we are deploring today.

No, what Virginia needs is not one good party, but two better parties. What Virginia needs is the competition which is the life of politics as surely as it is the life of industry and commerce and science and art. What Virginia needs is to teach both parties and all parties that they are made by the people——and that what the people have made, they can discipline and control——and, if need be— destroy.

The lesson history teaches is a moral one——for if a little prosperity would agree with the Republican party in Virginia there can be no doubt that an accurately measured dose of adversity would be beneficial to Virginia Democracy. In this particular campaign the Republican Party in Virginia stands for the moral issues——for the right principles—simply because in the days of adversity it has learned that the fear of the people is, for a political party, the beginning of wisdom.[6] When it forgets this lesson it will deserve in its turn to be forgotten.

For remember this always——the true safety of a Republic lies not in party loyalty, but in independence of conscience. There is an old charge, often repeated, that the people never have a worse government than they deserve because they can always have any kind of government that they want——whether or not this statement was ever true in the past, it is certainly true of Virginia in the present. If we desire and demand an efficient and progressive administration of our public affairs, we shall have it—and that speedily! If we demand that able, and independent men shall represent us—— men of public spirit and courageous acts——men who are not in-

6. The party's appearance was "lily-white"; its principles (repeal of the poll tax, election-law reform) meant to destroy white supremacy.

fluenced by party places and rewards——if we demand these men we shall not only secure them, we shall discover in a little while that the whole field of our political life has changed and grown better and richer. Try it once——vote once for the best men and the right principles, not for the old names and the ancient superstitions—— and then, having voted, stand aside and watch the public miracle that will occur. I do not ask you to vote always with The Republican Party——this would mean simply a change of masters, not an improvement of conditions. I ask you to vote in this coming election with the Republican Party because in this coming election that party stands for the right principles and offers you the ablest men. After that vote always for the right principles and the best men regardless of party names——until both parties will give you an equal choice of great issues.

For almost thirty years, ever since the Democratic control has been absolute and unquestioned, no man of independent thought and speech——no man who was not the lip servant of a hard and fast organization——has dared to aspire to high office in Virginia——or, if such a man has dared, he has been disciplined and defeated. A few naturally fearless men have tried to be independent——you know their names as well as I do——and you know also, as well as I do——the punishment that has followed and found them. Independence of thought has been banished from the public life of Virginia because independence of thought is the deadliest foe of a political tyranny——as of all other tyrannies. Principles have been ignored or disregarded because the only principle that underlies a political machine is the principle of perpetuity. And how many men of independent judgment will consent to serve as party supple-jacks that jump up and down and to and fro at the pulling of an invisible wire?

But in the final argument, in the last analysis of causes the responsibility returns to us——like curses that come home to roost. We are the people, and if we are in control of one political camp the fault is ours——the fault is mine and yours——and yours——and yours. If the resources of our State are neglected and wasted the fault is ours—the fault is mine——and yours——and yours——. If the roads of Virginia are the dismay of travellers and the schools of Virginia are the disappointment of educators—the fault is ours—the fault is mine and yours——and yours. The fault is yours and mine; the duty is yours and mine; the responsibility is yours and mine. The fault is yours and mine because we have made no effort to free ourselves from a tyranny of office-holders——because, in the manner of Brer Terrapin in the Uncle Remus stories we merely have "lounged around and suffered."[7] And we have made no effort to become free because we have been in fear of a name——in fear of our own imagination. If we could only realize that what we have been afraid of all along has been our own fear——that we have created a phantom and then given it a name and let it rule over us.

When I was a little child I was afraid of a number of things. I was afraid of the dark and spiders and bats and dentists and cows and men with long beards——but most of all I was afraid of the name of Mr. Mugglewuggle. Just as politicians have created for us an imaginary figure of terror, so my coloured mammy created for my wholesome discipline the awful image of Mr. Mugglewuggle. Whenever my conduct was not becoming in a perfect lady of the age of three or four, I was solemnly warned, just as politicians are warning us today, that if I "didn't look out and behave," Mr. Mugglewuggle would "pop up and get me yet."

Now for the last twenty or thirty years, the race question has been the Mr. Mugglewuggle of Virginia politics. Whenever we have grown restive under the absolute ruler of the Democratic Party we have been solemnly assured that "if we didn't look out and behave" and vote the Democratic ticket, the race question would "pop up and get us yet." And just as the happiest day of my infancy was the one on which I discovered that the terrible Mr. Mugglewuggle was but a name,——and that a name couldn't in any circumstance "get me"——so the happiest day politically in Virginia will be the one on which we realize that the race question is nothing more than the nursery bogey of an office holding majority. That a small and ineffectual minority such as the negro race in Virginia——without education, without experience in government, without property, and without influence of any sort, should constitute a serious menace to the established rule of the white people——is a proposition that could be advanced only by the Demo-

7. By Joel Chandler Harris (1848–1908); they first appeared in book form in 1880.

cratic Party in Virginia or to Alice in Wonderland.[8] "If you'll draw a long breath, and shut your eyes, you can believe anything," said the White Queen to Alice, and she sounds suspiciously like the Democratic Party in masquerade, "Why, sometimes I've believed as many as six impossible things before breakfast."

But the race question has been for so long the last refuge of aspiring politicians that now, since they have lost even the shadow of it, we may expect to find them resurrecting the dead bones of some other defunct superstition——or taking their stand behind that other scarecrow of the politically feeble minded——religious intolerance.

Today there is but one issue before the voters of Virginia——and that issue is the best and wisest administration of the affairs of the State. It is the duty of every Virginian——it is your duty and mine——to demand and obtain the best and wisest——the most efficient and economical management of the government of Virginia. It is the duty of every Virginian——it is your duty and mine——to vote with the party that pledges us the best, wisest, most efficient and economical management. There rests upon every voter a moral obligation to vote with the party which is right today——not with the party which was right yesterday——or may be right again tomorrow. For it is only by being right in the present that we can be sure of being right in the past and the future. And no party will be deserving of our support until it has learned that the people's motto is not "my party right or wrong," but "my party is the party that is right."

8. The poll-tax repeal and election-law reform proposed in Anderson's platform were promptly denounced by Democrats, who advanced the argument that such changes would greatly increase the black vote. Glasgow here is attacking the Democratic use of an improbable black rule as a fear tactic to split coalitions of blacks and whites with similar social needs. In the 1890s, conservative Democrats had used the same fear to destroy the Populist coalition, in which Glasgow had also taken a personal interest. In 1928, according to Donald J. Lisio's *Hoover, Blacks, and Lily-Whites* (1985), Anderson would persuade then candidate Herbert Hoover to de-emphasize race as a political factor, displace the Democrats who supported white supremacy, and, at the same time and unlike the Democrats, refuse to restrict black voting or to interfere with rights of blacks under the Constitution. His goal was to force Democrats to throw out their corrupt leaders and to campaign on real issues rather than racial fears and stereotypes. Anderson's strategy, however, required public silence regarding good intentions toward blacks. Lisio concludes that the Anderson approach was a "well-intentioned yet confused and compromising dream," one that backfired on Hoover.

We do not need statistics to tell us of the real conditions of the roads and the schools of Virginia. Anybody with a lead pencil and the multiplication table can make statistics, and anybody with another lead pencil and the multiplication table can refute them. What intelligent man or woman was ever converted or convinced by a column of simple numbers? "Figures never lie," remarked John Burns in the House of Commons, "but liars are sometimes good at figures."[9] And I pause here——lest there should happen to be a Democratic judge in my audience to beg you to observe that I am quoting from a speaker in the House of Commons, and that I have not called the State of Virginia or any candidate or either party—— names. For, in the words of the greatest orator of the ages, I hasten to add "they are all——all honorable men."

But we have no need of statistics, for whoever travels over the roads of Virginia bears visible testimony of their condition. There is an old song that runs,

> "Who is it travels the road so late?
> Hush, my child, 'tis the candidate!"

And if the roads were the Virginian ones, I have little doubt that the candidate is still travelling. I am not impressed by the statement that we make large appropriations for better roads when I find that, in spite of these large appropriations, the roads are no better. If the Democratic machine would devote a little of the energy it expends on the manufacture of political mud to the removal of the genuine substance, both our mental and our material avenues might be made more dignified as well as more comfortable. But, having overestimated, I suppose, the amount of mud it would take to bespatter Mr. Tucker——one of themselves, a faithful as well as a "deserving Democrat,"[10] the enterprising operators of the machine apparently decided to use the remainder, before it dried, on the Republican nominee——[11] neither one of themselves, nor a faithful and de-

9. John Burns (1858–1943), an English labor leader and Socialist, served in the House of Commons from 1892 to 1918.
10. Although Tucker ran as an independent Democrat, Trinkle beat him by 22,500 votes. In the general election, Trinkle went on to defeat Anderson by a two-to-one majority.
11. Henry W. Anderson vigorously aired important issues and put the Democrats on the defensive for their statewide apathy.

serving Democrat, but certainly a patriotic and public spirited son of Virginia.

But to return to the roads after this excursion into the underbrush, I should like to ask if those large appropriations are still hanging on the bushes by the wayside? The only difference I have been able to discover in the last five or six years in the Virginia roads is that whereas we used to ride or walk in a little pleasant shade in summer, we now are obliged to ride or walk in the sun. After every demand for good roads from the suffering public, the army of supervisors, inspired by that instinct to cut down or lop off which is peculiar to the masculine nature, appear to have attacked not the roads——but the trees. The finest roads in the world——the roads in England, in France, in Italy, and in many parts of our own country—lead through thick forests, with leafy boughs arching overhead,——yet the supervisors of our roads are evidently persuaded that the only way to build a road is to cut down a tree. "When I was in Virginia four years ago," a woman from New York said to me the other day, "almost every car bore a banner reading 'Vote for Davis and good roads.' You got your Governor, I see, but you didn't get your roads."[12]

As for our schools? Well, whoever travels about the counties of our State doesn't need statistics on education, for the unceasing complaints of indignant parents are much more instructive. Whether we stand forty-three in a list of forty-eight States, according to the latest published report, or thirty-four in a list of forty-eight States, according to the opinion of the Inspector of Public Instruction (a sincere and able man, I understand)——we still appear to stand in a place where we ought not to be. Wherever we are standing at present, it looks as if we had a long and rough road to travel before we reached the top.

As for any practical plans for the improvement of industrial and social conditions, these have come from the Republican Party alone. In all questions relating to the public welfare—to compulsory education, to mothers' pensions, to the general improvement of working conditions and the care for the needy Confederate sol-

12. Westmoreland Davis won the 1917 gubernatorial race in a unique three-candidate campaign, in which Davis took an antiprohibitionist stance; the other two candidates split the prohibitionist vote.

diers, the Republicans, not the Democrats, have taken the enlightened and progressive point of view. In its attitude toward the needy and the dependent, the Democratic Party recalls to my mind an account I read once in New York of a "banquet of prosperous exporters, who ate and drank until the small hours of the morning. Before the affair was closed," ran the account, "one of the gentlemen arose and said: 'Mr. Toastmaster, As we sat here around this table spread with the good things of life, all we could eat and all we could drink, my heart went out to the poor people of New York City, the women who have not enough clothing, the children who have not shoes to wear or books with which to go to school, and I move you, Mr. Toastmaster, that we now rise and give three cheers to the poor.'" I do not doubt that the Democratic Party will rise at any moment to give three cheers for mothers!

Just here, before I leave this subject, I should like to make acknowledgment of one great reform which has been accomplished by the administration of Governor Davis. For many years——all through my Father's life, I know——humane and enlightened Virginians worked in vain to make Virginia legislators [aware?] that the chief end of punishment is not to make more criminals, but to make fewer, not to harden, but to regenerate. In one short administration the present Governor has accomplished a reform for which many benevolent spirits have laboured in vain. A prison system that was in some respects mediaeval has been changed, I understand, into a modern institution——and for this progressive movement Governor Davis is entitled to the gratitude of all fair minded Virginians, regardless of creed or party. Yet, in spite of his genuine contribution to civilization has not Governor Davis shown an inclination to possess his own will a little too openly to please the organization to which he belongs? How long——this is both a question and a prophecy——will he be permitted to occupy a high place in the Democratic Party, which has disciplined and broken to harness far more recalcitrant spirits than he has proved himself to be?

Let us turn away from the present a moment and look back on the simple grandeur of Virginia's past. There triumphant figures move against a background of events which is like a brilliantly woven tapestry——or like the splendid pageantry of a Virginia forest in autumn. One and all these august figures were not bound, but free. One and all they looked not backward but forward. One and all they broke with tradition when the choice was between tradition and freedom. One and all they followed not a dead star, but a living one——the flaming vision of truth. Washington, Marshall, Jefferson, Henry——these were dynamic spirits, not static. These great Virginians were not content to rest on the laws and the civilization that their fathers had made. One and all they marched onward toward new worlds to conquer——toward the promise of better things—— toward the Great Perhaps of tomorrow.

And yet as majestic as these figures appear against that glowing background of the past, there is another who seems to me more sublimely heroic than any of these——one who fearlessly sacrificed the past to the future, tradition to freedom, and life to a cause which in the blind eyes of the world, was rejected. We search the pages of history in vain for another soldier whose genius can be measured with the spirit of Lee. Beside him Cromwell was a village tyrant and Napoleon a blustering braggart. Strong, temperate, serene, patient, confirmed in courtesy, without fear and without reproach, in the character of Lee alone man was near perfect and perfection loveable. However tragic the fate of the flag he followed, Lee himself was invincible. For the ultimate victory is one of the soul, and the battle of Armageddon is fought not on a plain of earth, but in the moral nature of man. It is perhaps asking too much of any country and any people that they shall rise to the standard of Lee. Most of us are for the moment—or at best for a single lifetime. Lee still lives not in time, but in eternity——not for yesterday or for today, but for that tomorrow which, like the Sabbath of the Lord, is without evening. It is asking too much of any people to expect [that they] rise to his height——yet it is not, I think, asking too much of Virginians to expect them to approach all questions and all convictions with that fair and open-minded tolerance which we derive from him as an inheritance. It is not asking too much of his people to expect them to decide public issues, not in prejudices or in passion, but with an equal and impartial judgment. If Lee could dignify and ennoble the horror of war, surely we, the heirs of his spirit, may dignify, even if we cannot ennoble the petty scramble of politics.

We may seek to lift the government of Virginia from a question of personalities and opinions to one of conviction and principle.

And remember—for this single fact animates all that I have said to you—I am not asking you to vote with any party in which you do not believe or for any cause of which you do not approve. I am asking only that you shall vote in freedom, not in mental bondage. I am asking only that you shall weigh the principles involved without prejudice and without sentimentality——and that after weighing them carefully, you shall vote as your better judgment and your conscience direct you. I hold no brief for the Republican Party. I hold no brief for any political party. The only brief I hold is for Virginia. I believe that the best interests of Virginia can be secured only by a temporary change of government——that the one way to bring back the old freedom and power of Virginia is through a proper balance of political power. The Republican Party is merely an instrument with which we can strike off the chains that have bound Virginia for thirty years or more——as the sleeping Gulliver was bound in innumerable threads by the Lilliputians.[13] For the true patriot is not the man who serves a party at the cost of Virginia; but the man who first, last and forever serves Virginia first. In the coming election, I shall vote neither as a Democrat nor as a Republican—but as a Virginian who places allegiance to Virginia and the welfare of Virginia above any other considerations.[14] I shall support the Republican platform in November, not because it is Republican, but because it is human——because it takes the human instead of the political point of view. I shall stand with the Republican ticket, in spite of habit and sentiment, because it does not follow the usual custom of selecting a list of office holders or party servants. I like the ticket because it recognizes the right of private judgment and individual opinion even in politics. I like it because it is composed not of men who think the same thoughts, but of men who think the best thoughts. Especially should this consideration appeal, I think, to women——

13. Jonathan Swift's (1667–1745) *Gulliver's Travels* (1726)
14. The race between Democrat E. Lee Trinkle and Republican Henry W. Anderson; a third party, an all-Negro ticket calling itself the "lily-blacks" and headed by John Mitchell, Jr., Negro banker and editor of the Richmond *Planet*, polled 5,000 of the 210,000 votes.

for women are less interested than men in the mere circumstance of party government and more interested in the public welfare and the conditions which surround the life of the family. I can say with all sincerity that the doctrine advocated by the Republican candidate for Governor is the logical development of the best political heritage of Virginia. That doctrine is both conservative and progressive——since it preserves the tradition of the past while it dedicates its constructive energy to the future.

And if we look back long enough, since that immortal moment when our first revolutionist, John Smith, turned triumphantly to judge his Judges, we shall find that the history of Virginia consists in a series of magnificent revolts against arrogant prejudice or unscrupulous power.[15] If we look back long enough we shall find that the high tradition of Virginia is the tradition of righteous revolution. For a revolution is not necessarily a change to more radical forms. It may be, like our own revolution, a return to reason——a release of the sober and conservative judgment of the people. Or it may be again the restoration of an ancient freedom that had been lost in the hour of common danger and common sacrifice. Such a revolution, as it seems to me, is the one that we are facing today——a revolution of opinion which means nothing more than the liberation from prejudice——which means nothing more than the recovery of that right of private judgment and independent political thought we surrendered when the safety of the State was endangered.[16] The moment is critical, not because we are facing fresh problems, but because it is always more difficult to recover an old right that has been lost than it is to demand and win a new one. The moment is critical because the longer we remain in mental subjection to an idea, the harder and the more bitter must be our fight to win freedom of thought. The moment is critical because, as a great English poet once warned us, "The man who is unwilling to fight for the truth may be forced to fight for a lie."

15. John Smith (1580–1631), the principal founder of the English colony at Jamestown in 1607, explored Virginia from 1607 to 1608 and was arrested upon his return to Jamestown by his enemies in the colony. Just before Smith was to be executed, a ship arrived with new settlers, who freed him.
16. Surrendered apparently when the war against the Union froze Virginia in a defensive posture later reinforced by resistance to Reconstruction.

The Novel in the South

Early in the dashing but decorous eighteen eighties John Esten Cooke published his *Virginia: A History of the People,* an important and delightful little volume which proved that the sword was more prolific than the pen in the Old South.[1] Slipped in among more serious considerations—for war, not letters, is the proper business of the historians—we find a few brief discussions of Virginia authors; and toward the end of the book a modest chapter is devoted to "Virginia Literature in the Nineteenth Century." After what he appears to regard as a consoling rather than an encouraging view, Mr. Cooke, who was a distinguished Southern novelist of his day, prudently decides to bury, not to praise, his Caesar.

"If no great original genius," he concludes, "has arisen to put the lion's paw on Virginia letters, many writers of admirable attainments and solid merit have produced works which have instructed and improved their generation; and to instruct and improve is better than to amuse. Whatever may be the true rank of the literature, it possesses a distinct character. It may be said of it with truth that it is notable for its respect for good morals and manners; that it is nowhere offensive to delicacy or piety; or endeavors to instill a belief in what ought not to be believed. It is a very great deal to say of the literature of any country in the nineteenth century."

That he lingers not to inquire but to moralize is sufficient proof,

This essay appeared in *Harper's Magazine,* CLVII (December, 1928), 93–100, and was partially incorporated into the preface of *The Miller of Old Church* that appears in *A Certain Measure* (1943). For the later version, she updated her list of southern writers discussed or mentioned to read as follows: John Esten Cooke, William A. Caruthers, Edgar Allan Poe, Thomas Jefferson, Joel Chandler Harris, Thomas Nelson Page, Charles Egbert Craddock, James Lane Allen, James Branch Cabell—all in the original version—plus William Gilmore Simms, George Washington Cable, Stark Young, Thomas Wolfe, William Faulkner, Allen Tate, Caroline Gordon, Marjorie Kinnan Rawlings, Hamilton Basso, Margaret Mitchell, and Clifford Dowdey—none of whom was in the earlier listing. Omitted were Amélie Rives Troubetzkoy, Mary Johnston, Margaret Prescott Montague, DuBose Heyward, Julia Peterkin, Paul Green, James Boyd, Frances Newman, Edith Summers Kelley, Julian Green, Conrad Aiken, Laurence Stallings, T. S. Stribling, Isa Glenn, Emily Clark, Dorothy Scarborough, Eleanor Carroll Chilton, Donald Corley, Berry Fleming, and Elizabeth Madox Roberts. Between 1928 and 1943, southern writing moved to a new plateau.

1. Novelist and historian of Virginia, John Esten Cooke (1830–86) served in the Confederate army, wrote *Surry of Eagles'-Nest* (1866) and other historical romances, as well as *Virginia: A History* (1883), which became a standard text in the public schools of Virginia.

were one needed, of Mr. Cooke's sterling piety and settled convictions. For it was a period when historians, like novelists, asked few questions and were able to believe, without prodigious effort, anything that was necessary. Speculation, when it flowed at all in the South, ran smoothly in the safest and narrowest of channels. Novelists, especially when they were historians also, were required to instruct and invited to please; but they were not allowed to interrogate. Why old Virginia, with a mode of living as gay, as gallant, as picturesque, and as uncomfortable as the life of England in the eighteenth century, created, not a minor *Tom Jones,* the crown of English fiction, but merely *Cavaliers of Virginia* and *Knights of the Horseshoe?*—this is a question which no Southern gentleman, however Georgian his morals or Victorian his manners, would have dignified with an answer.[2] A minor Fielding would have been, no doubt, too much to expect. But it would seem to the cold modern mind that almost any readers who devoured them so voraciously might have produced a native variety of Mrs. Radcliffe, of Miss Jane Porter, or even of Mrs. Charlotte Smith.[3] All these authors were with us in their solid bodies of masculine calf or modest feminine cloth. If our jovial grandfathers chuckled for a generation over *The Adventures of Peregrine Pickle,* our sentimental grandmothers shivered over *The Mysteries of Udolpho* and wept or trembled over the misfortunes of *Thaddeus of Warsaw.*[4] Yet, while sentiment effervesced as easily as soda water, the stream of creative energy flowed, as thin and blue as skimmed milk, into the novel that was "notable for its respect for good morals and manners." With the long inheritance of English tradition and culture behind it, why did

2. *Cavaliers of Virginia, or The Recluse of Jamestown* (1834–35) by William Alexander Caruthers (1800–1846), a historical romance of the Old Dominion. *Knights of the Horse-shoe* (1845), also by Caruthers, a traditionary tale of the cocked-hat gentry in the Old Dominion

3. Henry Fielding, the great eighteenth-century comic novelist whose works include *Tom Jones, Joseph Andrews,* and *Amelia;* Ann Ward Radcliffe (1764–1823), English poet and novelist born in London, whose novels of sensibility and psychological tension helped form the Gothic novel; Jane Porter (1776–1850), English novelist, whose works were published as companions to the Waverly novels of Walter Scott (1771–1832); Charlotte Smith (1749–1806), English poet and novelist born in London and authoress of *Emmeline, The Banished Man,* and *The Old Manor House*

4. *The Adventures of Peregrine Pickle* by Tobias Smollett (1721–71); *The Mysteries of Udolpho* by Ann Ward Radcliffe; *Thaddeus of Warsaw* by Jane Porter

the old South (and this is especially true of Virginia) provide almost every mortal dwelling except a retreat for the imagination of man?

It soon becomes clear that there are more answers than one to this question, and that each answer contains at least a germ of the truth. From the beginning of its history the South had suffered less from a scarcity of literature than from a superabundance of living. Soil, scenery, all the color and animation of the external world, tempted a convivial race to an endless festival of the seasons. If there was little in nature to inspire terror, there was still less in [the?] human not to awaken pity in the hearts of oak. Life, for the ruling class at least, was genial, urbane, and amusing; but it was deficient in those violent contrasts which enkindle the emotions while they subdue the natural pomposity of man. Even slavery, a depressing spectacle at best, was a slight impediment to the faith that had been trained to enjoy the fruits rather than to examine the character of peculiar institutions. Though in certain periods there was disseminated a piquant flavor of skepticism, it was a flavor that lingered pleasantly on the tongue instead of lubricating the mind. Over the greater part of the old South (and this applies forcibly to Virginia, where the plantation group was firmly united) a top-heavy patriarchal system was adjusting itself with difficulty to unusual conditions. While this industrial process required men of active intelligence, it offered little hospitality to the brooding spirit of letters. It is true that in the latter years of the eighteenth century much able writing in politics began to appear. Jefferson, who touched with charm and usually with wisdom upon almost every subject that has engaged the mind of man, created not only the political thought but the greater part of the Southern literature of his period.[5] After his death, however, and particularly with the approach of the Civil War, political sagacity withered beneath a thick increment of prejudice. Philosophy, like heresy, was either suspected or prohibited. Even those Southerners (and there were many of these in Virginia) who regarded slavery as an anachronism rather than an iniquity, and looked ahead reluctantly to a doomed social order, lacked either the courage or the genius that rides in the whirlwind and directs the storm. Before approaching disaster pleasure became not

5. Jefferson's public papers and *Notes on the State of Virginia* (1785), his only full-length book, constitute his major literary achievements.

merely a diversion but a way of escape. In the midst of a changing world all immaterial aspects were condensed for the Southern planter into an incomparable heartiness and relish of life.

For what distinguished the Southerner, and particularly the Virginian, from his severer neighbors to the north, was his ineradicable belief that pleasure is worth more than toil, that it is worth more even than profit. Though the difference between the Virginian and the far Southerner was greater than the distance between Virginia and Massachusetts, a congenial hedonism had established in the gregarious South a confederacy of the spirit. Yet in this agreeable social order, so benevolent to the pleasure-seeker and so hostile alike to the thinker and the artist, what encouragement, what opportunity, awaited the serious writer? What freedom was there for the literature either of protest or of escape? Here, as elsewhere, expression belonged to the articulate, and the articulate was supremely satisfied with his own fortunate lot as well as with the less enviable lots of others. Only the slave, the "poor white," or the woman who had forgotten her modesty may have felt inclined to protest; and these negligible minorities were as dumb and sterile as the profession of letters. And even if they had protested who would have listened? Even if they had escaped, either in fiction or in fact, where could they have gone? Complacency, self-satisfaction, a blind contentment with things as they might be: all these cheerful swarms, which stifle both the truth of literature and the truth of life, had settled like a cloud of honey bees over the creative faculties of the race. For the airy inquisitiveness that frolicked so gracefully over the surface of thought questioned the Everlasting Purpose as seldom as it invaded the barren field of prose fiction. Religion, which made so much trouble in New England, had softened in a milder climate to a healthful moral exercise and a comfortable sense of divine favor. A sublime certainty that he was the image of his Maker imparted dignity to the Southern gentleman while it confirmed his faith in the wisdom of his Creator. Although the venom of intolerance had been extracted but imperfectly, the Protestant Episcopal Church was charitable toward almost every weakness except the dangerous practice of thinking. Moreover, the civilization of the old South was one in which every member, white or black, respected the unwritten obligation to be amusing when it was possible and agreeable in any circumstances. Generous manners imposed a severe, if mute, restraint upon morals; but generous manners exacted that the artist should be more gregarious than sedentary. It is true that "Poe passed his early life in Virginia." Nevertheless, Mr. Cooke reminds us that "this great and somber genius was rather a cosmopolite than a citizen of any particular State."[6]

II

After the Civil War, pursued by the dark furies of Reconstruction, the mind of the South was afflicted with a bitter nostalgia. From this homesickness for the past there flowered, as luxuriantly as fireweed in burned places, a mournful literature of commemoration. A prosperous and pleasure-loving race had been thrust back suddenly into the primitive struggle for life; and physical resistance had settled slowly into mental repression. Already those desperate political remedies which, according to the philosopher, begin in fear and end in folly, were welding the Southern States into a defense and a danger. Out of political expediency there emerged a moral superstition. What had begun as an emergency measure had matured into a sacred and infallible doctrine. And among these stagnant ideas the romantic memories of the South ripened and mellowed and at last began to decay. That benevolent hardness of heart so necessary to the creative artist dissolved—if it had ever existed—into the simple faith which makes novels even less successfully than it moves mountains. To defend the lost became the solitary purpose and the supreme obligation of the Southern novelist, while a living tradition decayed with the passage of years into a sentimental infirmity. Graceful, delicate, and tenderly reminiscent, the novels of this period possess that unusual merit, the virtue of quality. Yet charming as they are in manner, they lack creative passion and the courage to offend which is the essential note of great fiction. The emotions with which they deal are formal, trite, deficient in blood and irony, and as untrue to experience as they are true to an attitude of evasive idealism. In the end this writing failed to survive because, though faithful to a moment in history, it was false to human behavior.

6. Edgar Allan Poe (1809–49) lived in Virginia from 1811 to 1815 and 1820 to 1827, in Baltimore from 1831 to 1834, in Richmond again during 1835–37; thereafter, he lived chiefly in New York and Philadelphia.

Yet, even with this serious defect, the first sustained literary movement in the South cannot be dismissed as undeserving of criticism. Had it been addressed to a race as self-sufficing both in literature and in the sphere of abstract ideas as the people of New England, much that is charming, if not vital, might have endured. But the new South, like the old, is self-sufficing only in the twilight region of sentiment. Always it has remained invulnerable alike to the written word and to the abstract idea. Though it gave its life for a cause, it was wanting in the subjective vision which remolds a tragic destiny in the serene temper of art. Not the word that stands, but the conversation that ripples has been always the favorite art of the Southerner. Never has his preference varied from the vocal sound to the printed letter. Content to borrow both his literature and his opinion of literature, he has clung through all his courageous history to the tender sentiments or vehement prejudices which are miscalled convictions. For instead of cherishing its own after the provident habit of New England, the South has hesitated to approach Southern writers until they also could be safely borrowed from that alien world in which all accredited Southern reputations are won. With diminishing fortunes, books became the first prohibited luxury; with increasing wealth, they have remained the last acknowledged necessity. "I am not really extravagant," remarked a Southern lady, with a virtuous air, "I never buy books."

Yet, in spite of this natural impediment to literature, the South in the nineteenth century was able to produce the incomparable folklore of *Uncle Remus*; and nothing better or truer than *Uncle Remus* has appeared in the whole field of American prose fiction.[7] It is not without significance, perhaps, that whenever the Southern writer escaped from beneath the paw of the stuffed lion into the consciousness of a different race or class, he lost both his cloying sentiment and his pose of moral superiority. Some literary magic worked as soon as the Southern novelist forgot that he had been born, by the grace of God, a Southern gentleman. The early dialect stories of Thomas Nelson Page are still firm and round and as fragrant as dried

---

7. The familiar folktales by Joel Chandler Harris (1848–1908), which began appearing in the Atlanta *Constitution* in 1876, were first published in book form in 1880.

roseleaves,[8] the humorous mountain folk of Charles Egbert Craddock are perennially fresh and delightful;[9] the simpler persons, portrayed without august idealism, of James Lane Allen,[10] are vital and interesting; the youthful romantic tales of Amélie Rives have exuberant vitality.[11] A little later, in the historical pageant of American fiction, Mary Johnston appeared to wear her fancy dress with a difference.[12] She also had grace, charm, quality, and the delicate touch upon manner as distinguished from manners. Moreover, as her books proved, Miss Johnston is endowed with the courage of her philosophy and the mystic rather than the romantic vision. Like Margaret Prescott Montague, another sincere artist, she has steadfastly refused to compromise with reality.[13]

Long and steep is the journey from John Esten Cooke in his happy valley to James Branch Cabell in his ivory tower.[14] Every step of the way has been won by a struggle; every struggle has widened, however imperceptibly, the boundaries of American fiction. To those of us who are and have been always in accord with the artistic impulse we are pleased to call Modernism it is a relief to find that the horizon even of the American novel is fluid, not fixed, and that

8. Thomas Nelson Page (1853–1922) wrote of antebellum and Reconstruction southern life in works once termed the "supreme glorification of the old regime." His contemporaries admired the dialect, the Negro characterization, the plantation tradition, the humor, and the romantic coloring of his stories.

9. Charles Egbert Craddock (1850–1922) was the pseudonym for Mary Noailles Murfree, whose stories and novels were peopled chiefly by rural southern mountaineers. Her collections include *In the Tennessee Mountains* (1884) and *The Bushwhackers and Other Stories* (1899).

10. James Lane Allen (1849–1925); Glasgow is probably referring to the characters in Allen's stories set in rural Kentucky: *A Kentucky Cardinal* (1894) or *The Kentucky Warbler* (1918), for examples.

11. Amélie Rives Troubetzkoy (1863–1945) wrote Elizabethan tales, featuring an Elizabethan idiom and manners attractive to her contemporaries. *Godey's Magazine* called her women "proud, selfish, handsome, alluring, lacking in womanly delicacy, and, above all things, desperately self-absorbed and inconceivably mean." Her sensually "scandalous" novel *The Quick or the Dead?* (1888) had once made Amélie Rives a *cause célèbre*.

12. Mary Johnston (1870–1936) was born and spent nearly all of her life in Virginia; she wrote historical romance novels depicting colonial and antebellum life in the state, including *To Have and To Hold* (1900), which sold more than 500,000 copies.

13. Margaret Prescott Montague (1878–?), short-story writer and novelist, published several stories in Emily Clark's *Reviewer* and a novel, *Deep Channel* (1923).

14. Glasgow may be poking fun at Cabell's sometimes aloof and haughty personality. Cabell was considered a pure escapist, to whom reality was both unpleasant and unimportant.

there is a way of escape from the artificial limitations of material and method.[15] It is fortunate for Mr. Cabell that he came not too far ahead of his time. It is fortunate that he is allied in his maturity with the general revolt against the novel of sterile posture and sentimental evasion. This fresh literary impulse in the South—which is merely a single curve in the broad modern movement toward freedom in art—has broken not only with its own formal tradition but with the well-established American twin conventions of prudery and platitude. For Mr. Cabell, spinning his perfect rhythms from iridescent illusions, is still in harmony with the natural patterns of life. Though he remains in the modern world and not of it, his genius is rooted deep below the concrete pavements of Richmond in the dark and fertile soil of Virginia's history. A long tradition and a thick deposit of human hopes and fears have flowered again in the serene and mellow disenchantment of his philosophy. Even the austere perfection of his art, with its allegorical remoteness and that strangely hollow ring which echoes the natural human tones of pity and passion, could have sprung only from a past that has softened and receded into the eternal outline of legend. Certainly it is an art which belongs by inheritance to the South, though it appears to contain no element that we may narrowly define as Southern except, perhaps, the romantic richness of its texture and the gaiety and gallantry of its pessimism. But its roots are firmly embedded, though they draw nourishment from nothing more substantial than fable. For even with a novelist of philosophy rather than of life there must be a fourth dimension in every fiction that attempts to interpret reality. There must be a downward seeking into the stillness of vision as well as an upward springing into the animation of the external world.[16]

And because this is true of every Southern novelist, and especially of those Southern novelists who are still to come, it is well to

15. The publication of *The Descendant* (1897) put Glasgow into the mainstream of modern fiction influenced by the scientific thinking of Charles Darwin (1809–82) and his followers; more recently, in short stories and especially in *Barren Ground* (1925), she had experimented with psychological and mythological materials in ways that suggest an interest in the ideas of Freud and Jung.

16. From her first Virginia novels through *Barren Ground* (1925) and *The Romantic Comedians* (1926), Glasgow had structured the action of her novels to follow, or deviate significantly from, the cyclic pattern of natural time, thus adding a fourth or universal dimension to the particulars of her "realistic" fiction.

remind ourselves that, if the art of the South is to be independent, not derivative, if it is to be adequate, compact, original, it must absorb heat and light from the central radiance of its own nature. The old South, genial, objective, and a little ridiculous—as the fashions of the past are always a little ridiculous to the present—has vanished from the world of fact to reappear in the permanent realm of fable. This much we have already conceded. What we are in danger of forgetting is that few possessions are more precious than a fable that can no longer be compared with a fact. The race that inherits a heroic legend must have accumulated an inexhaustible resource of joy, beauty, love, laughter, and tragic passion. To discard this rich inheritance in the pursuit of a standard utilitarian style is, for the Southern novelist, pure folly. Never should it be overlooked that the artist in the South will attain his full stature, not by conforming to the accepted American pattern, but by preserving his individual distinction. Sincerely as he may admire the flat and vigorous novel of the Middle West, he can never hope to subdue his hand to the monotonous soil of the prairies. That impressive literary movement has as little kinship with the Southern scene as with the stark poetic outlines which express so perfectly the frozen landscapes of New England. But in the vivid profusion of Mr. Cabell's art we find a genuine revelation of the beauty which, however neglected and debased, is indigenous to the mind and heart of the South.

It is easy to remind ourselves that this artistic inheritance was lost upon a race that has persistently confused emotions with ideas and mistaken tradition for truth. It is easy to remind ourselves that a logical point of view is almost as essential in art as it is in philosophy. But, like most other reminders, these are not only offensive but futile. After all, what the South has known and remembered was a lavish, vital, and distinctive society which, for want of a better phrase, we may consent to call an archaic civilization. Imperfect, it is true. For as long as the human race remains virtually, and perhaps essentially, barbarian, all the social orders invented by man will be merely the mirrors of his favorite imperfections. Nevertheless, there are arts, and the novel is one of them, which appear to thrive more vigorously upon human imperfection than upon machine-made excellence. Commercial activity and industrial development have their uses, no doubt, in any well-established society; but genius has been in even the most civilized periods a vagabond. And, with or without genius, the novel is more vital and certainly more interesting when it declines to become the servant either of sentimental tradition or patriotic materialism.

III

Every observant mind in the South to-day must be aware of what we may call, without too much enthusiasm, an awakening interest in ideas; and a few observant minds may have perceived in the rising generation an almost pathetic confusion of purpose. In the temper of youth we feel the quiver of expectancy and an eagerness to forsake the familiar paths and adventure into the wilderness. But where shall it begin? For what is it searching? Adaptable by nature, and eager, except in moments of passion, to conciliate rather than to offend, the modern South is in immediate peril less of revolution than of losing its individual soul in the national Babel. After sixty years of mournful seclusion, the South is at last beginning to look about and to coquet with alien ideas. With an almost disdainful air, the Southern mind is turning from commemoration to achievement. Noise, numbers, size, quantity, all are exerting their lively or sinister influence. Sentiment no longer suffices. To be Southern, even to be solid, is not enough; for the ambition of the new South is not to be self-sufficing, but to be more Western than the West and more American than the whole of America. Uniformity, once despised and rejected, has become the established ideal. Satisfied for so long to leave the miscellaneous product "Americanism" to the rest of the country, the South is at last reaching for its neglected inheritance.

At this point it may be wise for the prudent essayist to pause and approach his subject with caution. The recently invented noun "Americanism," which appears so mild and harmless in print, reveals itself to the touch as a dangerous appellation. No other word in our language arouses so easily the fierce possessive instinct of criticism. So sensitive, indeed, are the emotions aroused by this label that when I attempted to treat it lightly in a thin vein of satire, I was taken to task by a literal-minded lady who has still to learn that words are double-edged and not necessarily as flat as the paper on which they are written. Gravely she charged me with harboring what seems to be an "un-American" prejudice against a confusion of tongues. Yet nothing could be, in sober fact, more remote from my thought. On the contrary, I believe that America, if not the didactic term "Americanism," is big enough to include the diverse qualities in all the novels ever written by American novelists at home or abroad. Since the appearance of *Giants in the Earth*, I am disposed to add all the novels ever written by American novelists in any language; for Mr. Rölvaag has written a great and beautiful American novel in the Norwegian tongue.[17] I am told that excellent American novels may be written in Greek or even in Latin. Certainly, I see no reason why American novels, excellent or otherwise, should not be written in the English, or near-English, which, though incorrectly spoken, is still the native tongue of the South. But they will be written, it is safe to prophesy, by those Southern novelists who are concerned with the quality of excellence rather than with the characteristic of "Americanism."

For the Americanism so prevalent in the South to-day belongs to that major variety which, by reducing life to a level of comfortable mediocrity, has contributed more than a name to the novel of protest. After breaking away from a petrified past overgrown by a funereal tradition, an important group of Southern novelists has recoiled from the uniform concrete surface of an industrialized and democratized South. For the first time in its history the South is producing, by some subtle process of reaction, a literature of revolt. Consciously or unconsciously, the aesthetic sense that surrendered to the romantic life of the past, and even to the more picturesque aspects of slavery, is rejecting the standards of utility in art and fundamentalism in ideas. For, even though it is true that there has been an advance in the South of what the world has agreed to call education, there is a corresponding decrease in that art of living which excels in the amiable aspects of charm rather than in the severe features of dogmatism. If flexibility of mind has settled into earnest conviction, grace of manner has apparently hardened into a confirmed habit of argument. A new class has risen to the surface if not to the top. New prophets are creating new vices and denouncing

17. *Giants in the Earth* (1927) by Ole Edvart Rölvaag (1876–1931)

the old ones. It is this menace, not only to freedom of thought, but to beauty and pleasure and picturesque living, which is forcing the intelligence and the aesthetic emotions of the South into revolt. And it is this revolution of ideas that must inevitably produce the Southern novelists of the future.

Already a little band of writers, inspired by no motive more material than artistic integrity, is attempting a revaluation of both the past and the present, and subjecting the raw material of life to the fearless scrutiny and the spacious treatment of art. In the midst of a noisy civilization these writers are quietly evolving a standard for the confused mind of youth; and it is worthy of remark that in a higher degree than almost any other group of American artists they have retained a poetic quality of style in dealing with the pedestrian prose of experience. DuBose Heyward is writing with beauty and truth of a vanishing South.[18] Julia Peterkin is interpreting an alien race with beauty and truth and that something more which pierces deeper than even beauty or truth.[19] Paul Green is exploring a forgotten corner of life.[20] Burton Rascoe, a novelist by temperament, is illuminating the tragi-comedy of civilization.[21] James Boyd is infusing the precious quality of verisimilitude into the older historical patterns.[22] Frances Newman is evolving from her brilliant gifts a fresh and vivid criticism of life.[23] Edith Summers Kelley is depicting

18.   DuBose Heyward (1885–1940), born in Charleston, South Carolina, generally depicted the primitive Gullah Negroes of South Carolina and the Sea Islands. His most famous work, *Porgy* (1925), was adapted by Heyward and George Gershwin (1898–1937) into the opera *Porgy and Bess* (1935).

19.   Julia Peterkin (1880–1961), born in Laurence County, South Carolina, was a novelist and short-story writer whose works were influenced by African folklore and the Gullah dialect. Her *Scarlet Sister Mary* (1928), a novel of Gullah Negroes, won the Pulitzer Prize.

20.   Paul Green (1894–1981), American playwright and novelist, set nearly all of his works in his native North Carolina; his play *In Abraham's Bosom* won the 1927 Pulitzer Prize.

21.   Burton Rascoe (1892–1957), American journalist, editor, and critic, worked for such publications as *Newsweek, Esquire,* Chicago *Tribune, McCall's,* and New York *Herald Tribune.* As literary editor, he was quick to hail new or obscure talent (James Branch Cabell dedicated *Jurgen* to him).

22.   James Boyd (1888–1944) was born in Pennsylvania but, when he was thirteen, moved to North Carolina, the home of his ancestors. His novels are all historical, covering different periods of American history, and are notable for their naturalness, careful realism, and fidelity to fact.

23.   Frances Newman (1883–1928), American novelist and librarian, won the first O. Henry prize in 1924. Her novels stirred the public because of her extraor-

with power and insight the "poor white class" of the South.[24] Julian
Green is translating his early repressions into vivid French novels.[25]
Conrad Aiken is drifting in his foreign technic among the sea islands
of consciousness.[26] Laurence Stallings is revolting in forms of art
from the hypocrisy and the cruelty of an embattled idealism.[27] T. S.
Stribling is applying a modern realistic treatment to that romantic
melodrama so dear to the backward heart of the South.[28] Isa
Glenn[29] and Emily Clark are flavoring severe studies of manners
with a delicate mint sauce of satire.[30] Eleanor Mercein Kelly is seeking an appropriate background for the most ancient illusion.[31] Dorothy Scarborough is blending the old sentiments with the newer

---

dinary style (long, intricate sentences; esoteric allusions; complete absence of
dialogue) and her controversial subject matter, as in *Hard-Boiled Virgin* (1926).

24. Edith Summers Kelley (1884–1956), Canadian-born novelist who lived
throughout the United States, called herself a "farmer's wife." Her novels include
Weeds (1923) and *The Devil's Hand* (written in 1924 but not published until 1974).
She was also secretary for Upton Sinclair's (1878–1968) communal living experiments at Helicon Hall.

25. Julian Green was born in Paris (1900) less than a year after his American parents from Virginia and Georgia had moved to France. He wrote only one short story
originally in English and spent all but a few years of his life in France until the fall of
France in World War II, when he came to Virginia. His many French novels, including *Adrienne Mesurat* (1927), *Leviathan* (1929), and *Moira* (1950), are usually somber psychological studies.

26. Conrad Aiken (1889–1973), poet, novelist, and short-story writer, used psychoanalytic theory to create intensely subjective and subtle characters. In 1929, he
won the Pulitzer Prize for his *Selected Poems*.

27. Laurence Stallings (1894–1968), born in Macon, Georgia, is known more for
his motion picture and dramatic work than for his novels. He dramatized *The Big
Parade* and *Old Ironsides*, which led to his position as editor in chief of Fox Movie-
tone System. With Maxwell Anderson (1888–1959), he wrote the play *What Price
Glory?* (1924).

28. Thomas Sigismund Stribling (1881–1965) wrote generally of small-town
southern life, in works so realistic that many contemporary readers labeled his characters as degenerates. He won the Pulitzer Prize in 1932 for his novel *The Store*.

29. Isa Glenn (b.1888), daughter of an Atlanta mayor and cousin of James
McNeill Whistler (1834–1903), used the experiences and background of her travels
through the Orient and South America for her early novels. Her works include *Heat*
(1926), *Southern Charm* (1928), *Transport* (1929), *A Short History of Julia* (1930),
and *East of Eden* (1932). At her best, she was compared to Willa Cather (1873–1947)
and Glasgow.

30. Emily Clark (1892–1953) was founder and editor in chief of the *Reviewer*
from 1921 to 1924.

31. Eleanor Mercein Kelly (1880–1968) was born in Milwaukee but used various
backgrounds as settings for her books: Kentucky, Spain, Moorish Africa, Syria, Cor-
fu, and so on. She was primarily a storyteller of the old local color school.

psychology.[32] Eleanor Carroll Chilton is pursuing the mystery of dreams through a forest of shadows.[33] Among the later arrivals in the trampled field of prose fiction, we may discern unusual promise in such writers as Donald Corley, who was born in Georgia but inhabits the airy Kingdom of Magic,[34] and in Berry Fleming, who has steeped his first novel in the strong and mellow wine of adventure.[35] Even the "complete plunge" into consciousness, that immersion in the rhythm and change of being which remains the greatest contribution of modernism, has extended the horizon without lessening the sense of form in several Southern novelists.

Though it may be unfair to include Elizabeth Madox Roberts in this group of writers, it is not difficult to detect a Southern warmth and exuberance beneath the veracious Middle Western method of *The Time of Man* and *My Heart and My Flesh*.[36] In the latest work of Miss Roberts, if we look below a superficial "modernist" manner, we find all the depth of color and softness of texture which, either by virtue or by courtesy, we have assigned to the South. For whatever her position or her alignment may be in American letters, her books are saturated with that native essence of blood and tears, of vehement living, which exists in modern America merely as the effluvia of a decaying romantic tradition. But the essence of blood and tears, like some thwarted romantic yearning at the heart of reality, flows from the provincial into the universal experience.

32. Dorothy Scarborough (1877–1935) collected mountain ballads and Negro folksongs and wrote (for her Ph.D.) *The Supernatural in Modern English Fiction* (published 1917), still the standard in that field. Her novels depicted the hardships of southern plantation life, as in *In the Land of Cotton*.

33. Eleanor Carroll Chilton (1898–1949) was born in Charleston, West Virginia. Her poetry and novels were once appreciated for distinction of style, mystical views of nature, and personality analysis.

34. Donald Corley's (1886–1955) *The House of Lost Identity: Tales and Drawings*, was published in 1927, with an introduction by James Branch Cabell.

35. *The Conqueror's Stone* (1927), the first novel by Berry Fleming (b. 1899), was an adventure story set in the Carolinas in 1766.

36. Elizabeth Madox Roberts (1886–1941) was born near Springfield, Kentucky, in the "Pigeon Roost" country of which she wrote. She infused much poetry into her fiction, especially into the speech of her characters. *The Time of Man* (1926) was a moving study of Kentucky hill-dwellers. Her second novel was *My Heart and My Flesh* (1927).

IV

And so it would seem that the qualities which will unite to make great Southern novels are the elemental properties which make great novels wherever they are written in any part of the world: power, passion, pity, ecstasy and anguish, hope and despair. For it is as true in literature as in wars that with the imponderables lies the real force. The universal approach to the novel is not without but within; and the way to greatness leads beyond manner, beyond method, beyond movements, to some ultimate dominion of spirit. Even style, the essence of great literature, is not a manufactured film but a vital fluid.

And what does this mean, after all, except that the South must look to inward inspiration rather than to outward example? It is well to have an American outlook; it may be better to have what is called an "international attitude of mind"; but the truth remains that great novels are not composed of either an outlook or an attitude. Even to demand a return to aesthetic values in fiction will not help unless we have values more genuine and profound than purely aesthetic ones. And what will it profit a writer to look within if he has not accumulated an abundance of vital resources? It has become a habit in both English and American criticism to remark that the South contains a wealth of unused material for prose fiction, which means only that a sense of tragedy and heartbreak still lingers beneath the vociferous modern "program of progress." Wherever humanity has taken root there has been created, it is needless to point out, the stuff of great novels; and this is true of the South in the exact measure that it is true of every other buried past upon earth. But it is even truer that wherever the predestined artist is born his material is found awaiting his eye and his hand. All that is required, indeed, for the novel would appear to be a scene that is large enough to hold three characters, two passions, and one point of view.

In the Southern novelists of the past there has been an absence not of characters, not of passions, but of a detached and steadfast point of view. What the novel lacked was not only clearness of vision but firmness of outline. For even the treasure of the inward approach may be wasted upon a writer who does not possess the practical advantage of the outward eye; and it is essential that the look within should be that of the artist, not of the lover. If the Southern novelist of the commemoration period was submerged in the stuff of life and incapable, therefore, of seeing his subject steadily and whole, the fault was not in the material, but in the novelist's inevitable loss of perspective. To be too near, it appears, is more fatal in literature than to be too far away; for it is better that the creative writer should resort to imagination than that he should be overwhelmed by emotion. And so it is only since the romantic charm and the lover's sentiment have both passed away from the South that the Southern novelist has been able to separate the subject from the object in the act of creation. It is only with the loss of this charm and the ebbing of this sentiment that he has been able to rest apart and brood over the fragmentary world he has called into being. For this is the only way, it would seem, in conclusion, that great novels, in the South or elsewhere, will ever be written. This was the way of Fielding with English life; it was the way of Hawthorne with the past of New England; it was the way of Proust with his world; it was the way of Tolstoy or Dostoevsky with his universe.

An Experiment in the South

Emily Clark is one of those unusual and engaging writers who are able to reconcile a social manner with a literary conscience.[1] She has wit, charm, discrimination and that rare endowment, quality.

In her latest volume, "Innocence Abroad," she relates the adventures—I had almost written escapades—of a lighthearted little magazine which, though it never paid a contributor, lived for nearly four years on the ripest fruit of the literary landscape. "How you are able to get such good stuff without paying for it," wailed Burton Rascoe, "will always be the despair of other editors!"[2] Yet, oddly enough

This essay, a review of Emily Clark's *Innocence Abroad*, appeared in New York *Herald-Tribune Books*, March 22, 1931, pp. 1, 6.

1. Clark tells in *Innocence Abroad* of her experiences as editor in chief of the *Reviewer* (1921–24).

2. Rascoe was literary editor of Chicago *Tribune*, *McCall's*, New York *Herald Tribune*, and other publications.

"The Reviewer," which was born in 1920, at a party in Richmond, when somebody remarked, "Let's start a little magazine," seems to have died almost as plainly of too many contributors as of too few subscribers.[3] Not many magazines, big or little, have carried a more distinguished list of names on their covers; and, incredible as it appears, these distinguished names actually "furnished an equivalent of cash payments to the young obscure writers whom we hoped to launch." Yet a magazine cannot depend, not wholly, upon either the important and established or the young and obscure. Contributors may be satisfied with "an equivalent of cash payment"; but printers, who deal in actual values and are superior to equivalents, have been always more or less inclined to make trouble for literature. For printers prefer real subscribers to literary associations, and real subscribers, in the South, as elsewhere, demand reams of paper in exchange for their money.

I nowadays regret to confess that when I first heard of the project I could feel no enthusiasm. True, the experiment stirred me with the thrill of a forlorn hope; but I failed to perceive that there is always room for another forlorn hope in the South. All my life I had been visited by legitimate or illegitimate descendants of the "Southern Literary Messenger"; and I differed, it appeared, from every other Southerner in failing to cherish the memory of that departed periodical.[4] Moreover, it seemed to make so little difference whether the magazines one did not read were published in New York or New Orleans. But once again, and this was very soon made clear to me, I was mistaken because I had not recognized the smiling features of an opportunity. The time was ripe for an endeavor "to encourage and arouse the South." Even if the South did not want another little magazine, there was not the slightest doubt, after the first six months, that another little magazine in the South was one of the urgent needs of the North. Within a year, a new grand army, composed of admonitions and bearing the body of Mr. Menck-

---

3. The *Reviewer* was a literary periodical published from 1921 to 1924 in Richmond, Virginia, and from 1924 to 1925 in Chapel Hill, by the University of North Carolina Press. The editors and publishers included Clark, Cabell, and Green.

4. The *Southern Literary Messenger* was a literary magazine from 1834 to 1864, founded in Richmond. It was edited by Edgar Allan Poe from 1837 to 1843.

en's "The Sahara of the Bozart," crossed the Potomac.[5] Everybody was willing to give a contribution, or, at least, to give good advice as the equivalent of a contribution.

As Howard Mumford Jones, a thoughtful observer, has said recently:[6] "The continuing affliction of Dixie is to be that part of the country to which anybody can give advice. Southerners are supposed to thrive on it (they do, Mr. Jones). From the founding of Jamestown to the present day, they have, I believe, received more gratuitous counsel than have residents in any other portion of the Republic. In 1606, when 120 men set sail to settle in Virginia, 'Master Hunt, our preacher,' so the record runs, 'counseled that heterogeneous company with the water of patience and his godly exhortations.' Well-meaning persons have been imitating him ever since."

But counsel was not all from without when Emily Clark, with the assistance of Mary Street[7] and Margaret Freeman[8] and Hunter Stagg,[9] began yet another experiment in long-suffering. Thomas Nelson Page advised them that there was a field in the South for "a real Review conducted on sound business principles," and that there was "not room for any other kind."[10] William Cabell Bruce agreed with him that the Review should be "properly financed, and with an occasional good article on political and social topics."[11] H. L. Mencken, who inclined naturally to violence, warned the four

5. H. L. Mencken's article first appeared in the New York *Evening Mail* on November 13, 1917. His remarks on the South drew many replies (for example, from Gerald White Johnson, who called Mencken's remarks "outrageous").

6. Howard Mumford Jones (1892–1980) was born and raised in the Midwest but taught for many years in the South before moving to the University of Michigan and Harvard. In 1927, he published *America and French Culture, 1750–1848*.

7. Mary Dallas Street (1885–1957), associate editor for the *Reviewer* when it first appeared, also contributed twenty-seven pieces to the journal. She published her first novel, *At Summer's End*, in 1936.

8. Margaret Freeman (1893–1982), contributing editor for the *Reviewer* when it first appeared, later became the wife of James Branch Cabell.

9. Hunter Stagg (1895–1960), literary editor for the *Reviewer* when it first appeared. Later, Stagg became editor with Emily Clark.

10. In 1920, Page was near the end of his life (he died in 1922); at the time he was working on a series of lectures on Dante for the University of Virginia and reworking an antebellum novel, *The Red Riders*, completed in 1924 by Rosewell Page.

11. William Cabell Bruce (1860–1946), American biographer and United States senator from 1922 to 1928, was born in Virginia and practiced law mostly in Maryland. He was an editor for the *University of Virginia Magazine* and Pulitzer Prize winner for his biography of Benjamin Franklin in 1919.

editors that it would be "useless to attempt a compromise. You must arm yourselves and take to the highroad, ready to cut throats whenever it is necessary. The thing must be done boldly, and, in order to get a crowd, a bit cruelly." This last piece of advice sounds so familiar, the accents are so unmistakably oratorical, that it is hard to understand why it did not prevail. Certainly, there could be no surer recipe "to encourage and arouse the South" than a literary lynching conducted on sound principles and attended by a picked company of political and social topics. In comparison, the efforts of Walter H. Page, of Howard W. Odum, of Edwin Mims, must appear as unostentatious as evolution.[12] However, when Mr. Mencken advised taking to the highroad and cutting throats, he had not seen the gentle editors of "The Reviewer."

There followed four successful years, in which almost every well known American writer assisted in the experiment and "The New York Times" blandly recorded that "The Reviewer" was "blazing a way through the literary sand flats of the South." Then, before the sand flats could be cleared, Miss Clark resigned as editor in chief, and there came the end. Although Mr. Mencken confessed privately " 'The Reviewer' is the only magazine in America that interests me," and Mr. Hergesheimer declared publicly that he found "The Reviewer" more "appealing" than the starving children of Europe, there came the end.[13] Another forlorn hope in the South had gone down in the kind of defeat that is victory.

With philosophic detachment, Miss Clark writes:

> The magazine lived a year in North Carolina. That, I believe was long enough. Little magazines should not outlive their job, and the day of little magazines is, very surely now dead. There is no further need of

12. Three leading spokesmen for the New South. Walter Hines Page (1855–1918), journalist and novelist, founded the Raleigh *State Chronicle*, edited the *Atlantic Monthly*, and established *World's Work*. His novel *The Southerner* appeared in 1909; from 1913 to 1918, he was Wilson's ambassador to the Court of St. James. Howard W. Odum (1884–1954), the South's most notable sociologist in the first half of the twentieth century, founded the *Journal of Social Forces* in 1922; in the 1930s he was the leader of the Southern Regionalists. Edwin Mims (1872–1959) taught English at several universities including Vanderbilt, the University of North Carolina at Chapel Hill, and Emory; from 1906 to 1909, he was joint editor of the *South Atlantic Quarterly*.

13. Joseph Hergesheimer (1880–1954), American novelist born in Philadelphia, was known for his sarcastic and cynical wit; he was also a contributor to the *Reviewer*.

them, since even the most experimental work is now eagerly investigated by established editors and publishers. The South, especially, is as definitely a field for literary exploitation today as New England long ago, or the Middle West ten years ago, when "The Reviewer" was born. DuBose Heyward recently said to me that in the current world of letters it is almost as chic to be a Southerner as to be a Negro.[14] And I believe he spoke with accuracy.

It was, I think, Frances Newman who remarked: " 'The Reviewer' is indicative of the course that Southern literature will probably take when Southerners cease to be too proud to write."[15] Her prophecy may be, as Miss Clark observes, "fairly accurate." Yet a reader who enjoys both Swift and Addison, and believes that diversity is more important than direction in Southern letters, may well hesitate to assent.[16] Though "Jurgen" may remain the supreme achievement in American fiction, it is doubtful if the ultraviolet rays of Poictesme will lie quite so deeply over the literary scene of the future.[17] All the difference between youth in the autumn of 1921 and youth in the spring of 1931 may be measured by the space that divides the fashion of sophistication from the fashion of immaturity. In the early twenties few writers, especially young writers, were immature by preference; and the conversational style so happily described as "baby talk" was still in its infancy. The lost generation had not returned, though it was already beginning to exercise the right of every lost thing to be vocal. What nobody prophesied or imagined was that the lost generation would presently find itself in a reversal of the situation. In Southern fiction today it is

14. The "New Negro" movement and the Harlem Renaissance associated with Claude McKay, Jean Toomer, Countee Cullen, and others, as well as Heyward's *Porgy* (1925), all preceded (and helped prepare the soil for) the great explosion of southern writers that occurred between 1929 and 1931 and continued for several decades thereafter. Glasgow, Cabell, Green, John Crowe Ransom (1888–1974), Allen Tate (1899–1979), and William Faulkner (1897–1962) were also literary forces in the early 1920s and contributors to the emerging renaissance.
15. Newman wrote *The Hard-Boiled Virgin* (1926) and *Dead Lovers Are Faithful Lovers* (1928).
16. Jonathan Swift wrote scathing satires containing scatalogical details, whereas the essays of Joseph Addison (1672–1719) are models of eighteenth-century propriety and decorum.
17. *Jurgen* (1919) by James Branch Cabell immediately gained international attention when Cabell's publisher was summoned to appear in court for violating New York's pornography laws. His exoneration proved to be a milestone for freer treatment of human sexuality. Poictesme is the fictional setting of *Jurgen*.

safer to be immature than to be sophisticated; and the nursery school of raw-head-and-bloody-bones, an offspring of sentimentality seduced by sadism, is still a favorite with reviewers. Since, however, death, not arrested development, is the only finality, it would seem that even "baby talk" must either grow up or decay.[18] Fashions in fiction appear to change as quickly as fashions in dress. Another decade and another reversal of the situation may sweep us beyond the imminent Victorian revival into the sadder and wiser realm of moral ideas. Certainly, the return of "Peter Ibbetson" and the awakened interest in the Brownings as lovers lend at least a shade of color to what may appear an extravagant prophecy.[19] For Peter Ibbetson and the Brownings as lovers could have flourished nowhere, but in the realm of moral ideas.

Moreover, a close observer of things Southern may detect, in the spring of 1931, the beginning of a literary movement which owes as little to the nursery bugbear of Raw-head-and-Bloody-bones as it owes to the sentimental decadence of the early '90s. Signs are not wanting that Southern tradition in its native purity, before it softened and decayed, may furnish material, as well as inspiration, to a new assortment of novelists. Two important first novels of 1930, "The Tides of Malvern," by Francis Griswold, and Gerald Johnson's "By Reason of Strength" sprang from this original source.[20] And it was the finer Southern tradition that inspired the clear amber prose of Stark Young in his authentic novels of the deep past, "Heaven Trees" and "River House."[21]

So the sanguine critic who believes in the infallible discrimination

18.   Glasgow seems to have in mind the syrupy speech of southern heroines, the use of southern vernacular, and the violence of southern characters, including Faulkner's. Attacks on the violence of southern literature would continue to place her further from the mainstream as the 1930s wore on. Glasgow's deafness prevented her from exploring the advantages of vernacular speech.

19.   *Peter Ibbetson* by George du Maurier (1834–96) described du Maurier's childhood and school days. Rudolf Besier's (1878–1942) *The Barretts of Wimpole Street*, a popular play of 1930, had revived interest in the Brownings.

20.   Francis Griswold's (b. 1902) first novel was *The Tides of Malvern*, a story of a South Carolina family. It was followed by *A Sea Island Lady*, in 1939. Gerald Johnson (1890–1980) gained renown in the 1920s and 1930s as a journalist and biographer, working for the Greensboro *Daily News* and later with H. L. Mencken at the Baltimore *Sun*. His fiction depicted southern religious frenzy, racial prejudice, and poor whites.

21.   Stark Young (1881–1963), noted drama critic, journalist, novelist, and playwright, wrote four southern novels between 1926 and 1934, including *Heaven Trees* (1926), *River House* (1929), and *So Red the Rose* (1934). He also contributed an essay

of posterity (a faith I do not share) may place his hopes in shifting styles and dream of a future age so civilized that it will find truth to art or nature more exciting than the strain of violence or of sentimentality which so often distorts that truth. Yet, since we ourselves must have existed once merely as a mistaken literary hope of the past, it seems scarcely reasonable to expect better taste in the future than we display in the present. After all, it takes not only a writer but a reader to make a book; and "The Reviewer" proves again that there are more writers than readers below the Potomac. True, we are told that this was different "when classics were written and a collection of books made a library." But the conviction that the only good readers are dead readers is not, unfortunately, confined to the South. It was Charles Lamb, not James Branch Cabell, who cried: "Damn the age. I will write for antiquity!"[22]

In its brief existence "The Reviewer," which was always hospitable to the unknown, printed the earliest work of several notable writers. Paul Green was among the contributors; and the plays of Paul Green are as deeply real as any American writing. Though he is not, as Miss Clark says, "a literary man in any conventional connotation of that phrase," he has been, since his first published work, an encouraging event in the South. When almost every successful novelist feels obliged to write at the top of his voice, it is pleasant to remember that Paul Green is still working quietly "in the elemental," among his kinsmen the tall pines of North Carolina. DuBose Heyward sent his first prose work to the magazine, and, as everybody knows, DuBose Heyward has written, in "Porgy," an American classic. Then there were the early sketches of Julia Peterkin, whose distinguished story is "one of the brilliant chapters of Southern literary history."[23] It is possible, it is, indeed, probable

---

to the agrarian manifesto *I'll Take My Stand: The South and the Agrarian Tradition* (1930).

22. Charles Lamb (1775–1834) made the statement when a sonnet he had written was rejected (Letter to B. W. Procter, January 22, 1829).

23. Green's first contribution to the *Reviewer* was "Aunt Mahaly's Cabin" (April, 1924). He later became an editor when the magazine moved to Chapel Hill. Heyward's *Porgy* was adapted for drama and opera, the music for the opera written by George Gershwin and renamed *Porgy and Bess*. The earliest contributions to the *Reviewer* by Peterkin were "From Lang Syne Plantation" (October, 1921), "Imports from Africa" (January, 1922), and "Studies in Charcoal" (March, 1922). Her novels include *Black April* (1927) and *Scarlet Sister Mary* (1928).

that "The Reviewer," which had "blazed a way through the literary sand flats of the South," cleared also the only short cut to success for a Southern novelist across the then unexplored and unexploited province of Black-face.

Too much cannot be said in praise of Miss Clark's intelligent handling of her material. In an age when the popular manner in biography is a rude manner, she approaches her difficult task with urbanity and humor. If she is without malice, she is without sentimentality. One feels that she has told the truth, though she has prudently refrained from telling the complete truth. She writes in a clear, emphatic style which transmits not only the color but the very sparkle of personality; and this gives her book a superficial resemblance to certain amusing French memoirs.

"Innocence Abroad" is a gay and fascinating chronicle of a successful failure.

Opening Speech of the Southern Writers Conference

When I was asked, as the only woman on this committee, to bid you welcome to Virginia, I modestly replied that women come before men only in shipwreck.[1] But Mr. James Branch Cabell, who imposes his duty upon me, is constrained to illustrate his theory that after fifty the only thing worth doing is to decline to do anything. I, on the contrary, believe quite as firmly that the longer one lives in this world of hazard and escapes disaster, the more reckless one should become—at least in the matter of words. Did not Defoe,

This speech exists only in a manuscript that contains two parts or drafts, marked "Very Rough," and a fragment of a third. Newspaper reports show that passages from both drafts and the fragment were delivered at the Southern Writers Conference, which took place October 23–24, 1931, in Charlottesville, Virginia. Unless otherwise obvious, the brackets in the text indicate passages marked through yet still legible.

1. The Southern Writers Conference at the University of Virginia was attended by thirty writers. The central committee of the conference consisted of Glasgow (whose idea the conference was), Cabell, Archibald Henderson, DuBose Heyward, Stark Young, Paul Green, and Thomas Wolfe. (Young and Wolfe, however, did not actually attend the conference.) The central committee was responsible for selecting other writers to be invited to the conference.

the father of us all, wait until his adventurous sixties before he dared to write, in *Moll Flanders*, the things that can be said only in print?[2]

Now, as I glance over this *Round Table* I rejoice to find how elastic the term Southern writer may become when it is properly stretched. It isn't necessary to be born in the South in order to become a Southern writer. It isn't necessary even to take the trouble to live here. All that one requires, is the open and eager mind of what I prefer to call the world writer. And because you are not only Southern writers but world writers, you bring to our literature the diversity which is life, not the standardization which is the death of creation. A few years ago every Southern writer fell naturally—or was supposed to fall naturally—into a single class—a kind of Swiss Guard of Defense. But now, thanks to this healthful diversity, we are convincing even those who are not Southerners that the South is more than the South—it is a part of the world. Always, I suppose, the arrogant planter and the classic colonel will return as hardy annuals of journalism. [For I am inclined to believe that when the cockroach or the Japanese beetle finally inherits the earth, he will find that journalistic labels are the solitary survivors of the machine civilization.]

But for the rest of us, the gesture of defense has been so long discarded that we have lost even the art. To defend a civilization would seem to us as impertinent as to defend time. Certainly, the South needs defenders as little as it needs apologists. The Southern scene, as we use it today, is a simply shifting pattern which transmits the colour and movement of life. For the chief concern of the Southern writer, as of every [other?] writer, is life—even though he may have learned long ago that life itself is indefensible. We are, I think, less interested in any social order past or present than we are in that unknown quality which we once called the soul and now call the psychology of mankind. Into this world of psychology we may look as into a wilderness that is forever conquered and yet forever virgin. Here and there, we may see our own small trail which leads on to that vanishing point where all trails disappear. Yet the

2. Cabell was fifty-two in 1931, Glasgow was fifty-eight; Defoe published *Moll Flanders* in 1722, when he was about sixty-two.

merest glance into this wilderness must teach us that there is not one truth alone but many truths. Somewhere,—I have forgotten where—I have read a Persian proverb which says, "Many kinds of truth are acceptable to Allah, the Merciful, but the whole truth is not one of them."

There is, for example, what we have agreed to call the truth of life. Then there is that vastly different truth, the truth of art, which includes history and fiction. This, of course, is merely a way of saying that modern psychology or the Theory of Relativity or both together have demolished our conception of truth as an established principle superior to and apart from the thinking subject. We no longer think of truth as a fixed pattern outside of ourselves at which we may nibble for crumbs as mice at a loaf. All of you who write fiction must have felt the shock of finding that when we break off a fragment of the truth of life and place it, without shading and shaping, into the truth of fiction, it sheds a meretricious glare of unreality. And many of us have tried at least once to be so supremely honest that we have taken a single character or incident or even a phrase directly from life—only to be told that this single character or incident or phrase is the one false stroke in an otherwise truthful portrait of experience.

And it is because we have learned this in our work that writers are so very tolerant of other truths than their own. All we ask of any writer is that he shall be honest with himself, that he shall possess artistic integrity. Beyond this, we are perfectly willing, I think, to leave to each individual writer the choice of his own particular subject. For it is the unconscious, not the conscious, will that chooses for us our subject, and over the unconscious we cannot exert prohibitions. But it is this conviction——the conviction that artistic integrity is the only essential——that enables us to enjoy so many varied aspects of truth. We can enjoy, for example, not only the books that are painful, but, in a lesser degree (since we are citizens of a Republic that has been called (and rightly, I think) the masochist among the nations), we are still able—(or, at least some of us are able)—to enjoy the books that are pleasant. Because of this conviction we ask of Mr. Cabell the Cabellian truth, or aspect of truth, and not the truth of Mr. Stark Young or Mr. Allen Tate or Mr. DuBose

Heyward[3] or the different truth of Mr. Sherwood Anderson or Mr. Stallings or Mr. Thomas Wolfe.[4] [We see also the subtle truth of Miss Isa Glenn as clearly as we see the [flattering?] truth of Mr. John Peale Bishop—or the quiet truth in that fine new novel *Penhally*.[5] For to the honest novelist, I think, all truth is welcome so long as, like Allah the Merciful, he is not asked to accept the whole truth from any mortal.]

[By this time, you have observed, no doubt, that I have carefully avoided the subject of our general discussion. Candidly, I have little interest in publics. Like presidents, they fail to impress me because I so seldom agree with them. Even when a public appears in Roman dress on the stage, I immediately suspect that it [is] not there for any good, but for purposes of assassination. So I find but one approach to this topic, and that is with the question: How much or how little should a writer participate, as we may say, in his own public?]

When I was asked, as the only woman on this committee, to welcome you to the Round Table, I demurred because I was brought up to believe that women come before men only in shipwreck.[6] And I was perfectly confident that there will [be] no rocking of the boat on this delightful occasion. For never in my experi-

---

3. Cabell's works at this productive time include *Between Dawn and Sunrise* (1930), *Some of Us* (1930), and *The Certain Hour* (1929). Young's most recent works were *The Torches Flare* (1928), *River House* (1929), and *The Street of the Islands* (1930). At this time, Tate was busy with biographical narratives: *Jefferson Davis: His Rise and Fall* (1929) and *Stonewall Jackson, The Good Soldier* (1930); *Poems: 1928-31* would appear in 1932. In 1931, Heyward published two works: *Brass Ankle, A Play in Three Acts* and *Jasbo Brown and Selected Poems*.
4. Sherwood Anderson (1876–1941) published *Hello Towns!*, a collection of sketches written for newspapers, in 1929; and *Perhaps Women*, impressions of factory life, in 1931. *Dark Laughter* (1925) represented his artistic maturity. Laurence Stallings published his novel *Plumes* in 1924. "Vale of Tears," a short story, appeared in 1931. *What Price Glory?*, a play written with Maxwell Anderson (1888–1959), was produced in 1924. Thomas Wolfe (1900–1938) published his first novel, *Look Homeward, Angel*, in 1929.
5. Glasgow is probably referring to the subtle criticisms of "southern charm" in Glenn's later novels. John Peale Bishop (1892–1944) published *Many Thousands Gone* (1931), a book of stories; poems had appeared in *Green Fruit* (1917) and *The Undertaker's Garland* (1922). *Penhally* (1931) was the first novel by Caroline Gordon (1895–1981).
6. What follows seems to be an alternate draft of the speech. It begins much like that above, then moves in a different direction.

ence of committees or parties, have I seen so many persons in one room that I was eager to meet and to know better.

The most charming thing about this gathering is the way it proves once for all, that one can be a Southern writer without being a Southerner. It isn't necessary even to arrange to be born in the South. The only requirement, it appears, is the abiding interest in life everywhere with which every writer worth his salt is provided before he looks about him and reluctantly—for was it ever otherwise?—dips his pen into the ink. When I was a young girl, trying desperately, and with a sinking heart, to get my first book accepted by a publisher, I remember that a very well-known and well-thought-of critic of the late nineties remarked to me with that slightly supercilious air which was then the fashion with intellectuals, "There are writers and there are Southern writers. WE want only writers;" and despairingly, I replied, "But I [don't want Southern nor Northern writers, I want] am a world writer." For this is what pleases me most in this Round Table. It is composed of the elements of the world. We may go into not only romance and realism—— faded old terms, but that sounder realism which is romantic and that sounded [*sic*] romance which is realistic. For in my opinion, no literature in any country, not even in Europe, to which American has for so long played the part of a literary Little Orphan Annie,[7] can grow and mature except through diversity. In the world of ideas the apollonian [*sic*] and the Dionysian spirits are eternally alive and eternally hostile.[8] Maturity lies not in conquest but in ceaseless struggle and in endless reversals of the situation. And believing this so heartily, I welcome change and conflict and abhor standardization as the earliest sign of death and decay. Always I have felt that it is absurd to say that one prefers the past to the present, the old ways of writ-

---

7. The comic strip character (created by Harold Gray) that first appeared in 1924. In 1931, Annie and her guardian, "Daddy Warbucks," went broke with everyone else in the Depression, suffered and learned through the hardships, and were rewarded with wealth again. Earlier, in James Whitcomb Riley's (1849–1916) 1885 poem "Little Orphant Annie," the title character was a live-in housekeeper who told the children moralized "witch-tales" that end with the warning: "An' the Gobble-uns'll git you / Ef you / Don't / Watch / Out!"

8. Glasgow's library included H. R. Orage's *Friedrich Nietzsche: The Dionysian Spirit of the Age* (1911) as well as Nietzsche's *Beyond Good and Evil* and *Thus Spake Zarathustra*.

ing to the new; or the new to the old. Always, I have asked of a book only that it shall be a good book of its kind. Always, I have been willing to leave to a writer the choice of subject to which his temperament has impelled him. For if literature has one virtue it is the virtue of hospitality. There is room for all in the world of letters, and it is safe to assert that the style which occupies the almshouse today will be attired tomorrow in the red and purple——or at least ermine—of authority. And so, having read all your books and liked most of them——though naturally I have liked some of them more than others——I can welcome you with pleasure and pride in your achievement not only as Southern writers but, as my friend of the late nineties would say, as writers. Not only, I feel, are you convincing the South, which sorely needs convincing, that books are more significant [than] smokestacks, you are proving beyond argument [that the] South is in the world and Southerners are people.

As for the immediate discussion, I admit shamelessly that I am more interested in the Southern writer than I am in a public which seems to me to be composed either of words or of a sanguine illusion. [What Southern writers may be, I am perfectly convinced that there is no public.]

I am interested in American literature for what it says and even more I am interested in it for what it does not say——in an age when what we used to call the conspiracy of silence has been broken. If I might have chosen the topic for discussion, I should have avoided the Southern writer and his public, especially since that public is usually situated far away from the South, and have tried to discover why America which suffered so little from the world war in fact should have suffered more deeply in spirit than the defeated countries. It is historically and eternally true that in material defeat there is a spiritual victory. For Germany alone is producing today a literature of pity——and without pity can great books be written? Or is it true, as some psychologists assert, that America, being the most feminine of civilizations, is the masochist among nations? Is this why we enjoy abuse and scorn sympathy in our books? For what does it prove that of all the books written since the war only two are rich in compassion, and that these two, *The Case of Sergeant Grischa* and *The Road Back*, should have come out of Germany?[9] Has the South forgotten defeat? Has it forgotten its heritage of laughter and tragic passion? Who can answer. How does any one know? A year ago, a German professor said to me, "Germany is learning compassion," and I answered, "America is learning brutality."[10] For it is perfectly true that if I were asked by a young writer to point out the quickest road to success in American letters, and especially in Southern letters, I should say, if only half in earnest, "Be brutal. If you have a genius, be brutal. If you have not genius, be more brutal. For the only safe substitute for genius in American literature is brutality."

Why should this be true? Well, the Lord alone could answer, and he will certainly not do so. Perhaps, because we were once too sentimental, we have become like the infant experimented upon by the behaviourists, who was afraid not only of his favorite white rat, but of every other toy he had played with in his innocence, and even of his bottle of milk. Because we cherished our white rat of sentimentality too dearly, have we grown to fear sentiment, which is only another name for pity and understanding. Have we forgotten, in our terror and humiliation, that pity and understanding are the only qualities that justify man's tedious ascent from the troglodyte and perilous descent from the tree-tops. Shall Germany win the intellectual conquest because she is able to see the whole of life in defeat while we can look only as far as the disaster of a physical victory.

And since the most difficult thing on earth is to say what one really means in a little speech, I should like to add that I, who fought sentimentality and prudishness in my youth, who was a convicted heretic in an age when all books were written to win favour with Du Maurier's ubiquitous young person, have never flinched before the barest of truths——not even before that whole truth which was said to be unacceptable to Allah.[11] Only let us learn from Dostoyevsky

9. *The Case of Sergeant Grischa* (1928) by Arnold Zweig (1887–1968) is the central novel of a triptych, "A Trilogy of the Transition." *The Road Back* (1931) is by Erich Maria Remarque (1898–1970).

10. The elections of September, 1930, propelled Adolf Hitler and his Nazi party into power; they gained from only 12 seats to 107 seats in the Reichstag. Hitler, originally the object of ridicule and idolatry, became the key figure in German politics.

11. George du Maurier, author of the enormously popular *Trilby* (1894). All three of his novels—the other two are *Peter Ibbetson* (1891) and *The Martian* (1897)—are drawn from his experiences as a child and as a young man.

that if nothing is more terrible than life, nothing is more pitiable. Love may go; sex may go, and not stand upon the order of its go-ing——but, as Russia knew yesterday and Germany has discovered today, pity survives. Otherwise, the machine age may as well destroy itself while it prepares the world for the insect. For is not the insect the only living creature that is perfect as a machine?[12]

A young girl in the late nineties, I began life as a champion of the oppressed. As a protest against evasive idealism and sentimental complacency, I made the protagonist of my first novel the illegiti-mate son of an illiterate "poor white."[13] Always, I was in the skin of the fox at every fox hunt and in the skin of the yellow dog under the wagon at every village fair. Only, in the last few years, since there has been a reversal of the situation, and it has become not only fashionable but snobbish to be lowly and despised and re-jected, I find my sympathy shifting to that outcast from the machine civilization—the well-bred person.[14] The only distinction is that I think fine breeding springs from the mind and heart, not from ar-rested tradition. Two at least of the best bred persons I have known were laborers in the soil. The most perfect manner I have ever known was that of an old gentleman who was colored, and this manner was the natural result of simplicity and consideration for others. But in America today, the well-bred persons occupy very much the position of the Kulaks in Russia.[15] They have committed more than a crime; they have committed a blunder. Now and then, when the crowd scatters, we see them scurrying, like terrified pe-destrians, to take cover beneath "the mucker pose." For nobody, not even Mr. Sherwood Anderson, of the overflowing heart, has a word to speak in their favor.

12. A final illegible sentence seems intended to guide the meeting back to the subject of general discussion. A separate fragment, which was included in Glasgow's talk according to a newspaper summary, develops a theme she often expounded on elsewhere, sometimes using similar words: her shift in empathy from the "lowly and despised" to "the well-bred."
13. Michael Akershem, in *The Descendant* (1897)
14. She probably has in mind General David Archbald, the protagonist of her next novel, *The Sheltered Life* (1932).
15. Prosperous farmers considered by the Communists as having excessive wealth; they were denounced as oppressors of less fortunate farmers and were fined or had their land confiscated or were even executed.

I have always liked Goethe's remark that the assassination of Caesar was in very bad taste.[16]

[Before the war would have been an abolitionist.]

[Behaviorist, trained to be President of the U.S.A. We clung to our white rats.][17]

16.   While discussing "Romans" in Part II, *On Theory of Color* (1810), Johann Wolfgang von Goethe (1749–1832) describes the murder of Caesar as "the most atrociously absurd deed ever perpetrated."—translated by Hermann J. Weigand.

17.   These final notes to herself indicate that Glasgow probably extemporized on themes not fully developed in the written speech.

A Memorable Novel of the Old Deep South

If there were a state of security, either artistic or economic, in American life it would seem that Mr. Stark Young had attained it in this ripe and beautiful work.[1] In the beginning I recommend "So Red the Rose" to the many rebellious readers (they must by this time form our latest revolutionary movement) who feel that they have learned all they need to know about degeneracy, including its successful exploitation in Southern fiction.[2] Some critics, I am aware, may object that this book is written from the point of view of the Southern planter and does not, therefore, survey the past from the flat proletarian angle.[3] But these people had a point of view. They paid a great price for that privilege. When the necessity arose they sacrificed life itself for a way of living. Certainly they are entitled to be heard in their own defense. They merit at least a share

This essay, a review of Stark Young's *So Red the Rose*, appeared in New York *Herald-Tribune Books*, July 22, 1934, pp. 1–2.

1.   Young published *So Red the Rose* (1934) at Scribner's.

2.   As in Erskine Caldwell's (1903–1987) *Tobacco Road* (1932) and *God's Little Acre* (1933). "Corncob Cavaliers" (below) may refer to the corncob pipe of many southerners, but specifically to William Faulkner's *Sanctuary* (1931), in which Temple Drake is raped with a corncob (hence the reception of the novel as scandalous). "Futilitarian" may also refer to Faulkner, whose early novels are strongly deterministic.

3.   In August, 1932, Clifton Fadiman (b. 1904) had published, in the *New Republic*, a review of Glasgow's *Sheltered Life* so scathing and so obviously left-wing in conception that, the following September, the magazine published a second review—this time by Stark Young. Fadiman's political unfairness wounded Glasgow deeply.

of the attention we pay to the sodden futilitarians and corncob cavaliers of the literary South.

"So Red the Rose" is the best of Mr. Young's novels. It is, moreover, in my judgment the best and most completely realized novel of the Deep South in the Civil War that has yet been written. The penetration is unerring; the light falls straight on the subject. Although the technique is realistic and liberal and serves more to transmit the essence than to present a stiff and formal pattern of history, there is outward as well as inward verisimilitude. Thus the book gives an impression, rare in American literature, of being rooted not only in a special sense of time and place but in some larger habit of mind, some abstract fidelity.

The many phases of Southern life and relationship are gathered here into a single created form; the characters and the types, the social mingling and drinking, the pleasure in horses, the changing relations with the Negroes, the religious varieties, and love conceived in family terms as well as in the stress of individual emotion. There is an amplitude of substance which may (and probably will) displease admirers of the telegraphic style in fiction[4] as much as it will delight the true believer in the novel of character and manners. For the essence of social life in the South, old or new, is in this feeling of abundant vitality and animation, in the closely multiplied effects, in the perpetually shifting surface over an illusion of permanence. The conversations, so light and natural at first, and apparently meaningless, deepen into a kind of sustained rhythm, an exactitude that proceeds from within outward. In the midst of careless remarks about nothing in particular something arises, or is spoken, which by the time the scene is over has brought a lump to the throat. These simple words or acts, falling in the hour of catastrophe, are woven into the very stuff of experience.

There comes a point in every novel when, if it is to survive, it must overflow regional boundaries and achieve universal validity. Regional tributaries carry us only so far into life, and for the complete plunge we must return to the source. On the surface "So Red

---

4. Possibly refers to the style of Hemingway and his imitators. Hemingway's recent works included *Winner Take Nothing* (1933), a collection of short stories; and *Death in the Afternoon* (1932), a book about bullfighting. Glasgow's library included *Men Without Women* (1927).

the Rose'' is a novel of the Deep South, where the border psychology of Virginia plays as small a part as does the Puritan conscience of Massachusetts. This is the South, not of Jeffersonian heritage, which paid lip-homage at least to plain living and high thinking, but the South of camellias and cape jasmines, of double galleries and latticed pavilions, of lingering French influences and French furniture, of reckless gallantry and passionate commemoration. Even when they have forsaken their plantations the leading characters still belong to the planter class, with the planter loyalties and traditions. The scene is the old Natchez neighborhood, with the places of lovely names: Portobello, Montrose, Green Leaves, Magnolia Vale, Bowling Green, Cliffton. Yet beneath the regional spirit and atmosphere there is an integrity of structure which identifies these people with human beings in every age in any part of the world.

The story begins in a tranquil stream, with innumerable bright and shallow impressions. Living must have been like this, we tell ourselves, convinced, in the double galleries and the blue latticed pavilions. Still, for the first two chapters, with a world in confusion and alarm below our windows, we may pause to wonder if life anywhere at any time could have been so spacious and serene and harmonious. In looking back after the end we see that this subdued brilliance is created in part by the skillful arrangement of light and shadow and is used, as art uses life, to thicken the long twilight of the perspective.

Outside, beyond the music and dancing and lighthearted voices, we hear a constant vibration, now near, now distant, scarcely louder at first than the humming of bees in the meadows. While we are still unaware of its significance the vibration approaches and suddenly the storm breaks in the sky where only a few dark clouds were visible. Within this rim of disaster the Bedfords of Portobello, the McGehees of Montrose, and all the other persons, white or black, in these crowded pages appear of full stature but are never magnified beyond the semblance of life. They are round and not flat, and, like all living things, they change and grow and develop. Little by little, feature by feature, with a slow accretion of detail, we come to know all these men and women not as characters in a book but as acquaintances in the flesh.

There are the older men and the younger, two generations contrasted. There are the two girls—Lucy, a spirit moving inward, and Valette, who responds to life as openly and naturally as the growing world does to the sun. There is Miss Mary Cherry, the loving spinster, "an Amazonian in buckram," disquieting at moments to overrefined sensibilities, who was and still is an integral part of the Southern scene, if not of Southern tradition. There is William Veal, the Montrose butler, who represents an entire race of Negroes as distinct and individual as the planters themselves. One and all, the characters are created with understanding and sympathy and with that quick sense of humor which sharpens the firm edges between sentiment and sentimentality.

Young Edward McGehee, the most appealing figure in the book, becomes the symbol of youth sacrificed in war, as youth is always sacrificed in war, as youth is always sacrificed to the abstraction we call, according to our habit of mind, either an ideal or an illusion.

"The Southern country that Edward loved remained. 'And I go with it,' he thought; for he was one of those people who follow something inner, some compulsion like a cloud; something in him was like the balancing of the clouds.

"In the young soul there is a certain universal element by which causes and events are simplified and weighed so that they take a form that is like what eventually time will give them. The report of events that later history gives is often only what they were to the youth who were in the midst of them. And so at this moment Edward could not but have believed that his feeling was right about these things. If he had consciously thought in those terms he would have seen himself as the prophecy of what would some day be the story of this Southern cause."

Mr. Young shows clearly that this agrarian society was doomed by its virtues as well as by its faults to destruction. All this grace of living, the product of romantic thought and feeling, sinks into our consciousness and we ask ourselves why these happy planters did not make a green isolation in the South and let the rest of the world speed by to nowhere on the wings of the dynamo. But the planters had everything, it appears, except the sense to perceive that slavery, in name at least, had become an anachronism and that romance and gallantry were lost causes—or merely old fashions. Or did they perceive it and choose deliberately to go down to defeat as champions of the lost?

Directly in the road of the industrial revolution, which would introduce its own slavery, and the leveling process that followed in the name of democracy, it was inevitable that the Old South should be "liquidated" before the new system could establish its own standards, its own realism, its own inequalities. The question was not one of right or wrong, of better or worse, but of economic expediency. Moral pressure is so unusual in human development that it appears only as fanaticism in the candid pages of history.

Hugh McGehee, an example of the Southern type at its best, saw this as plainly as we see it nowadays from a different approach to disaster. Beyond the spacious living in his strangely circumscribed world another world waited to take from the planters what the planters had taken from the pioneers and the pioneers from the Indians. "There was still a world of the piney-woods whites, the squatters, the people from back among the bayous, the people on their way to the West. Natchez-under-the-Hill was still a proverb for vice all over America and even in Europe the place most of all where met fantastic river romance, scum, and all that the frontier had spelled. But neither of these, the rough frontier nor the human dregs of the river, concerned the town of Natchez itself nor the society of the great plantation houses." That touches perhaps the hidden ulcer not only in that old society but in all social orders everywhere. The human dregs in the lower depths have seldom concerned them.

"So Red the Rose" has, in the true sense of that abused word, an epic quality. Not an individual Southerner but the collective spirit of the South is the protagonist. The shadow of destiny is always larger than the pattern before us. One never loses the feeling that there are momentous issues involved. This effect is multiplied by Mr. Young's admirable handling of actual encounters. The air is thick with the reverberations of war, yet the battles are not near enough to be seen. We do not go with the soldiers into the midst of the fighting. What we learn of the conflict filters through the agonized imaginations of characters not in the field, or through moving incidents related from memory. Although we miss the exact medical chart, the precise physical reactions to killing and the lust of it, we gain in emotional and spiritual insight. And seldom has the suffering of the civilian population of the South been so vividly and so truthfully depicted. I can recall few more heartbreaking passages in modern fiction than those that describe Agnes McGehee's journey to bring home the body of her son after the Battle of Shiloh.[5]

"There was an early dinner and Agnes set off with William Veal on the seat of the spring wagon. Work in the fields near the house had stopped, and a crowd of Negroes gathered at the entrance gate to watch the departure; they were silent and stood with their heads bare as William Veal drove out. He wore an old pair of riding gloves that Lucy had brought him, and looked straight ahead down the road. Mrs. Bedford had stayed on, and she and Lucy, when they had said goodbye and the wagon had started, went back from the lawn up the gallery steps and stood watching. Everywhere was green. The trees and shrubs, the garden, the orchard, stood under a bright sky, with soft clouds like summer drifting round its rim. For a time you could hear the sound of the wagon as it went along the road, then suddenly it was the doves calling. In some field, some wood or grove, the doves called."

And later, after the return, when three coffins rested on chairs on the front gallery and saucers of charcoal stood on the floor beneath them, Mrs. Bedford tells Valette of the journey. "Well, they wouldn't let Agnes go on the field, 'twas night already. But old William Veal stole out there. And he went over the field, feeling all the hair of the dead till he found Edward, he knew him by his hair. You know how fine it was. And then, after they left Jackson last night, it was so dark that they stopped at a house and got one of those piney woods people to ride ahead of them on a white horse. So they could follow along the road. That's how dark it was. So the man rode ahead on those blind roads and they followed."

I have quoted this passage in full because it contains the essential qualities of imaginative literature: simple fidelity to truth, the strong quiet pulse, like the pulse of life itself, and the sudden light that brings a deeper understanding and an enlargement of vision.

---

5. April 6–7, 1862; the first great bloody conflict of the Civil War, fought at Pittsburg Landing in Tennessee, and won by Union General Ulysses S. Grant

In time of general disintegration, when stupidity, cruelty, vulgarity and mere empty violence are all glorified in our fiction; when, as Santayana has said, "Many critics and philosophers seem to conceive that thinking aloud is itself literature,"[6] it is well to be reminded that a novel must have a spirit as well as a body, that literature is more than a vocation, it is an affair of the heart.

6. George Santayana (1863–1952), Harvard University philosopher and author, probably the contemporary American thinker Glasgow most admired. He expresses related ideas in *Reason in Art*, Vol. IV of *The Life of Reason* (5 vols., 1905) and discusses the relationship between thought and poetry in *Three Philosophical Poets* (1910). The quote appears in "The Intellectual Temper of the Age," *Winds of Doctrine: Studies in Contemporary Opinion* (1913); he is discussing the irresponsibility of reason in an age when reason itself has come to worship "evolution, instinct, novelty, action."

Virginia Historical Portraiture, 1585–1830: An Introduction

Any group of approximately two hundred pictures, assembled on whatever principle, is obliged to present more than one interesting aspect. The general history and the biography interwoven with the portraits reproduced in this volume are adequately treated in other parts of the text. It follows, therefore, that the single purpose of this comment is to consider what these portraits reveal of the art of which they are an expression. For painting has a history of its own consisting of things more important than stories, piquant or otherwise, of its practitioners; and this history, whenever it is present at all, provides an essential means of understanding an age or a nation. A succession of portraits like this, involving as it does so many justly and unjustly celebrated persons, and covering a memorable period of time, becomes an authentic, if fragmentary, record of the art that it represents. And it so happens that, for the countries and periods embraced in the scheme of this volume, portraiture does actually constitute the most significant manifestation of painting.

This essay introduced *A Memorial Volume of Virginia Historical Portraiture, 1585–1830*, ed. Alexander Wilbourne Weddell (Richmond, 1930). The expertise on art and the style suggest Glasgow received assistance from editor Weddell in composing the piece.

It is obvious that our survey must be restricted to the art as it was practised in England and in those countries which were to become the United States of America. The French portraits in this book tell us very little about painting in France. There is charm in the fresh color and free brush work of Lagrenée's Lafayette,[1] and Van Blarenberghe's Rochambeau is an amusingly keen reading of character.[2] But the French works are too few and scattered to afford a basis for any general remarks.

As definitely, then, as we may agree, this collection may be considered to represent England from about 1575 to about 1750, and America from before 1700 to somewhat beyond 1850.[3] The period of overlapping was that in which occurred the initial transplantation of art by immigrant painters. Later there was a renewed effort made by the native-born to import technical training, and this was followed, in several instances, by modification toward an art that was to become specifically American.

Among the more than thirty portraits, all of English men and women (excepting Pocahontas), painted in England between 1575 and 1700, only one may be attributed to an English artist with any reasonable degree of certainty.[4] Probably the Earl of Pembroke is the work of William Dobson; but an elegance and fluency so obviously borrowed from Van Dyck are, for that very reason, scarcely to be called English.[5] Of the half-dozen anonymous examples, the portrait of Lieutenant-Governor Dinwiddie alone looks as if it may

1. The painting of the French leader, who volunteered to assist the American cause when he was only twenty, was brought to this country by a member of the De Ganes family who was expelled from France, at the time of the *coup d'état* of Napoleon III, for opposing Napoleonic policy.

2. The portrait of General Rochambeau (whose forces together with those of Washington, Lafayette, and De Grasse laid siege to Yorktown and Gloucester, Virginia, in September, 1781) is perhaps by Henri Désiré Van Blarenberghe (1734–1812). Rochambeau died in 1807 at the age of eighty-two.

3. From England before 1750, the volume includes portraits and biographical sketches of Queen Elizabeth, Sir Walter Raleigh, Sir Francis Drake, Henry Wriothesley, and others. From America before 1850, the volume includes George Washington, Patrick Henry, Daniel Boone, Thomas Jefferson, James Madison, and others.

4. The painter who portrayed the Indian maiden Pocahontas is unknown.

5. The painting is William Dobson's (1610–46) portrait of Philip Herbert, 4th Earl of Pembroke (1584–1650); among his long list of activities and achievements, Herbert was a member of the council of the Virginia Company that chartered Jamestown. Dobson's resemblance to Sir Anthony Van Dyck (1599–1641) in style is due to Van Dyck's personal efforts and recommendations to the king, which raised Dobson from relative obscurity to the sergeant-painter of Charles I.

be an English work.[6] During this period of one hundred and twenty-five years England had fine miniaturists in the two Hilliards and the two Olivers;[7] but in painting generally she was still conforming to the fashion of importation which had been introduced fifty years before by the younger Holbein.[8]

In literature also England had sought her models on the continent, though her eager reading of other languages had merely inspired her to write masterpieces in her own. So intensely creative, indeed, was this awakening of the national genius in literature that there was little surplus energy left for the imagination in other fields. Yet, even if it is true that the English mind is innately suited to literature and innately unsuited to pictorial or plastic art, it must be conceded that in painting, if not in sculpture (that lost province for the Anglo-Saxon genius), England became, after Kneller,[9] sufficiently impressive to hold her place in the world. Only it must not be forgotten that during the sixteenth and seventeenth centuries painting in England, overshadowed by the court beauties of Sir Peter Lely[10] and the ten reigning sovereigns of Sir Godfrey Kneller, was in no sense a genuinely native art. On the contrary, it was an art practised there in the continental manner by foreigners.

Moreover, the foreigners who painted in England from 1575 to 1700 were all, with the exception of Rubens and Van Dyck, below

6. Robert Dinwiddie (1693–1770), born in Scotland, was appointed lieutenant-governor of the colony of Virginia; his chief activity during his tenure was protecting the English colonies from French expansionism, even precipitating the outbreak of the French and Indian War by sending twenty-one-year-old George Washington to French commanders to protest the occupation of British territory. The artist is unknown.

7. Nicholas Hilliard (1547–1619) and his son Lawrence Hilliard (no dates) are probably the two referred to here. Nicholas was the portrait painter to Queen Elizabeth, James I, and Mary Queen of Scots. He is especially noted for his miniatures; his son chiefly lived and painted on his father's laurels. Isaac Oliver (1556–1617) and his son Peter Oliver (1601–60) were also miniaturists of some renown. Isaac was a pupil of Nicholas Hilliard and painted many of the same popular figures of the time; his son Peter is said to have surpassed him in talent and skill.

8. Hans Holbein, the Younger (1497–1543), was born in Germany; when he went to England in 1532, he took with him the German school of Renaissance art, leaving no real successor behind.

9. Godfrey Kneller (1646–1723) was born at Lübeck but studied painting in Amsterdam, Rome, Venice, and elsewhere; there was scarcely a person of note in his day that he did not paint. When he died, a monument was erected to him in Westminster Abbey with an epitaph by Alexander Pope.

10. Sir Peter Lely (1618–80) was born in Westphalia but went to England in 1641, where Charles II eventually appointed him his principal painter.

the first rank in any school.[11] It may be surmised that Rubens would never have visited England at all had he not been sent there in the course of a patriotic ambassadorial mission; and it is probable that Van Dyck's long stay at the Court of Charles I was owing to his conviction that Flanders was scarcely wealthy enough to maintain both Rubens and himself at the same time. Thus, so long as England did not produce her own painters, she was obliged to be content with less than the best, since it is seldom that the best is obliged to travel in search of a living. For example, both Tintoretto and Veronese were in the full tide of production[12] at the time that Federigo Zuccaro made his visit to London;[13] and after 1600, when various minor Flemings and Dutchmen were depicting the English, the burghers and gentry of those countries were immortalized by Rubens, Hals, and Rembrandt.[14]

But if England was content to have no painters of her own and to harbor foreigners of lesser talent, she was not without an independent taste in matters of art. While Italy was still maintaining her great decorative tradition, while France was producing her classic landscape, while Holland was exploring the pictorial romance of common life, England was firmly insisting on the portrait. Zuccaro's continental reputation was based upon his immense and flamboyant frescoes;[15] but in England he was put to work at por-

11.   Peter Paul Rubens (1577–1640) served as an ambassador, between 1621 and 1630, for the Spanish Hapsburgs, who controlled Flanders. In 1629, he was called to England by Charles I and was largely responsible for the peace treaty of 1630 between Spain and England. He returned to Flanders in 1630. Sir Anthony Van Dyck was at the court of Charles I from 1632 to his death.

12.   Jacopo Robusti (aka. Tintoretto) (1518–94) and Paolo Cagliari (aka. Veronese) (1528–88) were the last of the great Venetian masters; both painted on a huge scale. By the time Zuccaro went to England in 1574, both Tintoretto and Veronese were acknowledged masters with most of their great works already completed.

13.   Federigo Zuccaro (1543–1609) was born in Italy, where he painted for Pope Pius IV in the Belvedere and the Vatican. He went to England in 1574, where he is said to have painted portraits of Queen Elizabeth, but he returned to Rome and later established the Academy of St. Luke for painters.

14.   Frans Hals (b.1580?–1666) is known for his portraits of the Dutch middle class in Haarlem. Rembrandt van Rijn (1609–69) painted many portraits of important citizens in Amsterdam.

15.   In the Belvedere, he painted *The History of Moses and Pharoah*, *The Marriage in Cana*, and *The Transfiguration*. With his brother, Taddeo Zuccaro (1529–66), he painted other large works in the Vatican and at the Villa Farnese. His best-known works are *Dead Christ Surrounded by Angels*, in the Borghese Palace, and *Man with Two Dogs*, in the Pitti Palace.

traits alone; and the other foreigners were portrait-painters exclusively. A secular and essentially matter-of-fact art, portraiture, as admired and afterwards practised by the English, seems to have been a sanguine expression of the national character. It was also an inheritance brought away by the emigrants to America, where, affected by different religious and economic conditions, it comprised the whole of painting for nearly two hundred years.

Among the portraits that span the century and a quarter composing the first act of this historical pageant, the supreme quality of design, in the complex sense that word has acquired in modern art criticism, virtually does not exist. The word is used now to denote not only the natural balance of composition, but the arrangement of line, space, texture, color, and form, into an emphatic three-dimensional volume. Yet in these early portraits, wherever volume is rendered, the subject is almost invariably placed in an otherwise empty canvas. Occasionally a head will be constructed with fair success and the rest of the body will be allowed simply to flatten out into the background. Even when accessories are arranged more or less into an active element of the whole, this success is never pushed out to the very edge of the frame until every square inch of canvas is given its correct value and made to hold its own in the visual counterpoint.

But, if we overlook these deficiencies, there is much of interest in this earliest group of portraits associated with Virginia. The Lady Somers by Paul Vansomer, not very competent technically, is yet engaging in the studied awkwardness of arrangement;[16] it is more than a step away from the true portrait in the direction of the Dutch figure-piece, in which the person becomes little more than an object over which light descends. Kerseboom's Robert Boyle, harsh in drawing and dry in texture, is the inadequate execution of a reason-

16. The reputation of Lady Somers has been overwhelmed by that of her sea-roving husband, Sir George Somers (1554–1610), an admiral of the British fleet in the struggles against the Spanish Armada. In 1606, he was named second in the list of grantees of the first Virginia Charter, and in 1609 under the second Charter, was appointed "Admiral of South Virginia" (as opposed to "North Virginia" or New England). He died in Bermuda attempting to secure food for the struggling Jamestown settlement. Paul Van Somer (1576–1621) was one of the chief painters in James I's reign.

ably good idea of the way a state portrait should be composed.[17] Gheeraerts shows himself, in the Robert Cecil, capable of a lively treatment of costume; but this sort of skill appears less important than his reading of character in the Sir Walter Raleigh. Once past the surprise of seeing gray hairs on a man whom most histories perpetuate as a brilliant and dashing youth, one perceives the fitness of these tragic eyes in the face of him who wrote the magniloquent apostrophe to Death.[18]

In occasional examples, such as the Captain George Percy, character delineation triumphs over an incomplete technical equipment;[19] though in the present group, such delineation seems to be most often associated with the minute manner of craftsmanship practised by the painters of the Low Countries. De Geest's fourth Lord de la Warr[20] and Janssen Van Ceulen's Prince Henry contain a good measure of silvery atmospheric tones in the light falling directly on the heads;[21] but these workmen show themselves to be

17. Robert Boyle (1627–91) became the best-known scientific man of his time. With his considerable wealth and association with the leading scientists in England, he built laboratories and developed instruments that enabled his experiments to make major breakthroughs in physics and chemistry. When he died, he left a considerable fund for the education of Indian youth in the newly chartered College of William and Mary. J. (Johann?) Kerseboom's portrait of Boyle was sent to William and Mary by Boyle's son; Kerseboom died in London in 1708.

18. Robert Cecil (1563?-1612), Earl of Salisbury, a preeminent statesman for both Queen Elizabeth and James I, attained his highest position of treasurer in 1608. His name heads the list of subscribers for the second Virginia Charter. In this collection, it is not Gheeraerts' painting of Cecil but Federigo Zuccaro's. Marcus Gheeraerts' (1561?-1635 or 1562-1636) portrait of Raleigh appears in this volume. Sir Walter Raleigh (1554-1618) is shown at a great age and was probably painted during his imprisonment in the Tower of London or shortly after his release. "Apostrophe to Death" was the last section of Raleigh's *History of the World*.

19. George Percy (1580-1682), one of the most prominent of the original Jamestown settlers, served as the president of the Council of Virginia during its earliest and darkest hours. He became governor of Virginia until 1612, when he returned to England, never to return to America. The artist of the portrait is unknown, but it was painted in England and never brought to America.

20. Henry West (4th Lord de la Warr) led an undistinguished life and died in 1628 at the early age of twenty-five. He is chiefly remembered as the son of Thomas West (3rd Lord de la Warr), who was the first governor and captain-general of the colony of Virginia. The artist is probably Wybrand de Geest (1592-1659), a pioneer Dutch painter of individuals and family groups.

21. Henry Frederick, Prince of Wales and son of James I, died at the early age of eighteen in 1612. Nothing is known of the history of the portrait before its purchase in the early 1920s. The artist is probably Jan Janszen van Ceulen, Amsterdam painter, *ca*. 1672.

school portraitists rather than thoughtful painters by refusing to extend the light into an opaque background. Mytens exhibits both talent and craftsmanship in the handling of his Henry Wriothesley.[22]

Technical skill and character interpretation are more evenly balanced in the work of Sir Peter Lely, although in composition it is often cramped and stiff—rarely spacious and serene with the ease of Van Dyck. Colonel John Page retains an aristocratic air in spite of heavy-handed restoration by Eastman Johnson;[23] where Lely was precise in detail and painted thinly, the restorer has smothered the details with thick pigment, has covered up a rococo fineness of workmanship with a saucerful of Düsseldorf varnish. The main strength of Lely's two royal portraits lies in the rendering of personality. Charles II appears flippant and slightly sinister, and William III is depicted with the exact personal traits mentioned in the biographical sketch of him—self-contained gravity, a habit of silence, and more than a trace of sullenness.[24]

In Sir Godfrey Kneller, the baroque qualities of elegance and display have definitely triumphed over the interpretation of character. His craftsmanship does not lack cleverness, but the emphasis upon laces and embroideries and other stuffs is no compensation for the decline in perceptive power. Where Van Dyck had style, and Lely had at least a manner, Kneller had only a mannerism.

And at length, well after the opening of the eighteenth century, there appeared in England a great school of native-born portrait-painters. Masters of living texture, of vibrant blues and reds, such later men as Reynolds, Gainsborough, Romney, Hoppner, and Law-

22. Henry Wriothesley (1573–1624), 3rd Earl of Southampton and the object of Shakespeare's dedication in the *Rape of Lucrece*, was not only a prominent English aristocrat but also an active organizer in the early colonization of Virginia and the treasurer for the Virginia Company. The portrait by Daniel Mytens remained in the hands of a descendant of Wriothesley, "through the male line for ten generations."

23. John Page (1627–92) was known as "The Immigrant" because he was the first of his family, the powerful and wealthy Pages of Middlesex, England, to come to Virginia. He owned the "Middle Plantation," which is present-day Williamsburg, Virginia. Eastman Johnson (1824–1906) was known for scenes of homey American life.

24. The portrait of Charles II in this volume was one of a number of portraits of him painted by Lely, his official court painter. William III ended the rule of the House of Stuart. His support of education in Virginia led to the Royal Charter for the College of William and Mary. This portrait was probably painted in 1677 while William was still Prince of Orange; the background is probably Lely's conception of the capture of Naarden or Bonn in 1673.

rence, painted a more engaging humanity, and certainly a fairer womanhood, than this prosaic world has to show.[25] With the exception of the fine portrait of the Earl of Dunmore, there are no characteristic examples of the English school in this collection.[26] And so we pass on reluctantly to Mason Chamberlain's picture of the young Thomas Nelson, in which an unusual blond color scheme and a precise clarity of drawing point to some distant French influence.[27] But by this time, it is needless to say, the colonies had begun to supply their own painters as well as the subjects for portraiture.

There are portraits dating from before 1700 about which too little is certain for them to be assigned definitely as yet either to England or to Virginia. Only one of these works may be safely assigned to the Colony, even though its painter is not known. The picture is that of the young Mann Page I.[28] Technically it is harsh in color and rigid in drawing, but the shapes into which the child's dress and arms are disposed make a pattern of decided energy. The portrait has an undeniable honesty and a rough vigor which still command respect.

It is from just such starting-points that scholarship, whether of the antiquary or the connoisseur, pushes out its investigations, gradually increasing the area of knowledge and legitimate conjecture. There is no reason why itinerant painters should not have been at work in Virginia well before the end of the seventeenth century. Indeed, they must have been here then; their works are still here to prove it. New investigations and a watch over fresh material turned up in archives and old homes may be expected to yield more

25. Joshua Reynolds (1723–92), Thomas Gainsborough (1727–88), and the others took the tradition of Van Dyck and modified it to a romantic view of life and nature against the artificiality of the Continental baroque and rococo styles.

26. This portrait of John Murray (1732–1809), 4th Earl of Dunmore, was painted by Joshua Reynolds. Murray, a relatively poor Scots nobleman, was assigned to service in America, where he had the misfortune of being assigned as governor of Virginia just before the outbreak of the revolutionary war in 1772.

27. Thomas Nelson, Jr. (1738–1789), was a signer of the Declaration of Independence, governor of the Commonwealth of Virginia, and major-general in the revolutionary army. The portrait was painted in 1754 when he was sixteen years old and studying at Cambridge University. Mason Chamberlin (1727–87) was a London portrait painter who never "flattered" his subjects.

28. Mann Page I (1691–1730) was the grandson of Colonel John Page. This portrait by an unknown artist was probably painted before Page was sent to England in 1706 to attend Eton and Oxford.

facts and possibly even a name or two. For it must be remembered that even the material already available concerning Virginia's early history has not been subjected to scrutiny by competent persons searching specifically for information about paintings and painters. When that is done, something tangible may be placed beside similar material from New England and New Netherlands.

By the middle of the eighteenth century, among the increasing numbers of canvases that are still anonymous, there are others to which makers' names may be attached.[29] The outstanding painter of the time is unquestionably Charles Bridges, who must have painted some portraits of Virginians in England before he crossed the ocean for his lengthy period of work on this side.[30] The study of his work has not yet reached the point where his full merit may be recognized; but whenever his name is cleared of the less competent and consistent portraits by which it is now burdened, it will take its rightful place in the first line of pre-revolutionary painters in America.

In this volume, his style may be observed in the pictures of President and Mrs. Lewis Burwell, Lieutenant-Governor Spotswood, and Lucy Parke.[31] He shows himself, on the whole, quite courtly in tone and accomplished in craftsmanship. He has considerable mastery of textures, finding an evident pleasure in the sheen of satins and the elaborate detail of embroidery. All this is more easily perceived in his men than in his women; society was evidently in the pheasant-cockatoo stage, when the males had the advantage in fine feathers.

29. These include portraits of Thomas Lee (1690–1750), president of the council in Virginia; William Nelson (1711–72), a president of the council and one of the largest landed proprietors in the colony; and Robert "King" Carter (1663–1732), known as "king" because of his immense possessions and overwhelming influence in the Virginia colony.

30. Charles Bridges (fl. 1724–40) was an Englishman who painted in Virginia between 1735 and 1740, in the style of Lely and Kneller.

31. Mary Willis Burwell's (m.1736) husband, Lewis Burwell (1710–52), was a descendant of Robert "King" Carter (1663–1732) and eventually ascended to the presidency of the council of Virginia. Alexander Spotswood (1676–1740), born in England, became the most famous of colonial governors; his fame and popularity sprang from his traversing of the Blue Ridge Mountains, his efforts in developing the iron industry in Virginia, and his restorations of the Capitol and the College of William and Mary. Lucy Parke Byrd (m. 1706, d. 1716), wife of William Byrd II (1674–1744), died at an early age after gaining a reputation as one of the great romantic celebrities in Virginia. This painting was done in London shortly before her death and was originally attributed to Sir Godfrey Kneller.

Of more technical importance, however, than his textures was Bridges' skill in attaining animated patterns over his canvases. Even more noticeable is his figure construction; his men especially exist very substantially within their clothes and back into the shadows. His drawing is by no means perfect, but it is more than good; his color has variety from canvas to canvas, and a real unity upon each one taken alone. In short, he shows himself a true inheritor and successful practitioner of the baroque tradition as that was brought into English paintings by Lely and Kneller. Though not the equal of Lely, he can bear comparison with Kneller to his own advantage. It is true that he is not so fluent as Kneller; but he exhibits a greater thoroughness and a better grasp upon individual character.[32] These qualities in portrait painting are worthy of respect and hold our interest; and on the strength of them, Bridges will emerge into the general history of art in America as the most vivid and adequate perpetuator of Virginia's early eighteenth-century society.

After Bridges, both in time and ability, comes Wollaston. Among the numerous examples of his work, the three portraits of Mr. and Mrs. Warner Lewis and their children may be taken as typical in every way.[33] They show that he, like Bridges, was fond of the sheen of stuffs, and that he was not so skillful as his predecessor in rendering them. There is variety of color in the clothes he paints, but he does not equal Bridges in managing his color relationships. In the faces there is a self-conscious animation quite impartially bestowed by the painter upon all his sitters. Even more affected is the facial construction; eyes, nostrils, mouths, and chins are made into a series of repeating slants from both sides down to a central line. When the features have consistent texture and solidity, the hands and fingers positively curl with elegance beyond the power of flesh and bone. In a poor painter such repetition would become tiresome, if not intolerable; that is the effect, for example, of looking at

32. The qualities Glasgow admires in painters reflect her own commitment to realistic detail and representation in writing.

33. Warner Lewis was born in 1720 in Gloucester County, Virginia, and later served as colonel in the revolutionary war. His wife was Eleanor Bowles Gooch Lewis, and his children were Warner II and Rebecca. The artist most likely is John Wollaston (1738–75) of London, who painted in the United States between 1749 and 1767.

many pictures by Wollaston's contemporary, the Bostonian, Joseph Badger, with their leathery textures and indifferent drawing.[34] But Wollaston's limitations of manner remain interesting, even amusing, because he was a really good painter, because he had a real feeling for the manipulation of his medium.

A portrait by Blackburn, who is definitely associated with New England in the history of our painting, may serve as the reminder of all that was going on in that region. His superb Governor Amherst is exceptional not only in its own painter's work but in all the work of its time in New England.[35] Lord Amherst's American activities were all in the North, so it is fitting that he should have been portrayed by an artist who worked there also. And no more than Lord Amherst himself did the New England painters of the day—not even the poor ones like John Greenwood; certainly not Feke or Copley—journey to Virginia.[36] The interests of the two places were still too divergent to compel much intercommunication, and consequently all manifestations of culture, including painting, remained in each case a strictly regional affair.

All the New Englanders just mentioned, except Blackburn, were native-born, but not yet has any portrait by an American appeared in this group of Virginians. Nevertheless, these portraits are legitimately termed American. Not only were they painted from and for Virginians in Virginia, but the artists who painted them have no place elsewhere in the history of their art. They and their works belong here or nowhere; they are to be cherished by us or by no one.

In John Hesselius, however, there comes a painter who was born

34. Joseph Badger (1708–65) was born in Charlestown, Massachusetts, and died in Boston. About eighty portraits by him have been identified.

35. Sir Jeffrey Amherst (1717–97) first came to America as major-general of the British forces with the intention of breaking the French power in North America. After conquering Canada and gaining a peace treaty, he was appointed governor and commander in chief of Virginia but resigned these posts and returned to England when he could not suppress Indian uprisings. Joseph Blackburn was born in England but worked in America from 1754 to 1762, when he painted about eighty portraits.

36. John Greenwood (1727–92) was born in Boston and died in England. His American portraits were all painted before 1752. Robert Feke (1705–50) was born in Oyster Bay, Long Island, but painted in Newport, Boston, Philadelphia, and New York. John Singleton Copley (1738–1815) was born in Boston and was greatly influenced by the art of Benjamin West (1738–1820). Like West, he went to England in 1774 and never returned to America. Critics of his time ranked his portrait work close to that of Reynolds and Gainsborough.

in the South with which his professional fortunes were bound up.[37] Unfortunately the problems involved in the relation between his work and his father's, between the work of both of them and that of others, are more complicated than the intrinsic worth of the work itself can well bear. In any event, profitable discussion of his individuality as a painter must be based upon more material than is available in this volume.

Shortly before the Revolution a certain John Durand was working in Virginia.[38] The prevailing flatness of his figures and the occasional awkwardness of detail in his drawing are redeemed by a very personal if restricted sense of mellow tones, and his work remains in the memory with unfading charm. About this time also appears the curious name of Cosmo Medici.[39] The portrait which carries that name as its maker is one of the genuine, though minor, discoveries brought about by the exhibition at *Virginia House.*[40] The laboriously applied pigment manages to conserve a veraciousness and a feeling for character which rise superior to mere quaintness.

Charles Willson Peale, to whom John Hesselius had given his first instruction, marks a double change coming over the art of painting in America.[41] It alters from colonial to republican, from regional to

37.   John Hesselius (1728–78) was born in Annapolis, Maryland, and was the first teacher of Charles Willson Peale (1741–1827). Few of his works have been identified. His father, Gustavus Hesselius, a noted artist from Sweden, came to America in 1711 and settled near Wilmington, Delaware. John Hesselius' early portraits were painted in Philadelphia before 1750.

38.   John Durand, a portrait painter of whom little is known, save that he painted many portraits in Virginia between 1750 and 1775

39.   Nothing is known of a painter named Cosmo Medici, but War Department records show "that one Cosmo Medici served in the Revolutionary War as Captain of a company designated Captain Cosmo Medici's 3rd Troop and Captain Cosmo Medici's Company of North Carolina Light Dragoons." The portrait is a painting of Mrs. Lucy Gray Briggs, wife of Captain Howell Briggs of the English army. On the back of the canvas is printed "Cosmo Medici Pinxit September 24, 1772."

40.   Most of the paintings reproduced in this volume appeared at an exhibition held at Virginia House, a palatial structure constructed of materials from the ancient Priory of Saint Sepulchre of Warwick, England. The Virginia House is near Richmond, overlooking the James River. The exhibition was sponsored by the Virginia Historical Society and took place between April 26 and May 27, 1929.

41.   Peale, born in Maryland, was considered the best artist in America from 1774, when Copley left for Europe, to 1793, when Gilbert Stuart (1755–1828), West's greatest pupil, returned to America after his European training. Peale founded the first art school in America (in Philadelphia), founded the first museum in the United States, and organized the first successful art exhibitions. He was also a pupil of Benjamin West.

national. Increased intercommunications, developed by the political and economic necessities of the revolutionary period, wiped out sectionalism in painting. As Washington, the Virginian, becomes a national possession and is painted by everybody, so does the art itself drop its geographical differences and become uniform in practice.[42] The colonial stiffness of pose and rigidity of composition are supplanted by a new ease and naturalism, even as the brilliancy and elaborateness of costume are subdued to a degree of soberness and simplicity. Although the average of professional competency attains a decidedly higher level, it does so by means of the technical formula imported direct from eighteenth-century England.

Stuart learned his craft in the same school, yet his preëminence in American painting is owing in large measure to the extent of his departure from the habit of that school.[43] To a degree rarely surpassed by any member of it, Stuart caught the individualities of the people he portrayed. He was an accomplished technician most of the time, but his supreme merit is his eye for personality.

As we pass on, the name of Stuart evokes that of another and younger artist whom he aided and encouraged. It is to be regretted that Thomas Sully is represented by only two pictures; an early study of Judge Peter Lyons, and the charming Byronic head of Peyton Randolph, the younger.[44] Certain it is, however, that Sully's portraits possess a charm of coloring and a grace of outline which distinguish them from most contemporaneous work. And this facility seemed to remain with him until the last; for pictures painted by

42. Charles Willson Peale painted fourteen portraits of Washington alone. Among other artists who painted Washington were Rembrandt Peale (1778–1860), the son of Charles Willson Peale; Gilbert Stuart; John Trumbull (1756–1843); and Joseph Wright (1756–93).

43. Gilbert Stuart, born in Rhode Island, traveled to London, where he was discovered and trained by Benjamin West. He was considered America's greatest portrait painter. Because the personality of his subject was his greatest concern, he used simple backgrounds to emphasize the subject; his unusual technique arose from his inability to control his hand, which always shook.

44. Peter Lyons (1734–1809), born in Ireland, came to Virginia under the persuasion of his uncle to practice law; he became president of the Virginia Supreme Court in 1803. The portrait was done in January, 1806. Peyton Randolph, the younger, remains an obscure figure, who died at an early age and is overshadowed by his politically active father, Governor Peyton Randolph of Virginia. Thomas Sully (1783–1872), born in England, came to America, where he came under the guidance of Stuart. Because there were as yet no art schools in America, he returned to England and came under the tutelage of Benjamin West. He died in Philadelphia.

Sully in his seventy-fifth year reveal much of his former art, and even at eighty he was still sought out to portray childhood and youth.

With Peale and Stuart, this procession of portraits has reached the point beyond which the story is familiar. As for the years after Stuart, what is told here simply confirms all that has been written again and again in the accepted histories of our arts. Portraiture, practised by men of declining skill, became subdued in the drabness of human costume and the bleakness of human life; after the middle of the century, it was debased by droves of minor workmen engaged in mistaken competition with daguerreotype and photograph.

But the message of widest import conveyed by these pictures from two hundred and fifty years is the never-to-be-forgotten truism that portraiture has been always primarily a craft and a trade. Consequently, the presence of higher qualities in any given example is somewhat in the nature of a free gift, since these qualities must originate on mental levels that lie deeper than those on which a trade can be plied, and vary with the temperament, even with the temporary mood, of their possessors. Whether a specific portrait will have technical merit depends upon the dexterity or the craftsmanship of the painter; whether it can have psychological value depends upon his ability to read character and his interest in the subject; whether it can attain high aesthetic importance depends upon the unpredictable factor of genius.

III The Novel as Voyage

Ellen Glasgow: An Interview

Miss Ellen Glasgow is an ardent American; she is still more ardently, a novelist. From a declaration of intense devotion to democracy and of belief in America in particular, she turned to just as eager a profession of faith in the novel as the literary form which must best express our people and our times. By way of establishing a first love, it might be added that Miss Glasgow thinks that the American democracy could be bettered by women's vote,[1] but holds that the novel can scarcely be improved upon as a form. Those who know the work of the author of "The Deliverance," and "The Wheel of Life," need not be told that Miss Glasgow has in mind the realistic novel.

Until two years ago Miss Glasgow could work only in her home in Richmond, Virginia.[2] Now she lives and writes almost entirely in New York City, in her apartment overlooking Central Park at West Eighty-fifth Street. It was there that the interviewer saw her, to ask her about her work.

"I have just finished a book," she answered. "I must go rather slowly about writing. I cannot write more than one book in two years.[3] That is not very many—I cannot understand how anyone can finish and publish two books a year regularly. It seems that one ought to give more of oneself to a book than that. For my own work, I should like to write each novel and keep it ten years before I publish it. But my friends tell me 'Of course that is impossible. You change so much in ten years—all would be different. You would be obliged to write it all over again.' I suppose that is true."

Miss Glasgow writes in her study, the windows of which open out high over the Park. There, in New York City, this woman, who

This interview appeared in New York *Evening Post*, February 19, 1913, p. 6.

1. Since 1909, Glasgow had been politically active in the struggle for female suffrage; see her essays in "Woman to Woman," the first section of this book.

2. During her most ardently feminist period, Glasgow lived from 1911 to 1915 in New York.

3. From 1898 to 1913, Glasgow's novels came out at roughly two-year intervals; thereafter the interval between books was closer to three years.

confesses her deepest admiration for the democracy of the West,[4] writes about the South—for virtually all of her novels have dealt with Southern life.

"I don't find it best to write about people or places when they are immediately before me," she said. "When I first came to New York, to live here for a time—it was two years ago—I expected to be here for six months of the year perhaps, and to do most of my work in Richmond. Actually, it turns out that I am now here about nine months of the year, and spend one month in Richmond. Even at the time I worked altogether there, however, I did not write the things immediately about me. One really must get at some distance and obtain a perspective, especially for realistic writing. I believe strongly in the realistic novel, but realism isn't a photographic reproduction of life. It is rather the truth of life portrayed—and in the novel, with an interpretation, for one must put oneself into the writing. In my present book, everything is taken wholly from actual life; it had all been in my knowledge and thoughts for ten years or more.

"All of my novels have been cast in the South. In this last book of mine, two or three chapters are set in New York City.[5] My idea was to tell the life story of a woman in the transitional period—the book begins in 1884 in the South. The years since then have been the period of transition—the change has come in that time from the old to the new."[6]

Miss Glasgow's novels have commonly dealt with the real, instead of the romantic South. Here she made a remark about the romantic literature of the South which she preferred not to be reported. As to her own plans for the future:

4.   Suffrage was granted to women in the United States in 1920; however, several western states had already granted women suffrage by 1913: Wyoming (in 1869, while still a territory), Colorado (1893), Idaho (1896), Utah (1896), Washington (1910), California (1911), Oregon (1912), Arizona (1912), and Kansas (1912).

5.   *Virginia*; the first review appeared in April, 1913.

6.   According to George Brown Tindall, in *The Emergence of the New South, 1913–1945* (1967), 1913, the year of this interview, marked the end of "half a century of Southern political isolation." In this year, Woodrow Wilson, a southerner by birth, was inaugurated as president; several members of his cabinet were southerners as well. Wilson's election climaxed the reconciliation of North and South called for by Henry W. Grady (1850–89) in his important speech "The New South," delivered to the New England Society in New York on December 21, 1886, calling for northern capital to develop a South ready to forget the "Lost Cause."

"I have in my mind the stories of several women," she said.[7] "I want to write several books, each taking the life story of one woman and working it out. I want to tell for one thing the story of the business woman who has been highly successful. She has always interested me. These are in my thoughts now—but I am resting for a short time. My last book was begun a day after the predecessor was finished; now I must rest.

"These books will not deal with problems.[8] I do not ever let a problem get into my novels—there is none, except, of course, as some problem of an individual life may present itself to the character. I am not concerned with any propaganda. A book should never serve any purpose but the telling of life as it is—being faithfully realistic.

"And realism is only the truth of life told, and is the writer's true business. Hawthorne was strongly realistic. He did not try to be pleasing or pleasant. He wrote things as he saw them."

"Hawthorne is your favorite author, isn't he?"

"Yes, I am sure that he is, of the American writers.[9] Of the English, I have no favorites—sometimes it is Hardy, sometimes it is Meredith. I change constantly. Three months in the company of one generally makes me desire a change."

In writing the stories of the several women referred to above, Miss Glasgow intends to avoid any effort to write of the "woman movement." She herself is an ardent suffragist.[10]

"Isn't that rather hard to keep out of your books?" I asked.

"Perhaps one can notice it," she answered; "but I am not conscious of it. No, that seems to me part of a propaganda, and I keep propaganda out."

7. A plan fulfilled in the trilogy of novels that tell the life stories of three women from different walks of life: *Virginia* (1913), a wife and mother; *Life and Gabriella* (1916), a successful businesswoman; and *Barren Ground* (1925), the tragicomic career of Dorinda Oakley, a successful farmer defeated in her emotions.

8. Although the three novels treat problems of women in marriage, business, and farming, they focus on the emotional and psychological struggles of individuals; in short, the books are more psychological than sociological.

9. It was unusual of Glasgow to mention Nathaniel Hawthorne (1804–64) or any classic American authors but common for her to include Thomas Hardy (1840–1928) and George Meredith, along with Fielding and Richardson, among her favorite novelists in English.

10. See her interview "Woman Suffrage in Virginia," in the first section of this book.

Even in the years when dramatization of novels was almost invariably the rule, Miss Glasgow never permitted the making of a play from one of her books.[11] She cares only for expressing herself in the novel form.

"No, I have never had the desire to write a play," she said. "I like the flow of the novel. It is the best expression of the people and the times. The drama cannot comprehend all of life as it is to-day. A larger canvas is needed to picture the greater complexity. The greatest drama was written in times when life was far more simple than it is now. The novel alone can take in its flow all of this complexity. I am ardently interested in the form of the novel. Its technique is more real."

"Do you care for the short story?"

"I know of nothing more exquisitely disagreeable than trying to write a short story," Miss Glasgow answered, laughing.[12] "At times I have thought that some of the ideas which I have and want to tell could be put into a short story. My ideas, though, seem always to present themselves to me as novels to be written."

11.   Although in *Virginia* the husband of the title character deserts her for an actress after he succeeds as a dramatist in New York

12.   This comment is ironic in that, between 1916 and 1923, a period when Glasgow's skill as a novelist subsided, she did some of her best, and most experimental, work in such short stories as "The Shadowy Third" (1916) and "Whispering Leaves" (1923).

"What Is a Novel?":
Contribution to a Symposium

What is a good story? My neighbor confides to me that she could not finish 'The Old Wives' Tale' because 'there is no story in it'; but, to my judgment, this novel without a story is the most interesting work of prose fiction written in our generation. To my neighbor, who, by the way, is a very intelligent person, only the unusual is worthy of print, while to my simpler taste a sincere transcript of

These paragraphs were Glasgow's contribution to "What Is a Novel? A Symposium Showing That It Is More Than 'A Good Story Well Told,'" in *Current Opinion*, LX (March, 1916), 198–99. The symposium included James Lane Allen, W. L. George, Rupert Hughes, W. J. Locke, and Kathleen Norris.

ordinary life is more exciting than melodrama. 'Treasure Island' is a good story well told, but it is not really a novel; 'Anna Karénina'— the greatest novel ever written in any language—is scarcely a good story;[1] and it is just here, I think, that the crisp definition of Dr. Phelps crumbles to pieces.[2]

That master of realism, Henry Fielding, was far more than a gifted spinner of tales; he was the greatest imaginative historian not only of his age but of English literature.[3] The plots in his books are buried beneath his vital criticism of life; and it is this criticism of life that makes his work an immortal heritage of English letters. For great fiction is great truth telling, and the true novel is not merely 'a good story well told'—it is history illumined by imagination.

1. *The Old Wives' Tale* (1908) by Arnold Bennett; *Treasure Island* (1883) by Robert Louis Stevenson; *Anna Karenina* (1875–77) by Leo Tolstoy

2. In a booklet titled *Twentieth Century American Novels* (1927), William Lyon Phelps writes, "I define an excellent novel in five words: a good story well told." A professor of English at Yale, he had been using the formula for many years in his *Scribner's Magazine* column, "As I Like It."

3. From Fielding, Glasgow apparently drew her own criterion for good fiction: "history illumined by imagination," which, she believed, set her work apart from surface realism.

"Evasive Idealism" in Literature: An Interview by Joyce Kilmer

What is the matter with American literature? There are many answers that might be made to this often-asked question. "Nothing" might be one answer. "Commercialism" might be another. But the answer given by Ellen Glasgow, whose latest successful novel of American manners and morals is *Life and Gabriella*, is "evasive idealism."[1]

I found the young woman who has found in our Southern States themes for sympathetic realism rather than picturesque romance temporarily resident, inappropriately enough, in a hotel not far from Broadway and Forty-second Street.[2] And I found her to be a

This interview by Joyce Kilmer first appeared in the New York *Times Magazine*, March 5, 1916. Kilmer reprinted it in his *Literature in the Making* (New York: Harper and Bros., 1917), from which the present version is taken.

1. *Life and Gabriella* (1916)

2. Glasgow had moved her furnishings back to Richmond in 1915.

woman of many ideas and strong convictions. One strongly felt and forcibly expressed conviction was that the "evasive idealism" which is evident in so much of our popular fiction is in reality the chief blemish on the American character, manifesting its baleful influence in our political, social, and economic life. Miss Glasgow first used the term "evasive idealism" in an effort to explain why contemporary English novels are better than contemporary American novels.

"Certainly," she said, "the novels written by John Galsworthy and the other English novelists of the new generation are better than anything that we are producing in the United States at the present time.[3] And I think that the reason for this is that in America we demand from our writers, as we demand from our politicians, and in general from those who theoretically are our men of light and leading, an evasive idealism instead of a straightforward facing of realities. In England the demand is for a direct and sincere interpretation of life, and that is what the novelists of England, especially the younger novelists, are making. But what the American public seems to desire is the cheapest sort of sham optimism. And apparently our writers—a great many of them—are ready and eager to meet this demand.

"You know the sort of book which takes best in this country. It is the sort of book in which there is not from beginning to end a single attempt to portray a geniune human being. Instead there are a number of picturesque and attractive lay figures, and one of them is made to develop a whimsical, sentimental, and maudlinly optimistic philosophy of life.[4]

"That is what the people want—a sugary philosophy, utterly without any basis in logic or human experience. They want the cheapest sort of false optimism, and they want it to be uttered by a

---

3. Recent English novels included Joseph Conrad's *Chance* (1913); Arnold Bennett's *The Regent* (1913) and *The Price of Love* (1914); Hugh Walpole's *Fortitude* (1913) and *The Duchess of Wrexe* (1914); John Galsworthy's *The Dark Flower* (1913) and *The Freelands* (1915); D. H. Lawrence's *Sons and Lovers* (1913) and *The Rainbow* (1915; suppressed). Recent American novels ranged from Booth Tarkington's *The Turmoil* (1915) and *Seventeen* (1916); to Willa Cather's *O Pioneers!* (1913) and Edith Wharton's *The Custom of the Country* (1913); to Theodore Dreiser's *The Titan* (1914) and *The "Genius"* (1915).

4. A lay figure is a "jointed model of the human body used by artists to show the disposition of drapery."

picturesque, whimsical character, in humorous dialect. Books made according to this receipt sell by the hundreds of thousands.

"I don't know which is the more tragic, the fact that a desire for this sort of literary pabulum exists, or the fact that there are so many writers willing to satisfy that desire. But I do know that the widespread enthusiasm for this sort of writing is the reason for the inferiority of our novels to those of England. And, furthermore, I think that this evasive idealism, this preference for a pretty sham instead of the truth, is evident not only in literature, but in every phase of American life.

"Look at our politics![5] We tolerate corruption; graft goes on undisturbed, except for some sporadic attacks of conscience on the part of various communities. The ugliness of sin is there, but we prefer not to look at it. Instead of facing the evil and attacking it manfully we go after any sort of a false god that will detract our attention from our shame.[6] Just as in literature we want the books which deal not with life as it is, but with life as it might be imagined to be lived, so in politics we want to face not hard and unpleasant facts, but agreeable illusions.

"Nevertheless," said Miss Glasgow, "I think that in literature there are signs of a movement away from this evasive idealism. It is much more evident in England than in America, but I think that in the course of time it will reach us, too. We shall cease to be 'slaves of words,' as Sophocles said, and learn that the novelist's duty is to understand and interpret life. And when our novelists and our readers of novels appreciate the advisability of this attitude, then will the social and political life of the United States be more wholesome than it has been for many a year. The new movement in the novel is away from sentimental optimism and toward an optimism that is genuine and robust."[7]

5. Political corruption was rife in the United States during this period, especially in cities. New York, Philadelphia, Boston, and Chicago were all run by political machines, and substantial corruption existed in many other cities as well.

6. The essence of evasive idealism as shown in Glasgow's novels is the conscious or unconscious use of an illusion or ideal to distract one's own attention or that of another from a shabby reality; for example, in many of her novels, characters who focus on the "Glory of the Old South" do not face up to the realities of the present South.

7. Glasgow's novels of the next ten years—especially *Life and Gabriella* (1916), *The Builders* (1919), and, to a lesser degree, *Barren Ground* (1925)—are all flawed

"Then a novel may be at once optimistic and realistic?" I said. "That is not in accord with the generally received ideas of realism."

"It is true of the work of the great realists," answered Miss Glasgow. "True realism is optimistic, without being sentimental."

"What realists have been optimistic?" I asked.

"Well," said Miss Glasgow, "Henry Fielding, one of the first and greatest of English realists, surely was an optimist. And there was Charles Dickens—often, it is true, he was sentimental, but at his best he was a robust optimist.

"But the greatest modern example of the robust optimistic realist, absolutely free from sentimentality, is George Meredith.[8] Galsworthy, who surely is a realist, is optimistic in such works as *The Freelands* and *The Patricians*.[9] And Meredith is always realistic and always optimistic.

"The optimism I mean, the optimism which is a distinguishing characteristic of George Meredith's works, does not come from an evasion of facts, but from a recognition of them. The constructive novelist, the novelist who really interprets life, never ignores any of the facts of life. Instead, he accepts them and builds upon them. And he perceives the power of the will to control destiny; he knows that life is not what you get out of it, but what you put into it. This is what the younger English novelists know and what our novelists must learn. And it is their growing recognition of this spirit that makes me feel that the tendency of modern literature is toward democracy."

"What is the connecton between democracy and the tendency you have described?" I asked.

"To me," Miss Glasgow answered, "true democracy consists chiefly in the general recognition of the truth that will create destiny.[10] Democracy does not consist in the belief that all men are

---

by her attempts to graft positive endings onto basically realistic life stories. It is as though she were trying to write her way out of the limits of her own life story, which, in July, 1918, would include an attempt at suicide.

8. Meredith's later novels all show a heightened social awareness, an increased tendency to take a humane view of human stupidity and error, a strong preference for psychological rather than moral analysis, and a sharp focus on the underprivileged position of women (*e.g., Diana of the Crossways*).

9. *The Freelands* (1915), a story with an expression of belief in the land as "the very backbone and blood of our race"; *The Patricians* (1911)

10. The context indicates that Glasgow intended to say "that will *creates* des-

born free and equal or in the desire that they shall be born free and equal. It consists in the knowledge that all people should possess an opportunity to use their will to control—to create—destiny, and that they should know that they have this opportunity. They must be educated to the use of the will, and they must be taught that character can create destiny.

"Of course, environment inevitably has its effect on the character, and, therefore, on will, and, therefore, on destiny. You can so oppress and depress the body that the will has no chance. True democracy provides for all equal opportunities for the exercise of will. If you hang a man, you can't ask him to exercise his will. But if you give him a chance to live—which is the democratic thing to do—then you put before him an opportunity to exercise his will."

"But what are the manifestations of this new democratic spirit?" I asked. "Is not the war, which is surely the greatest event of our time, an anti-democratic thing?"

"The war is not anti-democratic," Miss Glasgow replied, "any more than it is anti-autocratic. Or rather, I may say it is both anti-democratic and anti-autocratic. It is a conflict of principles, a deadly struggle between democracy and imperialism. It is a fight for the new spirit of democracy against the old evil order of things.[11]

"Of course, I do not mean that the democracy of France and England is perfect. But with all its imperfections it is nearer true democracy than is the spirit of Germany. We should not expect the democracy of our country to be perfect. The time has not come for that. 'Man is not man as yet,' as Browning said in *Paracelsus*.[12]

"The war is turning people away from the false standards in art and letters which they served so long. The highly artificial romantic

---

tiny." Too often in her novels during the next decade Glasgow tended to identify "will" with "character," so that the endings of *Life and Gabriella*, *The Builders*, and *Barren Ground* seem willed into being—or to derive from the author's best wishes for her heroines; the endings do not, in truth, emerge from the deep core of the characters themselves. In short, Glasgow's ideology had prevented her from throwing off evasive idealism altogether.

11. In *One Man in His Time* (1922), Glasgow would effectively dramatize this conflict in the struggle between the enervated old Culpeper family and the energetic but vulgar new Vetch family.

12. Dramatic poem by Robert Browning (1812–89) published in 1835; the speech by Paracelsus continues: "Nor shall I deem his object served, his end / attained."

novel and drama are impossible in Europe to-day. The war has made that sort of thing absolutely absurd. And America must be affected by this just as every other nation in the world is affected. To our novelists and to all of us must come a sense of the serious importance of actual life, instead of a sense of the beauty of romantic illusions. There are many indications of this tendency in our contemporary literature. For instance, in poetry we have the Spoon River Anthology—surely a sign of the return of the poet to real life.[13] But the greatest poets, like the greatest novelists, have always been passionately interested in real life. Walt Whitman and Robert Browning always were realists and always were optimistic. Whitman was a most exultant optimist; he was optimistic even about dying.[14]

"Among recent books of verse I have been much impressed by Masefield's *Good Friday*.[15] There is a work which is both august and sympathetic; Mr. Masefield's treatment of his theme is realistic, yet thoroughly reverent. There is one line in it which I think I never shall forget. It is, 'The men who suffer most endure the least.'

"*Good Friday* is a sign of literature's strong tendency toward reality. It seems to me to be a phase of the general breaking down of the barriers between the nations, the classes, and the sexes. But this breaking down of barriers is something that most of our novelists have been ignoring. Mary Watts has recognized it, but she is one of the very few American novelists to do so."[16]

"But this sort of consciousness is not generally considered to be a characteristic of the realistic novelist," I said. And I mentioned to Miss Glasgow a certain conspicuous American novelist whose books are very long, very dull and distinguished only by their

13. Edgar Lee Masters' (1869–1950) *Spoon River Anthology* was published in 1915. Its realistic portraits of people in an Illinois village contrast with much of the verse of its time, which was dominated by lyrics on nature, love, and the goodness of life.

14. The optimism of Walt Whitman (1819–92) about death can be seen in "Out of the Cradle Endlessly Rocking" and "When Lilacs Last in the Dooryard Bloom'd." Whitman views death as a step toward rebirth and regeneration, and hence a part of the life process itself. The optimism of Browning is evident in such poems as "Abt Vogler" and "Rabbi Ben Ezra."

15. John Masefield (1878–1967), Poet Laureate of England, novelist, playwright, critic, military and nautical historian, published *Good Friday* in 1915 and *Good Friday and Other Poems* in 1916.

16. Mary (Stanbery) Watts (1868–1958), American novelist born on a farm in central Ohio. Her best-known work was *Nathan Burke* (1910).

author's obsession with sex.[17] He, I said, was the man of whom most people would think first when the word realist was spoken.

"Of course," said Miss Glasgow, "we must distinguish between a realist and a vulgarian, and I do not see how a writer who is absolutely without humor can justly be called a realist.[18] Consider the great realists—Jane Austen, Henry Fielding, Anthony Trollope, George Meredith—they all had humor.[19] What our novelists need chiefly are more humor and a more serious attitude toward life. If our novelists are titanic enough, they will have a serious attitude toward life, and if they stand far enough off they will have humor.[20]

"I hope," Miss Glasgow added, "that America will produce better literature after the war. I hope that a change for the better will be evident in all branches of literary endeavor. We have to-day many novelists who start out with the serious purpose of interpreting life. But they don't interpret it. They find that it is easier to give the people what they want than to interpret life. Therefore this change in the character of our novels must come after the people themselves are awakened to a sense of the importance of real life, instead of life sentimentally and deceptively portrayed.

"I think that our novels to-day are better than they were twenty-five years ago. Of course, we have no Hawthorne to-day, but the general average of stories is better than it was. We have so many accomplished writers of short stories. There is Katharine Fullerton

17. Theodore Dreiser (1871–1945) published *The "Genius,"* a novel about an artist named Eugene Witla, in 1915. Witla's experiences are very closely based on Dreiser's own life, especially his sexual promiscuity. In 1916 the novel was banned by the New York Society for the Suppression of Vice. H. L. Mencken circulated a petition, signed by many artists, writers, and editors, protesting the ban. Among those refusing to sign was Ellen Glasgow, who had not read the novel.
18. Glasgow was not alone in this view. For example, Stuart P. Sherman published, in the *Nation* in 1915, an essay on Dreiser, accusing him of possessing "a crude and naively simple naturalistic philosophy" and attacking him for his view that "man is essentially an animal."
19. The range of realists represented here indicates that Glasgow did not confine her conception of the movement to the recent critical realism and naturalism currents. Notably absent here is Thomas Hardy, who strongly influenced her earliest novels, and would again in *Barren Ground* (1925).
20. "Titanic" no doubt refers to Dreiser's novel *The Titan* (1914). Glasgow's accusation of Dreiser's failure to "stand far enough off" is probably based on the autobiographical nature of much of Dreiser's writing: *Sister Carrie* (1900) was based on the experiences of Dreiser's sister Emma; *Jennie Gerhardt* (1911) on his sisters Mame and Sylvia; and *The "Genius"* (1915) on his own life.

Gerould.[21] What an admirable artist she is! Mary E. Wilkins has written some splended interpretations of New England life,[22] and Miss
Jewett reflected the mind and soul of a part of our country."[23]

21.   Katharine Fullerton Gerould (1879–1944), American novelist, essayist, and
short-story writer born in Brockton, Massachusetts. Her writing career began in
1900, when she won a prize for the best story in the *Century*'s competition for college graduates. Her most recent collection of stories was *The Great Tradition* (1915).
22.   Mary Eleanor (Wilkins) Freeman (1852–1930), American novelist and short-
story writer born in Randolph, Massachusetts. She is credited with 238 short stories,
12 novels, a play, and 2 volumes of verse. Her best work appeared in *A Humble
Romance* (1887) and *A New England Nun* (1891), both collections of tales.
23.   Sarah Orne Jewett (1849–1909), like Mary E. Wilkins, was considered the last
of the great genre writers in New England. Her masterpiece was *The Country of the
Pointed Firs* (1895).

Literary Realism or Nominalism: An Imaginary Conversation

Characters.
[1] A Reader Who Has Turned. (This is not a joke. He reads. He has
    even read the Victorians in the original and unexpurgated.)
[2] An American Woman Who Has Never Seen the Middle West.

Scene
An American town in that small section which has not been men-
tally assimilated by the Middle West. An English reader of American
fiction would imagine that he was in France——or Italy——or even
South Africa——never in the United States. A house that is really
old. Eighteenth century furniture that is "real". A long porch with
white columns wreathed in honeysuckle and wistaria which has finished blooming. A flight of stone steps leading down into a garden
which is rosy with crepe myrtle and white and gold with Cherokee
roses. Two feathery mimosa trees where the humming-birds are
busy above a few late yellowish-pink blossoms. There are no
prairies in sight. No underclothes hanging on clothes'-lines. No
drug stores. Saddest of all, for the lover of modern fiction, there are
no "men in cuffless shirtsleeves with pink arm-garters." Yet, start

This dialogue, which dates from 1921, was first published as "'Literary Realism or
Nominalism' by Ellen Glasgow: An Unpublished Essay," ed. Luther Y. Gore, *American Literature*, XXXIV (March, 1962), 72–79. The present version is taken from the
manuscript in Alderman Library.

not, gentle reader, it is America. It is scarcely more than a stone's throw, as they count miles in the Middle West, from the place where American democracy was first established on this continent.

Time. A summer afternoon in the year 1921.

The Reader Who Has Turned. Generally speaking, of course, the glad philosopher is more objectionable than the sad philosopher. If I were obliged to choose between them——.

The American Woman Who Has Never Seen the Middle West. Oh, be explicit. Implication has gone to dust with the Great Victorians. The only vices we recognize today are restraint in speech and self-control in conduct.

The Reader Who Has Turned (preparing to sting). Well, to be explicit, if I were obliged to choose (which God forbid!) between Mrs. Gene Stratton Porter and Mr. Lewis, I should probably choose Mr. Lewis——.[1]

The American Woman. On the principle that an acrid taste is better than no taste?

The Reader. On the principle of truth, not of taste. Yet, after all, I am not sure. The orbits of Mrs. Porter and Mr. Lewis appear to lie at equal distances from the centre of reality. To borrow a word from philosophy and twist it to fit a special case, is Mr. Lewis' literary nominalism any nearer to the truth of experience than Mrs. Porter's sentimentality?[2] Is there veracity in any interpretation of life which treats only of names, not of realities? Nominalism, in a literary sense, it may be, but not realism.[3] The drug store may be a factor in

1. Gene Stratton-Porter (1863–1924) was an Indiana author of sentimental novels and nature studies written for girls; *Freckles* (1904), her most popular novel, tells of an Indiana boy who thinks he is an orphan until reclaimed by his wealthy father. In 1921, Sinclair Lewis (1885–1951) had recently published *Main Street* (1920) and four minor novels, but not yet *Babbitt* (1922). In 1930 the Minnesota novelist would receive the first Nobel Prize awarded an American author. Theodore Dreiser and Sherwood Anderson were other midwestern writers grouped with Lewis, especially by Mencken.

2. Glasgow seems to have in mind Lewis' habit of naming and describing particulars that do not refer to a general vision. Glasgow felt that, from Tolstoy, she had assimilated an aesthetic of "concrete universals," which allowed her to tie particulars to the general cycles of time: the patterns of the seasons and human development—birth, growth, maturity, decline, death, and, for the seasons, rebirth.

3. Glasgow here is distinguishing realism from positivism, the theory that positive knowledge is based on natural phenomena and their properties and their relations as verified by the empirical sciences. She is stressing the place of vision, or imaginative interpretation of experience, in knowledge.

American civilization; but it is not the most important factor, nor is ice cream soda 'the end of every man's desire.' And even sex, so dear to the heart, and so inexhaustible in artistic possibilities to the eye, of every writer who, in the language of the 'new school' belongs,—even sex is not the whole of human experience.[4] In the life of the normal American man sex is scarcely more than the poor relation of politics or finance. No, the trouble with the militant group is that it lacks a sense of proportion, it has no perception of what, if it were composed of painters, we should call 'values'; it recognizes no gradation of colour, no gradation even of light and shade; it paints life without its penumbra; it reproduces only the harsh surface—and it reproduces that violently.

The American Woman. Oh, don't be serious! Though we lose every other sense, let us keep the sense of comedy.

The Reader. No, I insist upon the importance of being earnest. For instance, what could be more serious than Mr. Lewis in a love scene? He is so serious that, like Mr. Hergesheimer,[5] he banishes 'the feminine nuisance' from his pages, and makes all his women merely gentlemen from the Middle West in strange attire. How many women, do you suppose, beyond the bounds of modern American fiction, would recognize this description of what in Victorian days was classified as 'a love scene'? 'His slightly pouting lips, his mastiff eyes, were begging her to beg him to go on. She fled from the steam-roller of his sentiment.' Does that awaken memories, realistic or romantic?

The American Woman (laughing). Oh, but nobody in the Middle West ever made love to me! Perhaps that is the way they are taught to do it in the 'new school.'

The Reader. The 'new school!' I really must interrupt. Now, I can forgive them for calling it a 'school'——whatever they mean by

4. Dreiser in *Sister Carrie* (1900) and *The "Genius"* (1915), Anderson in *Winesburg, Ohio* (1919), Lewis in *Main Street* (1920), and Cabell in *Jurgen* (1919) had begun the struggle to liberate American writing from the evasive treatment of sexuality. Glasgow's discussion of proportion and values participates in that evasion; but her resistance in part reflects an internal struggle inasmuch as *Barren Ground* (1925) and *The Romantic Comedians* (1926) represent her own breakthrough to a bolder treatment of sexual materials.

5. Joseph Hergesheimer of Philadelphia was the author of *Mountain Blood* (1915), contrasting the new rich with old Virginians of Highland stock, and of *The Three Black Pennys*, the story of several generations of a Pennsylvania family who establish an iron foundry.

that! I can even forgive them, though this is harder, for calling it 'American'. But I cannot bring myself to forgive them for daring to call it 'new'. I confess that I feel as resentful as if I had encountered the familiar British features of Mr. Arnold Bennett in Fifth Avenue,[6] and read beneath them an announcement that the enterprising photographer had invented 'a perfectly new face.' For I maintain, not only, (in the words of a great, and almost forgotten American),[7] 'that Shakespeare will never be made by the study of Shakespeare', but that an "Old Wives' Tale" will never be made by the study of Mr. Bennett.

The American Woman. Well, they can't help the fact that we are still in the imitative stage of development. Isn't Mr. Wells doing everything he possibly can to assist us to climb out of it?[8] And how could you expect anything else after all the hours when we have sat, rapt and motionless, afraid even to breathe, at the feet of any European infant intelligence that was old enough to stand up and lisp? Not that Mr. Wells and Mr. Bennett are infants——more's the pity. I wish they were, for then we might be sure of at least two giants in the next generation. I would rather read "The Outline of History" than any novel that has appeared since "The Old Wives' Tale"—and that is, you will admit, one of the Six Greatest English Novels.

The Reader. Oh, I admit it. I am always glad to make admissions of that sort! Mr. Bennett at his best (and he is not by any means always at his best) cannot be made better. You see I am that prehistoric literary bird—a Reader—the Pterodactyl or the Archaeopteryx of letters—and because of my archaic habits, I still recognize the intrinsic difference between the books that are Bennett and the books that are only Arnold. They have others, too, over there who have made the discovery (surprising in this generation) that life is not all surface——and that the whole of reality is not contained in the three dimensions. The realism of Hugh Walpole, for instance, (to mention only one of a dozen names) owes less to external detail

6. Arnold Bennett's *The Old Wives' Tale* was published in 1908.
7. Ralph Waldo Emerson (1803–82), in "Self-Reliance" (1841)
8. Glasgow's 1921 edition of *The Outline of History* by H. G. Wells is well marked.

than it does to a rich and deep spiritual consciousness.[9] "The Green Mirror", "The Captives" and even the enchanting "Jeremy" are all written with fidelity to life and with that note of pity which is the supreme gift of the Russian realists.[10]

The American Woman. If he were only not the Friend of all the World he might become the greatest of English writers. But he is smothered by his friends.

The Reader. One can always lose them by speaking the truth. At least he looks down into life, not merely at it——and this is the distinction between the realists and what I have called, for want of a more accurate name—the nominalists. If a stranger judged our country by the 'new school' (I refuse to apologize again to Mr. Bennett) he might be forgiven for mistaking the 'honk' of the Ford car for the voice of America.[11] Certainly he might assume that the national soul, manifested in shirt sleeves, fretted eternally over beer and silk stockings. How have they done it? I mean how have they compelled us to accept this deluge of mediocrity? How have they led——or driven——us into pretending that it expresses us? They tell us that it is the life of the Middle West; but if Mr. Lewis and his satellites treat of life anywhere, they never reach the blood——they never penetrate beneath the skin——for the elemental attributes are shared in common by humanity, and the Big City and the Small Town 'are sisters under the skin'.

The American Woman. I suppose it would be asking too much of a man to expect him to discern that it is, after all, a question of fashion. We have no literary criticism, merely reviews of fashions; we are primarily concerned with neither philosophy nor method, but with the tasteful display of either fancy dress or homespun. Our one permanent interest is in externals; and the first demand we make of our novelists is that they shall follow what the authors of

9. Walpole wrote *The Green Mirror* (1917), *Jeremy* (1919), and *The Captives* (1920).

10. Leo Tolstoy (1828–1910) had been her favorite since 1895, but her library also contained a good selection of works by Chekhov, Turgenev, and Dostoevsky, as well as scattered volumes by other Russian authors.

11. During this period, the Ford Model T was by far the most popular car in America. It was introduced in 1908; in 1913, Henry Ford began mass-producing it on an assembly line, allowing him to reduce the price greatly, thus making it immensely popular. It was not discontinued until 1927, when it was replaced by the Model A.

'fashion notes' in the daily press describe as 'the prevailing style'. A decade or so ago our publishers and our public alike would tolerate no scenery except that of countries that were never seen on land or map; today we demand, in as unfaltering accents, the small town and the corner drug store.[12] And yet you laugh at women because every skirt must measure exactly the same number of inches! Why, today a novel with a background of 'Zenda' (was that the name of the country or the hero?[13] I have actually forgotten!) would be as hopeless a problem to a publisher as a débutante in long skirts would be to a chaperon.

The Reader (sternly). How flippant your mood is!

The American Woman. I am fresh from Mr. Hergesheimer's newest fashion-plate.

The Reader. And I from Mr. Cabell's latest fable of suppressed desires.[14] But these writers are so fine that they are already a little old-fashioned; and I confess that I find the national weakness you make merry over both discouraging and depressing. How much really distinguished work has been sacrificed to the habit of a 'prevailing style' in fiction! Take the case of the South, for instance——and of the negro. There are two permissible fashions in which one may write of the negro in American fiction today——the fashion of the North which portrays him as a celestial victim in allegory, or the fashion of the South which presents him as the poetic figure of sentimental legend. The shadows of Uncle Tom and Uncle Remus are still falling across the American scene.[15]

The American Woman. Well, I give up Uncle Tom, but I cling to Uncle Remus. He is the Homer of the inarticulate.

The Reader. So do I cling to him. I cling to legends——but I cling

12. Life in small midwestern towns is the subject of Sherwood Anderson's *Winesburg, Ohio* (1919) and Sinclair Lewis' *Main Street* (1920).

13. In *The Prisoner of Zenda* (1894), by Anthony Hope (pseudonym of Anthony Hope Hawkins [1863–1933]), Zenda is a small town in the fictitious kingdom of Ruritania.

14. In 1921, Hergesheimer's most recent novels were *Java Head* (1919) and *Linda Condon* (1919); Cabell's latest were *The Judging of Jurgen* (1920), *Figures of Earth* (1921), and *The Jewel Merchants* (1921). In 1921, Cabell also published *Joseph Hergesheimer*.

15. *Uncle Tom's Cabin* (1851–52), by Harriet Beecher Stowe (1811–96), presented Tom, in James D. Hart's words, as "a noble, high-minded, devoutly Christian Negro slave," whereas Joel Chandler Harris' *Uncle Remus* (1880) takes a whimsical, lovable old former slave for its title character.

to them in their place. Now, I wish that some one would write truthfully about the negro as he is today in the South; but no one can as long as he is obliged to write under the shadows of Uncle Tom and Uncle Remus. A Southern woman, Sarah Barnwell Elliot, tried once——some years ago——in a short story called (if my memory doesn't betray me) 'An Incident'.[16] Nothing so true and strong and simple as that story has been written of the modern problem of the negro in the South—and yet, as far as I am aware, I am the only critic or reader who ever noticed it. But we are wandering from our point which was the national acceptance of the second-best—the apotheosis of the average. How have they forced it upon us?

The American Woman. It does not take an observant eye to perceive the medium by which they have forced it upon us. But, after all, why blame the nominalists? Is not their method simply a free adaptation from the romancers?

The Reader (becoming thoughtful). Ah, that explains so much! The romancers——and I suppose the name romancer applies to every writer who discerns that, though beauty may not be truth, neither is ugliness——the romancers, not the realists, began the great American practice of 'boosting'.[17] When, for instance, Mr. Joseph Hergesheimer, in his loud Olympian manner, and as disdainful as Jove of his infatuated feminine following, stoops to praise a fellow craftsman, is it natural paganism alone that inspires the grateful fellow craftsman to begin chanting the 'Hymn to Zeus'? And the felicitous Mr. James Branch Cabell? When his mercy 'droppeth as the gentle rain from heaven' on all of his contemporaries (with the exception of Mr. Henry Sydnor Harrison, whom it leaves high and dry on his violet bank)——is it not 'twice blest'——since quite obviously 'it blesseth him that gives and him that takes'?[18]

16. Georgia-born Sarah Barnwell Elliot (1848–1928) dealt realistically with Tennessee mountain people in *Jerry* (1891). Her collection of short stories, *An Incident and Other Happenings*, appeared in 1899. After 1902, she became extremely active in the woman suffrage movement but published no more fiction.

17. The method of real estate promotion that Lewis had satirized in *Main Street* (1920) and would again in *Babbitt* (1922), when imitated by novelists, became the practice of authors writing favorable reviews of, or glowing tributes to, one another, as Cabell did in *Joseph Hergesheimer* (1921) and *Of Ellen Glasgow* (1938) and as Glasgow did in her various reviews of Cabell's novels after 1924.

18. Tennessee-born Henry Sydnor Harrison (1880–1930) was a Richmond editorial writer before he turned to fiction in 1910. His tribute to his brother killed in

The American Woman. That is not 'boosting'. It is the law of literary reciprocity——the secret formula of all schools. And speaking of the schools, can you tell me what 'school of fiction' contains Booth Tarkington and 'Alice Adams'?[19]

The Reader (after a moment's thought). 'Alice Adams' is a school in itself. It is what all realistic fiction aspires to be——a moment of ordinary life imprisoned in crystal——a vivid experience seen more clearly and more intensely in art than we should ever have seen it in the actual world that surrounds us. Taken all in all, it is the most encouraging thing that has happened in modern American fiction—— or so at least it appears to one earnest reader. For sheer pathos—— the pathos of every day in which tears and laughter are mingled ——I can think of no other scene in modern fiction that equals the last evening of Alice's romance. The incomparable ending of Mr. Conrad's 'The End of The Tether' is more poignant——for here the laughter is left out, and the tragedy is so still that one seems to breathe in the pathos with the very air of the room.[20] But 'Alice Adams' is a true realism. It is the realism that may save us yet, 'in the teeth of all the schools' from what would seem an inevitable rebound to the romanticism of masquerades and mock heroics.

The American Woman. But he is not alone——Booth Tarkington, I mean. There are others.

The Reader. Others who are writing soberly——in the fear of God and of the English language? Yes, there are others who are often felt, but seldom heard beneath the shouting. They are interpreting life sincerely and sanely; and some day, when what we may call 'the fast set' in fiction has, like Mr. Lewis' characters, who never walk, 'bustled' and 'scampered' out of fashion, the hour of these quiet ones will begin to strike. Though none seems to me so finely realistic as the author of 'Alice Adams'——yet there are many names

---

World War I, *When I Come Back*, appeared in 1919. In 1921, his popular novel, *Queed* (1911), was dramatized.

19. This story of an ambitious middle western girl from the lower middle class would win Booth Tarkington (1869–1946) a Pulitzer Prize in 1922, as had his *The Magnificent Ambersons* in 1919. Alice's romance ends at a pathetic family dinner that turns her wealthy beau against her.

20. "The End of the Tether," published in the volume *Youth, A Narrative* (1902), ends with several people receiving news of the death of the hero, Captain Whalley, and their reactions to this news.

that come back to me; and in the teeth, not of the schools, but of Mr. Hergesheimer, I shall speak first of women. Mrs. Watts, (one of the quietest of the quiet ones) Mrs. Wharton, (in her latest book) Miss Zona Gale, Miss Cather, Mrs. Gerould, Miss——no, Mrs. Canfield——these women are giving us an interpretative realism which recognizes not merely the surface of existence, but the invisible influence and the fundamental realities.[21] The men? Well, perhaps your good friend, Mr. Hergesheimer will match my list with a better one of his own making.

The humming-bird has left the mimosa tree. The sunshine is fading from the crêpe myrtle to the alley, from the alley to the city, and from the city to the world. There is beauty here, but there is also tragedy and comedy——for beneath the fading sunshine there flows on beyond the garden and the alley and the city, that deep and narrow stream of universal experience which we have tried so futilely to interpret as human destiny.

21. These women had recently published the following books: *The Boardman Family* and *From Father to Son* (1918 and 1919, by Mary S. Watts); *The Age of Innocence* (1920, by Edith Wharton [1862–1937]); *Miss Lulu Bett* (1920, by Zona Gale [1874–1938]); *My Ántonia* (1918, by Willa Cather); *A Change of Air* (1917, by Katharine Fullerton Gerould); and *The Brimming Cup* (1921, by Dorothy Canfield [Fisher] [1879–1958]). Inasmuch as Glasgow had begun publishing at least half a decade before any in this group, she may here be defining a school of realistic women writers in which she could justly claim to be a leading, if not the leading, figure.

Uncertain Criticism

Surely nothing, except life, or love, is more uncertain than criticism. Even the writers we esteem as poets or novelists or prophets betray our confidence as soon as they pick up the rusty pruning-knife and attack the work of a confrère or even a classic. There is, by way of illustration, the superlative example of Mr. James Branch Cabell, an author so deserving that, without prodigious effort, he might become the anointed of the press and step into

This comment appeared in "Preferences of Four Critics," New York *Herald-Tribune Books*, April 15, 1928, p. 2. The others commenting were Virginia Woolf, G. B. Stern, and Rebecca West.

the comfortable shoes of "the Dean of American Letters."[1] Yet Mr. Cabell, who has proved his agility by escaping the Pulitzer Prize, continues to find that ill-matched pair George Moore and Jane Austen dull reading.[2] Well, any man, be he critic or confessor, may have the body of George Moore if only he will leave me the irresistible manner of Jane Austen. But while Mr. Cabell is in the very act of dismembering the realism of Mr. Moore, there is thunder on the left amid the ruins of literary Puritanism. The prophetic voice of Katharine Fullerton Gerould chants in the accents of Cassandra that it is impossible for her to write of Mr. Cabell because one cannot review what one has never been able to read.[3] Here, at last, resigning Mr. Moore to a more sanguine posterity, and pairing Mr. Cabell with the incomparable Jane, I have sufficient cause for a quarrel with anybody. Certainly there is no woman, living or dead, whose charms retain the perennial freshness of Jane Austen's; and Mr. Cabell is one of the few living writers to whom I apply the ambiguous epithet "immortal." Moreover, I relish the air of Poictesme so heartily that I may never be assigned, in the enjoyable society of Mrs. Gerould, to that very private and most particular inferno, where, beneath the magic symbols "Beyond Life" and "Straws and Prayer-Books,"[4] Mr. Cabell imperturbably roasts all those authors whom he fails to admire in company with those even less enviable authors who fail to admire him * * * When, therefore, I am invited to "mention—quite informally—a half dozen books which have seemed interesting during the spring," what better can I do than steal a band of roving but still bravely twinkling stars from Isabel Paterson?

1. Given the notoriety of *Jurgen* (1919), there is probably an element of friendly irony in this title when applied to Cabell. But with the defense of H. L. Mencken, George Jean Nathan (1882–1958), and others of the "smart set," Cabell had made the 1920s in America his own decade. In 1928, he was busy preparing the eighteen-volume collection of his works known as the Storisende Edition (1927–30).

2. George Moore (1852–1933), Irish novelist, essayist, and autobiographer, criticized for his rudeness, temper, meanness, and light regard for truth. Glasgow's library included *Esther Waters* (1922) plus three other titles by Moore, as well as a ten-volume edition of the novels of Jane Austen (1775–1817).

3. Gerould, who taught English at Bryn Mawr, had published *Lost Valley*, a novel set in New England, in 1922.

4. Poictesme was the mythical medieval country in which Cabell set his series of romances of Dom Manuel beginning with *The Soul of Melicent* (1913) and including *Jurgen* (1919). *Beyond Life* (1919) and *Straws and Prayer-Books* (1924) are volumes of criticism defending a fiction of allegory that interprets the dream of life.

* * *[5] For the books that seem most interesting to me have descended from other and distant springs. I have read for the third time Fielding's "Amelia," and for the third time I have agreed with Sir Walter Raleigh that "it may be doubted whether a figure so beautiful and at the same time so perfectly lifelike as Amelia has ever been drawn in the whole range of English prose fiction."[6]

When I look at the pile of spring catalogues I feel that I have read very few books of the year. However, a memorable volume, not to be classified, is "The Sun of the Dead," by Ivan Shmelov.[7] This is a profound human document, conceived in anguish, saturated with pity and terror. But it is dangerous to begin writing about Russians. * * * Let us turn to "Wintersmoon," by Hugh Walpole, a rich and vital book, with very real characters and a background that is steeped in the mellow glow of English tradition.[8] * * * Then there is Elinor Wylie's beautiful tragi-comedy of another poet who, like Coleridge, "hungered for eternity." "Mr. Hodge and Mr. Hazard" is a fantasy of pure loveliness, so fragile that it can bear no heavier burden than a delicate spirit of tragedy and a style that is flowerlike in texture.[9] . . . A glance at my table reminds me that I have enjoyed "The Brontë Sisters," by Ernest Dimnet, a sympathetic study of the most interesting women in literature; "The Skull of Swift," by Shane Leslie, a dramatic and brilliant book;[10] and "The Land," by V. Sackville-West, a refreshing epic of the soil, written for those who know and love the beauty of England, for those who feel with me:

The country habit has me by the heart,
For he's bewitched forever who has seen,

5. A novelist who wrote the "Turns with a Bookworm" column for the New York *Herald-Tribune Books*. The "stars" refer to Paterson's use of asterisks.
6. Henry Fielding's last novel (1751). Raleigh's comment appears in *The English Novel* (1894).
7. Glasgow read the translation of the novel by Ivan Shmelov (or Chmelev) (1873–1950) by C. J. Hogarth published by Dutton in 1927.
8. Sir Hugh Walpole's *Wintersmoon* (1928) follows the lives of two sisters, Janet and Rosalind Grandison.
9. A tale of English life during the 1830s (1928) by Elinor Wylie (1885–1928)
10. Ernest Dimnet's study of the Brontës was originally published in French in 1910 but was translated into English in 1928. Sir Shane Leslie (1885–1971) published *The Skull of Swift, An Extempore Exhumation* in 1928.

Not with his eyes but with his vision, Spring
Flow down the woods and stipple leaves with sun.[11]

* * * This poem I brought over from the autumn season, and I brought, too, Emily Clark's charming dry-points of a familiar scene "Stuffed Peacocks."[12] I am watching Emily Clark because she has a genuine gift and she ought to become an able American novelist, notwithstanding the major impediment of being so little American that she was rocked in the cradle of the Republic and reared to be a Southern lady. * * * And speaking of Southern ladies reminds me that I have waited in vain for Frances Newman's "Dead Lovers Are Faithful Lovers."[13] * * * On this note of anticipation I shall thank Mrs. Paterson's stars, and so come to an end.

11. Victoria Mary Sackville-West (1892–1962) first published *The Land*, "the mild continuous epic of the soil" through winter, spring, summer, and autumn, in September, 1926.
12. Clark, founder and chief editor of the *Reviewer*, collected seven satirical portraits of Richmonders in *Stuffed Peacocks* (1927).
13. Georgia novelist and author of *The Hard-Boiled Virgin* (1926); her second novel, *Dead Lovers Are Faithful Lovers*, appeared before her death in 1928.

Impressions of the Novel

For those of us who enjoy enterprise, modern fiction affords an agreeable, and not too hazardous, voyage of discovery. Since it was first disclosed that the novel could go forward by merely turning within, the whole dark continent of the mind has tempted every budding explorer.[1] Mystery is in the air, and this voyage, which is older than we like to believe, is enlivened by the delights as well as the dangers of all speculative adventure. When nobody has blazed the trail each explorer is free to follow any meandering rill that engages his fancy. Where the wilderness is virgin and the destination is imaginary there is less need to be circumspect. At its best the

This essay appeared in New York *Herald-Tribune Books*, May 20, 1928, pp. 1, 5–6.
1. In 1928, Glasgow was midway through her period of most intense psychological fiction. *Barren Ground*, her portrait of a sexually wounded woman, had appeared in 1925, followed in 1926 by *The Romantic Comedians*, her study of passion in an elderly male. Her next novel, *They Stooped to Folly* (1929), would explore the significance of the sexual liberation that came with World War I. *The Sheltered Life* (1932) would contrast the sensual needs of a young girl with an elderly man's need for a woman to confirm his idealism.

prospect is exciting; at its worst it is easily avoidable. Meanwhile, every stream, we feel, must flow somewhere, if only into a marsh. Every departure, however forlorn, clears the ground for space. Every experiment, every invention, is a sign not of decay but of the continual efflorescence of life. For the modern novel, we remind ourselves hopefully, has as many perspectives as there are green aisles in a forest.

But there are others who prefer solids to fluids even in metaphor, and who cling to what they feel to be the superior altitude of tradition. Democracy, which was designed to elevate the average, has succeeded, they point out, only in reducing excellence to a common plane of unimportance. Though they do not deny that a fairer social order may be worth any price, even the price of democratized art, they prefer that an industrial millennium should usher in rather than wait upon the complete vulgarization of legend and literature. Some of them, indeed, would rest content not only with smaller loaves but with fewer hyacinths as well, if they might keep the loveliness of Helen unprofaned by the appetites of Mr. Leopold Bloom.[2] To these lovers of the past, the ugly trail of the subconscious has besmirched every aspect, even the most innocent-looking, of contemporary fiction. All is lost but allegory, they sigh, and this even is menaced by the too hearty right hands of fellowship.

If we turn to the animated scene of the novel it soon becomes clear that there are as many arguments as there are methods of writing. The age is a vociferous one, and no prophet is without honor who is able to strike an attitude and to speak loud enough to make himself heard. True, the pulpit has become a sad impediment, and the friendly soap-box is no longer the last stand of patriotism. The nearer, indeed, the literary prophet comes to ground, the better chance he has of reaching the ears of authority. For when all is lost but allegory the first thing to disappear is a certain eminence in the angle of vision.

2.   Helen here resembles Poe's ("To Helen," 1831) more than Homer's; the latter often berates herself for yielding to Paris in an age when love of Helen could hardly have been profaned, for to the Greeks love was divine but not sacred in the Christian sense. Leopold Bloom is James Joyce's (1882–1941) modern Odysseus and protagonist in *Ulysses* (1922), where Helen is connected to Mrs. Kitty O'Shea, a "woman [who] brought Parnell low."

If the recent overflow has done nothing else, it seems to have washed away, temporarily at least, the firmly planted convention of the guarded point of view. To the critical faculty of Mr. Percy Lubbock and the punctilious art of Mr. James Branch Cabell a novel can be no stronger than the weakest link in its point of view.[3] A discreet range of vision has been always, and for some of us still continues to be, one of the safe rules in fiction. The great novelists of the past, even when they employed the roving point of view, have shown almost invariably that they were aware of the dangers of a too omniscient author. Richardson and Defoe both deferred, not precisely, indeed, nor with complete success, to what they regarded as a natural and logical restriction of vision;[4] and the habit of popping in and out of the head of any character, with the mechanical agility of a Jack-in-the-box, has been held in disfavor by the more scrupulous novelists. But as the novel approaches closer to actuality, it begins, like life itself, to enlarge its boundaries and extend its outlook. As the fresh impulse emerges, the old restraint of precept or pattern is shed like a chrysalis. For until there is a new triumph of form over freedom (and a reversal of the situation occurs in the celebrated conflict between the Apollonian and the Dionysian illusions), the novel, like the social order from which it springs, will frolic with the hallucination of liberty.

Of all those modern writers, prophets or novelists, whom we called modernists yesterday, Marcel Proust alone has evoked an entire world from the rich afterglow and the gossamer texture of memory. To achieve this miracle he has taken whatever he required from the past; but he has not required apparently that convention which forbade the novelist to angle for big fish in little streams. In "Du Côté de chez Swann" the youthful hero remembers things that a child could never know, or knowing with the surface of his thoughts, could not possibly understand.[5] Here, indeed, by one tri-

3. Percy Lubbock (1879–1965), historian and biographer, wrote the major analysis of point-of-view techniques in *The Craft of Fiction* (1921).
4. Richardson, in novels like *Clarissa*, used the epistolary form with little or no narrative intervention, allowing the letters to speak for themselves and qualify each other. Defoe, in novels like *Moll Flanders*, used first-person narrators whose visions and perceptions were obviously flawed and limited.
5. Marcel Proust (1871–1922) published *Du Côté de chez Swann (Swann's Way)*, the first of the seven parts of *A la Recherche du temps perdu*, in 1913. Glasgow's

umphant achievement, Proust has demolished, as far as his own genius is concerned, the twin conventions of the limited field of knowledge and the restricted point of view. Here again he has proved that rules, like codes, are made for those artists who are not strong enough to break them.

And what is true of Proust applies, though in a lesser degree, to the work of Virginia Woolf—surely the most interesting, if not the most robust, of contemporary English novelists. In her novels the point of view has dissolved into mist and the vision is as diffused, as transparent, as luminous as a shower in sunlight. Not the characters in "Mrs. Dalloway," but life itself, is the spectator.[6] Life, fugitive, variegated, erratic, has become both the observed and the observer. Among English and American novelists only Mrs. Woolf has succeeded with this method, if it may be labeled a method, of the magnified vision. Her style, when she uses it herself, is saturated with the quality of a distinguished mind. In the hands of her admirers it is besmeared with vulgarity.

But what is this modernism of which we hear so much and yet see so little that appears significant enough to arrest the attention?[7] Has the novel achieved a closer approach to what we persist in naming reality? Has fiction altered not only its external aspect but even its inner nature? Has it received the sanction of those humane impulses which have at last released psychology from its long imprisonment in the nursery and the asylum?

Much has been made in recent criticism of the bold modern plunge into subjective experience. In reading some of these eulogies of the new psychology one is almost persuaded that introspection is as modern as aviation and that reality was first discovered by Mr. James Joyce while he was looking over the shoulder of Mr. Leopold Bloom. But is the matter so simple as this? Compared with the

---

youthful heroine Jenny Blair Archbald (*The Sheltered Life*, 1932) also seems to know things "a child could never know."

6. In *Mrs. Dalloway* (1925), Virginia Woolf (1882–1941) employs a chain of point-of-view characters, an approach resembling one Glasgow would use on a smaller scale in chapters of *Vein of Iron* (1935).

7. An age of strenuous experience and experiment, of desperate uncertainty and inward searching, of talent and energy, that stretched from World War I down to the angry protests of the late 1960s. In literature, the major works included Joyce's *Ulysses*, T. S. Eliot's (1888–1965) *The Waste Land*, and, in the year following this essay, Faulkner's *The Sound and the Fury* (1929).

mental involutions of Mr. Joyce or Mr. Lawrence, the great English novelists may appear a simpleminded assemblage, interested, not in pathological symptoms, but in this, too, too solid flesh and other tangible substances.[8] Nevertheless, beyond the English novelists there are the Russian, and beyond the Russian novelists there is—eternity. When the Russian stream of consciousness overflows it is out of the actual into the universal experience. For the Russian genius, like the philosophy of Plotinus, is "the flight of the alone to the alone."[9] With Tolstoy or Dostoievsky the spring of the unconscious mind is not a sluggish outlet, as colorless as sand, but a fountain of images transfigured by a luminous spray of emotion.[10] No novelist, living or dead, with the possible exception of Dostoievsky, has equalled Tolstoy in his use of those tremulous and palely phosphorescent states between thought and sensation. Turn to those matchless pages in which Anna Karenina knows, without admitting the knowledge into her thoughts, that the end is approaching. Or to those illuminated scenes before the death of Prince Andrei, while the flickering tide of consciousness ebbs and flows and ebbs again into darkness.

Always in Tolstoy or Dostoievsky or Tchekov this overflow of impressions is living and illuminated; but when we look closer we find that the illumination is not from without but from within.[11] For the radiance streams from some central glow of the spirit. It is, we discover presently, with astonishment if we are not Russians, whom nothing surprises, the light of the soul. "It is the soul that is the chief character in Russian fiction," says Virginia Woolf in her penetrating study "The Russian Point of View."[12] But the soul is

8. The D. H. Lawrence that Glasgow knew—through *Sons and Lovers* (1913), *Women in Love* (1920), and *Aaron's Rod* (1922)—based his fictions on events in his own life and on his struggles to understand them by plunging into the depths of his mind.

9. Plotinus (A.D. 205?–70), born at Lycopolis in Egypt, was the chief exponent of the Neoplatonic philosophy. He is generally described as a "mystic" who developed Plato's teaching, and he appears to have had some knowledge of oriental philosophies.

10. Tolstoy describes Anna Karenina's resignation in *Anna Karenina* (1875) and Prince Andrei's death in *War and Peace* (1869). Fëdor Dostoevsky (1821–81) represents extreme states of guilt, lust, doubt, decadence, innocence, and madness in *Crime and Punishment* (1866), *The Brothers Karamazov* (1880), and other novels.

11. Anton Pavlovich Chekhov (1860–1904), dramatist and writer

12. In *The Common Reader* by Virginia Woolf (1925)

more than a character; more than any number of characters. It is the illumination that transfigures the world they inhabit.

And this soul, so powerful and yet so transparent, is not to us a familiar or even a recognizable attribute. It bears no kinship to that winged creature so ludicrously like a celestial dragon-fly which took flight, according to mediaeval piety, from the mouth of the dying. It has no close relation to virtue (for rectitude is often devoid of it), and it is little more concerned with religion than it is with a man's simple aspiration after immortality.

> Though you really are mentally afflicted (you won't be angry at that, of course; I'm speaking from a higher point of view, said Algata to Myshkin), yet the mind that matters is better in you than in any of them. It's something, in fact, they never dreamed of. For there are two sorts of mind; one that matters and one that doesn't matter.[13]

For the things that matter in Russian novels are those terrible attributes of the soul—love, pity, goodness, regeneration—all the diminished virtues which are more unmentionable than obscenity in modernist fiction.[14] The Russian novelists are unashamed not only of soul, they are unashamed even of innocence. This is the illumination that enkindles their obscure world and brings it to life. They have the courage to confront pain and evil and ugliness; and they have also that rarer courage which faces beauty and tenderness and truth even when it is not ugly. If comprehension is the supreme gift of Tolstoy, forgiveness is even more abundantly the presiding genius of Dostoievsky. More completely than any other novelist, more completely than almost any other human being in our modern age, he was inspired by the desperation of pity. His vision of life is spun, not like ours, of the thin negations of reason, but of the quivering radiance of dreams and the power of tragic conviction. There are incidents in his novels so vivid, so intensely transfigured that they borrow the colors and the texture of a rainbow looked at through tears.

It is true, of course, that Dostoievsky's genius was essentially Russian; and in Russia, where there is little freedom in the external

13. From Dostoevsky's *The Idiot*: Prince Lef Nicolaievitch Myshkin and *Aglaya Ivanova* (not "Algata")

14. A pattern explored by Christopher Blake, the protagonist of Glasgow's most "Russian" novel, *The Deliverance*, published in 1904

world, the most incredible things may occur in the novel. In our republic it is more convenient and certainly far safer to remember that an improper allusion to the spirit may cost an otherwise irreproachable American writer his fame as a realist. Not even Mr. Theodore Dreiser would risk his reputation in the society of beauty or goodness. Yet, since he suffered martyrdom for the natural man, Mr. Dreiser has been a kind of tutelary saint in American fiction, as superior to compromising associations as if he occupied a niche in a cathedral.[15]

However, it is only in the impractical profession of letters that we revere a saint who inhabits a niche. Notwithstanding our inordinate zeal for improving and reforming the body, we continue to treat the soul as an impoverished female relation who is welcome only so long as she makes herself useful about the house. With the soul that loafs or star-gazes or is slow to lend a hand in our legitimate business of making over the world we have as little patience as if it were both in fact and in theological fiction our deceased wife's sister. Love, joy, pain, pity are, for us, merely words that rhyme or do not rhyme. When we write them they look as flat and stiff as flowers in gold or silver on the illuminated margins of manuscripts. Even Fielding, the greatest of the English novelists, would have felt embarrassed in the presence of Dostoievsky's naked realities. Dickens and Thackeray, their rough edges polished by Victorian reticence, became bold enough about sentimentality; but sentimentality is further removed from the soul as the Russians discerned it than is the coarseness of Fielding. Now and then Meredith approaches, vehement, yet discreet; and there are passages in the Wessex tales when Hardy glances beneath the surface of consciousness and is too saddened by what he sees to stay for a second look.[16] Now and then Henry James has edged perilously near a spot where the crust is thin, but he maneuvers quickly back again to his artful devices for

15. In addition to having had *The "Genius"* (1915) suppressed for sexual frankness, Dreiser would be harassed in 1931 by defenders of purity in Kentucky who brought charges of adultery against him and a woman he identified as Marie Pergain; the adultery charges would receive widespread coverage by the nation's newspapers.

16. "Wessex," used by Thomas Hardy to designate the southwest counties of England, principally Dorset, which are the scene of his novels. Additionally, there is an individual work by Hardy called *Wessex Tales* (1888).

avoiding equally the improper and the profound. One feels that even if he had discovered the soul he would have waited too long for its references before he attempted to cultivate an acquaintance. Excepting always the consummate art, the only things that really mattered to him were the things that did not matter at all to Dostoievsky. Not an ocean alone, but a whole universe separates their social philosophy. To Dostoievsky art was merely the servant of life; but to Henry James all that the Russians called life was no more than the sacrificial victim of art.

Nevertheless, modern prose fiction, especially American fiction, owes a debt of gratitude to Henry James which, like most debts of this nature, probably will remain forever unsettled. More than any other writer or group of writers, he encouraged the American novel to discard its Little Lord Fauntleroy curls and velvet jacket and to wear the attire, even if it could not assume the demeanor, of maturity.[17] A master of deportment as well as an incomparable artist, he has left an influence which, wearing a trifle thin with time and the decay of moral quibbling, is still to be reckoned with in contemporary letters. Strether, who feared and rejected happiness because his "only logic" was that hair-splitting logic of the Puritan conscience (now happily discredited) which prompted him "not, out of the whole affair, to have got anything for myself," is the literary ancestor of a prolific if unvirile progeny. His most distinguished moral equivalent is the limp protagonist in Mrs. Wharton's delightful novel "The Age of Innocence" who fears and rejects life because " 'It's more real to me here than if I went up,' he suddenly heard himself say; and the fear lest that shadow of reality should lose its edge kept him rooted to his seat as the minutes succeeded each other."[18] This school of novelists, so foreign in manner and so Puritan in temperament, achieved the apotheosis of our evasive idealism.

17. Glasgow uses the title character from Frances H. Burnett's (1849–1924) novel (1886) and play (1888) to represent the adolescent optimism from which Henry James (1843–1916), in *The Ambassadors* (1903), *The Golden Bowl* (1904), and many other intellectually and psychologically demanding fictions, helped liberate American literature. Lambert Strether is the protagonist of *The Ambassadors*.

18. Newland Archer, a young lawyer who is a member of New York's high society. He falls in love with Ellen Olenska and considers running away with her but never does because he is bound by his ties of marriage and convention. Edith Wharton published the novel in 1920.

If we turn back from Henry James to Balzac, the most opulently endowed of all novelists, we find a scene as solid, as compact, as animated and as palely glittering as any world constructed of three dimensions and illumined by an artificial system of lighting. Unrelated to creatures more vital than themselves, the characters in "La Cousine Bette" appear completely convincing.[19] Only when we compare them with beings of a new dimension, capable of development and variety, does it occur to us to look for their labels. Then we find, to our disappointment, that it is easy to classify them. Conjugal devotion, senile vice, embittered virginity, avarice, love, lechery—all are vivid; all are adequately clothed as long as they look us in the face and do not attempt to turn around. They are appealing; they are vitally shaped and colored; they are as plump and rosy as those mechanical puppets that move and speak and have natural hair on their heads. Until we place them side by side with the actual human beings in "War and Peace" we should never suspect that they are not real because they are made exactly alike and only their names, their faces and the strings that work them are different. It is interesting, it is even significant that when Balzac made an earnest effort to portray the soul he wrote what is probably the worst novel ever written by a great novelist. "I am preparing a great and beautiful work," he confided to Mme. Hanska, adding in a later letter, "If the Lily is not a breviary for women, I am nothing. In it virtue is sublime and not at all wearisome." Poor Mme. de Mortsauf, who is meant to be "full of soul," remains to the last a mere posture of duty, and only in that despairing cry at the end does she awaken for a moment to life.

And even Proust, that intrepid explorer of personality, seems a little stiff and self-conscious when we unfairly detach him from his own literary tradition and measure him by Turgenev or Tolstoy. But we look in vain for labels in "A la Recherche du Temps Perdu."[20] This world is firmly rooted and symmetrical. It springs up

19. *La Cousine Bette* (1847) is one of the "scènes de la vie parisienne" and one of the key novels of *La Comédie humaine* by Honoré de Balzac (1799–1850). Mme de Mortsauf is the heroine of Balzac's novel *Le Lys dans la vallée*. Mme Hanska (1801–82), wife of the rich Russo-Polish Baron Wenceslav Hanski, was Balzac's great love after 1833, long before and after her aged husband died in 1841. Balzac and she were married shortly before his death in 1850.
20. A long, complex novel in seven sections, the last three published posthu-

directly from the soil of experience; it expands naturally, puts forth fresh buds and leaves, blossoms, and at last, in the appointed season, bears fruit which is colored like autumn and has the faint savor of decay. There are few more satisfying pleasures than reading Proust. When we have gone, we think, as far as Balzac or even Flaubert can take us; when we pause before a blind alley we may turn suddenly and find that we have mistaken the road. Hidden from us as we traveled, yet always within our reach there was an enchanting perspective of light and shadow; there was a whole new forest which Balzac and Flaubert had never discovered. This, we decide with fresh anticipation, is the advanced approach. This is what we meant, vaguely but hopefully, when we talked of pushing back the boundaries and extending the horizon of fiction. Then, releasing a few of these vivid persons, we place them beside Anna Karenina and Prince Stepan and Dolly and Natasha and the heavy Pierre,[21] and we hesitate again while we reflect that the Russian and the French methods are different and that, after all, there are two sorts of mind. Yet, is it true that one sort matters more in art than the other? Is it true that the greatest Russian novelists have plunged deeper into life, that they have brought up from the darkness some treasure of universal understanding and sympathy?

Who knows, indeed? What novelist, what critic is able to answer? The future alone, and perhaps not even the future, may diminish the problems and the predicaments of the novel. Meanwhile, one fact appears reasonably sure—illumination is, for us, a perilous medium and our fiction is as blind to what the Russian novelists mean when they speak of "the soul" as if it shared the infirmity of those fish of the *amblyopsidae* that are spawned without eyes.[22] It is true enough that in a social order where privacy is, perhaps, the single beatitude that is beyond price, this outward vision may be an advantage rather than an impediment. The pressure of external discomfort may have been always the first compulsion to the spiritual life. Where an inner retreat is not needed it is usually allowed to

mously. Each section represents a phase of Marcel the narrator's life, an experience forgotten or deadened by years, then restored to his consciousness by some trivial sensation.

21. Anna Karenina, Prince Stepan, and Dolly are from Tolstoy's *Anna Karenina*; Natasha and Pierre from his *War and Peace*

22. Includes the blind fish of Mammoth Cave and other caves of North America.

decline from a cell of prayer into a chamber of punishment. So, turning from the immaterial to the medical aspect of psychology, it is better by far that we should continue to burrow in the thick increment of science, after the earnest manner of children who try to reach China by digging their way straight through the earth. As long as we dig hopefully we are sufficiently enterprising for experiment and adventure; and the capacity for experiment and adventure is the bone and sinew of fiction. Only in stagnation is there decay, and a dignified, if not a glorious, immortality in the fossil case of a museum. For the trouble with all modernism is not that it is young, not even that it is strange, but that it must soon grow old and decrepit. When that happens and the method ceases to shock, when it becomes as familiar as Victorian aesthetics, it will be thrust from the limelight by some more nimble or more imprudent performance.[23] After all, no invention was ever bold enough to startle to-morrow. The sunflower of Oscar Wilde looks to us as faded and as brittle as a pressed leaf in a book;[24] and the mud of "Ulysses" will harden probably into clay before the stream of consciousness has run dry in the novel. More encouraging still to reflect upon, all that we consider profane and indecent to-day will be, without doubt, as stale as a dull rubric to the next generation of insurgent youth that sets out hopefully to demolish standards and discover life.

23. Glasgow here anticipates the late twentieth-century revolt called "post-modernism." Joyce's *Ulysses* (1922) has ceased to shock youth, but its craft and language still inspire young writers.
24. Oscar Wilde (1854–1900), champion of the aesthetic movement of the 1870s and 1880s in England, walked London streets in velvet knee breeches and velveteen coat and wearing an exotic flower in the buttonhole; see the poet Bunthorne in Gilbert and Sullivan's *Patience* (1881).

One Way to Write Novels

Nothing, except the weather report or a general maxim of conduct, is so unsafe to depend upon as a theory of fiction. Every great novel has broken many conventions. The greatest of all novels defies every formula; and only Mr. Percy Lubbock believes that

This essay appeared in *Saturday Review of Literature*, XI (December 8, 1934), 335, 344, 350. It later constituted much of the preface for *The Sheltered Life* and has appeared in various collections on the modern novel.

"War and Peace" would be greater if it were another and an entirely different book. By this I do not mean to question Mr. Lubbock's critical insight. "The Craft of Fiction" is the best work in its limited field, and may be studied to advantage by any novelist.[1] In the first chapter there is a masterly analysis of "War and Peace." Yet, after reading it with appreciation, I still think that Tolstoy was the best judge of what his book was about and of how long it should be.

This brings us, in the beginning, to the most sensitive, and therefore the most controversial, point in the criticism of prose fiction. It is the habit of overworked or frugal critics to speak as if economy were a virtue and not a necessity. Yet there are faithful readers who feel with me that a good novel cannot be too long or a bad novel too short. Our company is small but picked with care, and we would die upon the literary barricade defending the noble proportions of "War and Peace," of "The Brothers Karamazov," of "Clarissa Harlowe" in eight volumes, of "Tom Jones," of "David Copperfield," of "The Chronicles of Barsetshire," of "A La Recherche du Temps Perdu," of "Le Vicomte de Bragelonne."[2] Tennyson was with us when he said he had no criticism to make of "Clarissa Harlowe" except that it might have been longer.[3]

The true novel (I am not concerned with the run-of-the-mill variety) is, like pure poetry, an act of birth, not a device or an invention. It awaits its own time and has its own way to be born, and it cannot, by scientific methods, be pushed into the world from behind. After it is born, a separate individual, an organic structure, it obeys its own vital impulses. The heart quickens; the blood circulates; the pulses beat; the whole body moves in response to some inward rhythm; and in time the expanding vitality attains its full stature. But until the breath of life enters a novel, it is as spiritless as inanimate matter.

Having said this much, I may confess that spinning theories of fiction is my favorite amusement. This is, I think, a good habit to culti-

1. Lubbock's *The Craft of Fiction* was first published in 1921.
2. The novels by Tolstoy, Dostoevsky, Richardson, Fielding, and Proust emerged, in Glasgow's earlier essays, as parts of her canon of great novels by which others are to be judged. *David Copperfield* (1848–49) by Charles Dickens, *The Chronicles of Barsetshire* (1855–67) by Anthony Trollope (1815–82), and *The Vicomte de Bragelonne* (1850) by Alexandre Dumas (1802–70) appear in this list largely because of their size.
3. Ironic, given *Clarissa*'s extraordinary length

vate. The exercise encourages readiness and agility while it keeps both head and hand in practice. Besides, if it did nothing else, it would still protect one from the radio and the moving pictures and other sleepless, if less sinister, enemies to the lost mood of contemplation. This alone would justify every precept that was ever evolved. Although a work of fiction may be written without a formula or a method, I doubt if the true novel has ever been created without the long brooding season.

I have read, I believe, with as much interest as if it were a novel itself, every treatise on the art of fiction that appeared to me to be promising. That variable branch of letters shares with philosophy the favorite shelf in my library. I know all that such sources of learning as Sir Leslie Stephen, Sir Walter Raleigh, Mr. Percy Lubbock, Sir Arthur Quiller-Couch, Mr. E. M. Forster, and others less eminent but often more earnest, are able to teach me, or I am able to acquire.[4] Indeed, I know more than they can teach me, for I know also how very little their knowledge can help one in the actual writing of novels. If I were giving advice to a beginner (but there are no beginners nowadays, there is only the inspired amateur or the infant pathologist), I should probably say something like this:[5] "Learn the technique of writing, and having learned it thoroughly, try to forget it. Study the principles of construction, the value of continuity, the arrangement of masses, the consistent point of view, the revealing episode, the careful handling of detail, and the fatal pitfalls

4. Glasgow's library included Leslie Stephen's *English Literature and Society in the Eighteenth Century: Ford Lectures* (1903); Walter Raleigh's *The English Novel, Being a Short Sketch of Its History from the Earliest Times to the Appearance of Waverly* (1910); Percy Lubbock's *The Craft of Fiction* (1921); and E. M. Forster's (1879–1970) *Aspects of the Novel* (1927). Of these, Lubbock's and Forster's books are marked about equally and on many more pages than are the studies by Stephen and Raleigh. Sir Arthur Quiller-Couch's (1863–1944) *On the Art of Writing* (1916) is no longer among the books of Glasgow's library, which her sister Rebe Glasgow Tutwiler inherited after the author's death.

5. The tone here, one of mature wisdom patronizing untutored youth, will mark many of Glasgow's comments about the generation of novelists who emerged during the 1920s as part of the modernist revolt against the great nineteenth-century tradition of the English novel. It is risky, of course, to speculate about which writers she has in mind, but Thomas Wolfe's *Look Homeward, Angel* (1929) may have seemed to her the work of an inspired amateur and William Faulkner's *Sanctuary* (1931), or Ernest Hemingway's *Men Without Women* (1927), the products of infant pathologists. In 1934, she may also have been reacting to Erskine Caldwell's *Tobacco Road* (1932) and *God's Little Acre* (1933), or to the sensational dramatization of *Tobacco Road* (1933).

of dialogue. Then, having mastered, if possible, every rule of thumb, dismiss it into the labyrinth of the memory. Leave it there to make its own signals and flash its own warnings. The sensitive feeling, 'this is not right' or 'something ought to be different' will prove that these signals are working." Or, perhaps, this inner voice may be only the sounder instinct of the born novelist.

If this were a treatise on the art of writing, how simple it would be to pursue it to its logical end—to any end, indeed, except the one that must begin the essay I am requested to write. But Dr. Canby did not ask for an article on prose fiction.[6] He asked (intrepid spirit!) for the "highly personal statement" which Mr. James Truslow Adams aptly describes as "a flagrant offense against modesty."[7] And immediately (though I am aware that my method or the lack of one, is not of the slightest interest to any human being but myself) the logical end becomes only a turning-point, and the dignified theory of fiction dwindles into the way I write novels.

The truth is that I began being a novelist, as naturally as I began talking or walking, so early that I cannot remember when the impulse first seized me. Far back in my childhood, before I had learned the letters of the alphabet, a character named Little Willie wandered into the country of my mind, just as every other major character in my novels has strolled across my mental horizon when I was not expecting him, when I was not even thinking of the novel in which he would finally take his place.[8] From what or where he had sprung, why he was named Little Willie, or why I should have selected a hero instead of a heroine—all this is still as much of a mystery to me as it was in my childhood. But there he was, and there he remained, alive and active, threading his own adventures, from the time I was three until I was eight or nine, and discovered Hans Andersen and Grimm's Fairy Tales. Every night, as I was undressed and put to bed by my colored Mammy, the romance of Little Willie would begin again exactly where it had broken off the evening before. In winter I was undressed in the firelight on the hearth-rug;

6. Henry S. Canby (1878–1961), critic and editor of the *Saturday Review of Literature*, where this essay first appeared
7. James Truslow Adams (1878–1949), American popular historian, author of *The Epic of America* (1931) and *The March of Democracy* (1932–33)
8. Glasgow gives a fuller version of this episode in her autobiography, *The Woman Within* (1954).

but in summer we moved over to an open window that looked out on the sunset and presently the first stars in the long green twilight. For years Little Willie lasted, never growing older, always pursuing his own narrative and weaving his situations out of his own character. I can still see him, small, wiry, with lank brown hair like a thatch, and eyes that seemed to say, "I know a secret! I know a secret!" Hans Andersen and the brothers Grimm were his chosen companions. He lingered on, though somewhat sadly, after I had discovered the Waverly Novels;[9] but when I was twelve years old and entered the world of Dickens, he vanished forever.

In those earliest formative years Little Willie outlined, however vaguely, a general pattern of work. He showed me that a novelist must write, not by taking thought alone, but with every cell of his being, that nothing can occur to him that may not sooner or later find its way into his craft. Whatever happened to me or to Mammy Lizzie[10] happened also, strangely transfigured, to Little Willie. I learned, too, and never forgot, that ideas would not come to me if I went out to hunt for them. They would fly when I pursued; but if I stopped and sank down into a kind of watchful reverie, they would flock back again like friendly pigeons. All I had to do before the novel had formed, was to leave the creative faculty (or subconscious mind) free to work its own way without urging and without effort. When Dorinda in "Barren Ground" first appeared to me, I pushed her back into some glimmering obscurity, where she remained, buried but alive, for a decade, and emerged from the yeasty medium with hard round limbs and the bloom of health in her cheeks. Thus I have never wanted for subjects; but on several occasions when, because of illness or from external compulsion, I have tried to invent a theme or a character, invariably the effort has resulted in failure. These are the unnatural children of my brain that I should wish, were it possible, to disinherit.

It is not easy to tell how much of this dependence upon intuition may be attributed to the lack of harmony between my inner life and my early environment. A thoughtful and imaginative child, haunted by that strange sense of exile which visits the subjective mind when

9. Series of Scottish novels by Sir Walter Scott, including *Old Mortality* and *The Heart of Midlothian*
10. Glasgow's black nurse (*ca.* 1873–80)

it is unhappily placed (and it is always, apparently, unhappily placed or it would not be subjective), I grew up in a charming society, where ideas were accepted as naturally as the universe or the weather, and cards for the old, dancing for the young, and conversation flavored with personalities for the middle-aged, were the only arts practised. Several members of my family, it is true, possessed brilliant minds and were widely and deeply read; but all despised what they called "local talent," and my early work was written in secret to escape ridicule, alert, pointed, and not the less destructive because it was playful. There is more truth than wit in the gibe that every Southern novelist must first make his reputation in the North. Perhaps this is why so many Southern novelists write of the South as if it were a fabulous country. When a bound copy of my first book reached me, I hid it under my pillow while a cousin, who had run in before breakfast, prattled beside my bed of the young men who had quarreled over the privilege of taking her to the Easter German, as the Cotillion was called. Had I entered the world by way of Oxford, or even by way of Bloomsbury,[11] I might now be able to speak or write of my books without a feeling of outraged reserve.[12] And yet, in the very act of writing these words, my literary conscience, a nuisance to any writer, inquires if ideas were really free at Oxford, or even in Bloomsbury, at the end of the century, and if all the enfranchised spirits who babble of prohibited subjects nowadays are either wiser or better than the happy hypocrites of the nineties.

From this dubious prelude it might be inferred that I consider the craft of fiction merely another form of mental inertia. On the contrary, I agree with those writers who have found actual writing to be the hardest work in the world. What I am concerned with at the moment, however, is the beginning of a novel alone, not the end-

---

11. Centers of English intellectual and artistic life, including in recent decades such figures as Aldous Huxley, Lady Ottoline Morrell, Lytton Strachey, E. M. Forster, Katherine Mansfield, Clive Bell, Roger Fry, Virginia and Leonard Woolf, and, occasionally, T. S. Eliot. At times, Glasgow seems to have envied Virginia Woolf both her brilliant father, Leslie Stephen, and the cultural support of Bloomsbury.

12. This remark helps explain the grandiose, detached manner Glasgow adopted when she wrote the prefaces collected in *A Certain Measure* (1943), a tone in strong contrast to the frank, even self-pitying attitude that comes through in her autobiography, *The Woman Within* (1954).

less drudgery that wrung from Stevenson[13] the complaint, "The practice of letters is miserably harassing to the mind; and after an hour or two's work, all the more human portion of an author is extinct; he will bully, backbite, and speak daggers." For being a true novelist, even if one's work is not worth the price of a cherry to public or publisher, takes all that one has to give and still something more. Yet the matter is not one of choice but of fatality. Like the enjoyment of music, or a love for El Greco, or a pleasure in gardening, or the taste for pomegranates, or a preference for Santayana's prose, the bent of nature is either there or it is not there.[14]

For my own part, and it appears, however far I stray, that I must still return to "the highly personal statement," the only method I have deliberately cultivated has been a system of constant renewal. If novels should be, as Sir Leslie Stephen has said, "transfigured experience," then I have endeavored, whenever it was possible, to deepen experience and to heighten what I prefer to call illumination, to increase my understanding of that truth of life which has never become completely reconciled with the truth of fiction.[15] I do not mean by this that life should necessarily be eventful or filled with variable activities. Profound emotion does not inevitably bear "the pageant of a bleeding heart."[16] Several of the most thrilling lives in all literature were lived amid the unconquerable desolation of the Yorkshire moors. Yet it is doubtful if either the exposed heart of Byron or the brazen trumpet of D. H. Lawrence contained such burning realities as were hidden beneath the quiet fortitude of Emily Brontë.[17]

Because of some natural inability to observe and record instead of

13. Robert Louis Stevenson, in the first essay of *Virginibus Puerisque* (1881)
14. George Santayana, the philosopher and man of letters, had published *The Genteel Tradition at Bay* in 1931; *The Last Puritan* would appear in 1935.
15. Stephen was an English philosopher, critic, biographer, as well as father of Virginia Woolf.
16. In "Stanzas from the Grande Chartreuse," Matthew Arnold (1822–88) asked, "What helps it now, that Byron bore, / With haughty scorn which mock'd the smart, / Through Europe to the Ætolian shore / The pageant of his bleeding heart?" The reference is to the confessional element in Byron's poetry based on his own travels.
17. The references are to Byron's poetry of romantic suffering (as in "Maid of Athens, Ere We Part," 1810) and D. H. Lawrence's unrestrained style and sexual symbolism (as in *Aaron's Rod*, 1922) in contrast to qualities admired in Emily Brontë (1818–48), who with sisters Charlotte (1816–55) and Anne (1820–49) lived in the desolate moors.

create, I have never used an actual scene until the impression it left had sifted down into imagined surroundings. A theme becomes real to me only after it is clothed in living values; but these values must be drawn directly from the imagination and indirectly, if at all, from experience. Invariably the characters appear first, and slowly and gradually build up their own world and spin the situation and atmosphere out of themselves. Strangely enough, the horizon of this real or visionary world is limited by the impressions or recollections of my early childhood. If I were to walk out into the country and pick a scene for a book, it would remain as flat and lifeless as cardboard; but the places I loved or hated between the ages of three and thirteen compose an inexhaustible landscape of memory. Occasionally, it is true, I have returned to a scene to verify details, though for freshness and force I have trusted implicitly to the vision within. And just as my scene is built up from fragments of the past, whether that past existed in fact or in a dream, so the human figures, though not one of them has been copied from my acquaintances, will startle me by displaying a familiar trait or gesture, and I will recognize with a shock some special blending of characteristics.

Frequently, these impressions have been buried so long and so deep that I have entirely forgotten them until they float upward to the surface of thought. Yet they are not dead but living, and recover warmth and animation after the creative faculty has revived them. In the same way, half-obliterated images, events, or episodes, observed in moments of intense experience, will flash back into a scene or a figure; and this is equally true of the most trivial detail my memory has registered. For example, in one of the tragic hours of my youth I looked out of a window and saw two sparrows quarrelling in the rain on a roof. Twenty years or more afterwards, a character in one of my novels looks out of a window in a moment of heartbreak and sees two sparrows quarrelling in the rain.[18] And, immediately, light streamed back, as if it were cast by the rays of a lantern, into the unlit recesses of memory, and I felt the old grief in my heart and saw the rain fall on the roof and the two sparrows quarrelling.

18. Familiar birds, including sparrows, are a recurring feature of most Glasgow novels, so much so that one might speak of a "language of birds" (and other common animals) supplementing the frequently noted language of flowers.

Because everything that one has been or heard or thought or felt leaves a deposit that never filters entirely through the essence of mind, I believe that a novelist should be perpetually engaged in this effort to refresh and replenish his source. I am confident, moreover, that nothing I have learned either from life or from literature has been wasted.[19] Whatever I have thought or felt deeply has stayed with me, if only in fragments or in a distillation of memory. But the untiring critic within has winnowed, reassorted, and disposed the material I needed. Not until the unconscious worker has withdrawn from the task, or taken a brief holiday, and the characters have woven their own background and circumstances, does the actual drudgery of moulding the mass-substance begin. Even now, after the groundwork is completed and the subject assembled, I still give time and thought (brooding is the more accurate term) to the construction. I try not to hasten the process and to leave the invisible agent to flash directions or warnings. The book must have a form. This is essential. It may be shaped like a millstone or an hourglass or an Indian tomahawk or a lace fan—but a shape it must have. Usually a novel assumes its own figure when it enters the world, and the underlying idea moulds the plastic material to its own structure. More deliberately, the point of view is considered and selected, though this may, and often does, proceed naturally from the unities of time and place, or from one completely dominant figure. In "Barren Ground," a long novel, I felt from the moment Dorinda entered the book that there could be put one point of view. From the first page to the last, no scene or episode or human figure appears outside her field of vision or imagination.[20]

In "The Sheltered Life," where I knew intuitively that the angle of vision must create the form, I employed two points of view alone, though they were separated by the whole range of experience. Age and youth look on the same events and occasions, the

19. In his essay "The Art of Fiction" (1884), Henry James had described the novelist as one "upon whom nothing is lost"—as one who possesses "the power to guess the unseen from the seen." Glasgow is placing herself in that tradition of realism, as opposed to a more journalistic, merely reportorial tradition.

20. The point of view in *Barren Ground* (1925) is that of a third-person narrator who, though a social historian, is yet able to merge with the consciousness of Dorinda Oakley.

same tragedy in the end.[21] Between these conflicting points of view the story flows on, like a stream in a narrow valley. Nothing happens that is not seen, on one side, through the steady gaze of the old man, seeing life as it is, and, on the other side, by the troubled eyes of the young girl, seeing life as she would wish it to be. Purposely, I have tried here to interpret reality through the dissimilar mediums of thought and emotion. I have been careful to allow no other aspects to impinge on the contrasting visions which create between them the organic whole of the book. This convention, which appears uncertain, when one thinks of it, becomes natural and even involuntary when the work grows, develops, pushes out with its own energy, and finds its own tempo.

While I am at work on a book I remain, or try to remain, in a state of immersion. The first draft of a novel, if it is long, will take two years, and still another year is required for the final writing. All this time the imaginary setting becomes the native country of my mind, and the characters are seldom out of my thoughts. I live with them day and night; they are more real to me than acquaintances in the flesh. In our nursery copy of "Gulliver's Travels" there was a picture which seems, when I recall it now, to illustrate my predicament in the final draft of a novel.[22] Gulliver lies bound in threads while the Lilliputians swarm over him and hamper his struggles. So words swarm over me and hamper my efforts to seize the right one among them, to find the right rhythm, the right tone, the right accent. But here again intuition, or perhaps only a flare of organized memory, will come to my aid. Often, when I have searched for hours for some special work or phrase and given up in despair, I have awakened with a start in the night because the hunted word or phrase had darted into my mind while I was asleep.

Nevertheless, it is the act of scrupulous revision (the endless pruning and trimming for the sake of a sound and flexible prose style) that provides the writer's best solace even while it makes

21. The third-person narrator of *The Sheltered Life* (1932) usually filters the events of the novel through one of two points of view, that of Jenny Blair Archbald, at ages nine and a half and seventeen and a half, or that of her grandfather, General David Archbald, at ages seventy-five and eighty-three.

22. First published in 1726 by Jonathan Swift. Her library contained *The Works of Dr. Jonathan Swift, Dean of St. Patrick's, Dublin* (1758).

drudgery. Every literary craftsman who respects his work has, I dare say, this same feeling, and remains restless and wandering in mind until he has entered the right climate in the beginning and tracked down the right word at the end. Although my characters may develop traits or actions I had not anticipated, the scenes may shift and alter in perspective, and new episodes may spring out on the way, still the end shines always as the solitary fixed star above the flux of creation. I have never written the first word of the first sentence until I knew what the last word of the last sentence would be. Sometimes I may rewrite the beginning many times, as I did in "They Stooped to Folly,"[23] and sometimes (though this has actually occurred but once) a shorter book like "The Romantic Comedians," completely realized before pen was put to paper, may bubble over of itself with a kind of effortless joy. Yet in the difficult first chapter of "They Stooped to Folly" I could still look ahead, over a procession of characters that had slipped from my control, to the subdued scene at the end, while the concluding paragraph of "The Romantic Comedians" placed the tone of the entire book and accented the rhythm.

The final words to be said of any activity will always be, I suppose, was it worth what it cost? Well, the writing of fiction is worth, I imagine, exactly what digging a ditch or charting the heavens may be worth to the worker, and that is not a penny more or less than the release of mind that it brings. Although I may not speak as an authority, at least I can speak from long perseverance. I became a novelist before I was old enough to resist, and I remained a novelist because no other enterprise in life has afforded me the same interest or provided me with equal contentment. It is true that I have written only for the biased judgment within; but this inner critic has held an unattainable standard, and has infused a certain zest of adventure into what may appear on the surface to be merely another humdrum way of earning a livelihood. Still, to a beginner who is young and cherishes an ambition to be celebrated, I should recommend the short cut (or royal road) through the radio and Hollywood; and certainly more than one creative writer in search of swift economic security would do well to buy a new broom and to set

23. The novel Glasgow published in 1929, between *The Romantic Comedians* (1926) and *The Sheltered Life* (1932)

out for the next crossing. But, incredible as it may appear in this practical decade, there are novelists so wanting in a sense of the best proletarian values that they place artistic integrity above the voice on the air, the flash on the screen, and the dividends in the bank. There are others who possess an unreasoning faith in their own work; and there are yet others endowed with a comic spirit so robust, or so lively, that it can find diversion anywhere, even in our national exaltation of the inferior. To this happy company of neglected novelists, the ironic art of fiction will reveal its own special delights, and may even, as the years pass, yield its own sufficient, if imponderable, rewards.

In looking back through a long vista, I can see that what I have called the method of constant renewal may be reduced to three ruling principles. Obedience to this self-imposed discipline has enabled me to write novels for more than thirty years, and yet to feel that the substance from which I draw material and energy is as fresh today as it was in my first youthful failure. As time moves on, I still see life in the beginnings, moods in conflict, and change as the only permanent law. But the value of these qualities (which may be self-deluding, and are derived, in fact, more from temperament than from technique) has been mellowed by long saturation with experience—by that essence of reality which one distills from life only after it has been lived.

Among the many curious superstitions of the age of science there is the prevailing belief that immaturity alone is enough. Pompous illiteracy, escaped from some Freudian cage, is in the saddle, and the voice of the amateur is the voice of authority. When we turn to the field of prose fiction, we find that it is filled with literary skyrockets sputtering out in the fog. But the trouble with skyrockets has always been that they do not stay up in the air. One has only to glance back over the post-war years to discover that the roads of the jazz age are matted thick with fireworks that went off too soon. To the poet, it is true, especially if he can arrange with destiny to die young, the glow of adolescence may impart an unfading magic. But the novel (which must be conceived with a subdued rapture, or with none at all, or even with the unpoetic virtues of industry and patience) requires more substantial ingredients than a little ignorance of life and a great yearning to tell everything one has never known. When I remember Defoe, the father of us all, I am persuaded that the novelist who has harvested well the years, and laid by a rich store of experience, will find his latter period the ripening time of his career.[24]

Transposed into an impersonal method, the three rules of which I have spoken may be so arranged:

1. Always wait between books for the springs to fill up and flow over.

2. Always preserve within a wild sanctuary, an inaccessible valley of reveries.

3. Always, and as far as it is possible, endeavor to touch life on every side; but keep the central vision of the mind, the inmost light, untouched and untouchable.

In my modest way, these rules have helped me, not only to pursue the one calling for which I was designed alike by character and inclination, but even to enjoy the prolonged study of a world that, as the sardonic insight of Henry Adams perceived, no "sensitive and timid natures could regard without a shudder."[25]

24. Daniel Defoe was a representative self-made man of the eighteenth century. Unlike most of his contemporary writers, he was of low birth and rose to prominence through business enterprises. His fiction, which he began later in life, reflected his ethics of money and perseverance (*e.g., Moll Flanders*). Because Glasgow's finest novels came to her after she was fifty, she no doubt felt a kinship with Defoe.
25. These words conclude *The Education of Henry Adams: An Autobiography* (1906); the chapter is titled "Nunc Age (1905)." Adams lived from 1838 to 1918.

Heroes and Monsters

Thirty years ago, I objected to the evasive idealism in American novels.[1] Nowadays, I object to the aimless violence. Not that I

This essay appeared in *Saturday Review of Literature*, XII (May 4, 1935), 3–4. It was read to the Friends of the Princeton Library, April 25, 1935.
1. Glasgow's first novel, *The Descendant* (1897), had produced a sensation through its empathy for the angry and oppressed. In 1898, when Hamlin Garland (1860–1940) visited Glasgow in Richmond, the spokesman for the young radicals of Chicago and New York found her a young woman of "alarming candor" already possessed of the "bitterness of age." He predicted that she would progress in the reverse direction of most intellectuals, from despair to increased hope, rather than from youthful idealism to hopelessness. Here, Glasgow is citing her credentials for criticizing the realists of the 1930s.

oppose either evasiveness or violence as material for fiction, provided the whole cloth is not cut, as dressmakers say, on the bias, and draped round a lay figure in a uniform style. But whenever I watch the professional rebels against gentility basking in that lurid light so fashionable at present among the genteel, I remember with a smile the local thunder-storm that followed my first modest effort to overturn a literary convention.

Thus it occurs to me that the flavor of plain truth, culled from long and sometimes bitter experience, may not be unwholesome today. For of all the weeds that grow and run wild in Southern soil, plain truth is the most difficult to serve without sauce. Moreover, there does not exist in the South today, nor has there ever existed at any time, a treatment of truth in fiction so plain and broad that it could be called, with fairness, a school of realism. There are, no doubt, a few scattered realists, as lonely as sincerity in any field, who dwell outside the Land of Fable inhabited by fairies and goblins. But goblins are as unreal as fairies; and beneath the red paint and charcoal, Raw-Head-and-Bloody-Bones, is our battered old friend, Jack-the-Giant-Killer.[2] We remain incurably romantic. Only a puff of smoke separates the fabulous Southern hero of the past from the fabulous Southern monster of the present—or the tender dreams of James Lane Allen from the fantastic nightmares of William Faulkner.[3]

So I shall pass on while I toss a magnolia blossom to those intrepid novelists who have won fine Southern reputations in the North—the only climate, it appears, that has ever been favorable to Southern literary reputations. To confine myself to a few of the notable successes of the Spring, I congratulate Miss Chilton, Miss Roberts, Mr. Wolfe, Mr. Faulkner, Mr. Berry Fleming, Mr. Hamilton Basso.[4] I welcome Mr. Stark Young's glowing reaffirmation of cour-

---

2. Glasgow is suggesting, it seems, that the "realistic violence" of modern southern fiction (Raw-Head-and-Bloody-Bones) is, in truth, a disguise for the romantic heroism of nineteenth-century southern fiction (Jack-the-Giant-Killer).

3. James Lane Allen, from Kentucky, wrote the once popular love stories *A Kentucky Cardinal* (1894) and *The Choir Invisible* (1897). In 1935, William Faulkner was better known as the author of the "fantastic nightmare," *Sanctuary* (1931), than as the creator of the surrealistic *As I Lay Dying* (1930) and *The Sound and the Fury* (1929), though Glasgow owned early editions of all three.

4. All southern writers publishing novels in 1935, as follows: Eleanor Carroll Chilton (Mrs. Herbert Agar), *Follow the Furies*; Elizabeth Madox Roberts, *He Sent*

age in defeat.[5] I salute Dr. Freeman's superb life of Lee, which has restored not only pure biography to English letters, after a period of wild oats and light living, but even the obsolete word "duty" to the American tongue.[6] And nothing, I am persuaded, unless it is a recovered faith in Santa Claus, could confer greater happiness on a liberated world than the miraculous resurrection of the sense of duty. In a sultry age, when we need the tonic of a bracing literature, character has become a lost quantity in fiction, and we miss the full, clear, commanding note of the disciplined mind. Our very vocabulary whines or blusters.

Turning from the formal traditions in Mr. Young's book, which is more history than romance, to the inflamed rabble of impulses in the contemporary Southern novel, one asks immediately: What is left of the pattern? Has Southern life—or is it only Southern fiction—become one vast, disordered sensibility? Is there no Southern horizon beyond Joyce?[7] Where is that "immoderate past" celebrated in Mr. Allen Tate's loyal "Ode to the Confederate Dead"?[8] Has "the salt of their blood" oozed away in a flicker of iridescent scum on the marshes? Does defeat always appear nobler than victory? Or is the whole tedious mass production of degeneracy in our fiction—the current literary gospel of futility and despair—merely a single symptom of the neuroses inflicted on its slaves by the conquering dynamo?[9]

Already, I think, we have answered most of these questions. Not the South alone, but the whole modern world, after its recent bold escape from superstition, is in fact trembling before its own shadow. We are trying to run away from our shadows under the delusion that we are running away from the past. But it is useless to

Forth a Raven; Thomas Wolfe, *Of Time and the River*; William Faulkner, *Pylon*; Berry Fleming, *Siesta*; Hamilton Basso (1904–64), *In Their Own Image*

5. *So Red the Rose*, published in 1934

6. Douglas Southall Freeman (1886–1953), editor of the Richmond *News Leader*, won the Pulitzer Prize for his four-volume *R. E. Lee* (1934–35).

7. Thomas Wolfe's *Look Homeward, Angel* (1929) and *Of Time and the River* (1935) and William Faulkner's *The Sound and the Fury* (1929) and *As I Lay Dying* (1930) all bore the mark of James Joyce's *Ulysses* (1922).

8. Tate's major poem, begun in 1925, contains the phrase "the salt of their blood"; Allen Tate was born in Kentucky.

9. An echo of the opposition Henry Adams emphasizes, in *The Education of Henry Adams* (1906), between the force the Virgin of the Middle Ages stimulated and the energy the modern dynamo generates.

run away from the past as it is to run away from what we call life. Wherever we go, we still carry life, and that root of life which is the past, in our tribal memories, in our nerves, in our arteries. All we can do is to deny or distort the shifting semblance we know as reality. And so the fantasy of abominations has stolen the proud stilts of romantics. To borrow Mr. Gerald W. Johnson's amusing expression, Southern fiction "comes stepping high," as of old, only it is now stepping over a bog instead of a battlefield.[10] Farther away, beyond the authentic masters of horror, press and push the rows of ambitious amateurs, who imagine that they are realists because they have tasted a stew of spoilt meat. But it takes more than spoilt meat to make realism. It takes, among other attributes, a seasoned philosophy and a mature outlook on life.

For thirty years I have had a part in the American literary scene, either as a laborer in the vineyard or as a raven croaking on a bust of Pallas.[11] In all these years I have found that the only permanent law in art, as in the social order, is the law of change. Although it may be true that we cannot change human nature, history proves on every page, as Mr. John Chamberlain has observed, that we can and constantly do change human behavior.[12] I have seen fashions in fiction and in behavior shift and alter and pass away while we watched them. I have seen reputations swell out and burst with wind and shrivel up into damp rags of India-rubber. I have seen, not without sardonic amusement, the balance of power in American letters pass from genteel mediocrity with hair on the face to truculent mediocrity with down on the chest.

For these and other reasons, the last position I would assume is that of the lone defender of the human species in modern fiction. I needed no peep at war to teach me that we live among evils. I needed no "planned economy" to prove to me that these evils are of our own making. It may be true, as our more popular novelists assure us, that we are doomed. It may be true that all is lost to us but moral and physical disintegration, and we should hasten out, while it is

10. In 1935, North Carolina–born Gerald W. Johnson was an editorial writer for the Baltimore *Sun* and an iconoclastic critic of southern cultural poverty.
11. Saying "Nevermore," like Poe's raven, to the nostalgia for the dead past. Pallas refers to Athena.
12. John Chamberlain (b.1903) published *Farewell to Reform* (1932), a history of the progressive mind in America.

yet day, to gather in that rich literary harvest. This, I repeat, may be true. One may point to life and prove anything; it all depends on the pointing. And despair itself may be vital; it may be strong; it may be courageous; though only worms can survive the damp chill of negation. Few things, however, are more certain than this:—the literature that crawls too long in the mire will lose at last the power of standing erect. On the farther side of deterioration lies the death of a culture.

But, even so, when the worst has been written, it is not an ignoble fate—it is not an unhappy fate—to go down still fighting against the inevitable. That is a triumph of the will, not a surrender; and if nothing pleasanter may be said of the inevitable, at least it is worth fighting. Whatever contemporary fiction may think of love, the world has shown from the beginning that it loves fighters. Nor is the impulse toward something better, or at least different, confined to humanity; it runs back and forth through all nature. We are too apt to forget that the earliest recorded conquest over destiny was achieved by a fish. Nowadays, while we puzzle over the human mass movement back into the slime, it is well to remind ourselves of our first revolutionary ancestor, that "insane fish," so lovingly commemorated by Mr. James Branch Cabell, "who somehow evolved the idea that it was his duty to live on land, and eventually succeeded in doing it."[13] Surely that high exploit deserves a more appropriate memorial than sophisticated barbarism and the sentimental cult of corruption.

The revolutionary fish no longer leaps. Although the word Revolution is in the air, the true spirit is wanting. Instead, we breathe in a suffocating sense of futility. That liberal hope of which we dreamed in my youth appears to have won no finer freedom than an age of little fads and the right to cry ugly words in the street. Not for whims like these do men unite and live or die happily. The true revolution may end in a ditch or in the shambles; but it must begin in the stars. There must be bliss, as Wordsworth found, in that dawn, "with human nature seeming born again."[14]

I am not asking the novelist of the Southern Gothic school to

13. In his nonfiction books, *Beyond Life* (1919), for example, Cabell made splendid use of the comic potential of evolutionary theory.
14. *The Prelude* (1850), VI, ll. 339–41; by William Wordsworth

change his material.[15] The Gothic as Gothic, not as pseudo-realism, has an important place in our fiction. Besides, I know too well that the novelist does not choose his subject; he is chosen by it. All I ask him to do is to deal as honestly with living tissues as he now deals with decay, to remind himself that the colors of putrescence have no greater validity for our age, or for any age, than have—let us say, to be very daring—the cardinal virtues. For, as a great modern philosopher has written: "An honorable end is the one thing that cannot be taken from a man."[16]

15. Faulkner's *Sanctuary* (1931) or perhaps Erskine Caldwell's *Tobacco Road* (1932) would likely have come to a reader's mind in 1935.
16. This idea is expressed by George Santayana, in different words, during a discussion of Browning in "The Poetry of Barbarism," from *Interpretations of Poetry and Religion* (1900); kindred positions are taken by Santayana in *Reason in Religion*, Vol. II of *The Life of Reason* (5 vols., 1905).

Elder and Younger Brother

The subject of the relation of the scholar to the imaginative, or creative, writer is one upon which I have speculated, at intervals, ever since I decided, on my seventh birthday, that my native heath was the field of American letters. Although the novel is my chief preoccupation, to which I was dedicated, or doomed, by some malicious godmother who hung over my cradle, it is not, and has never been, a solitary pursuit. Or, perhaps, I express my meaning more precisely when I say that, in my judgment, the province of the novel is the entire range of human experience and the vast area of mortal destiny. I am involved therefore, through imagination at least, in every human activity, and among these varied interests I regard with peculiar envy the part of the scholar—by which I mean not the diligent collector of old bones, but the earnest seeker after the good and the true.

Thus, when I speak of scholarship I think of an agency that is vital and living. Just as I cherish the Greek name for a philosopher, lover of wisdom, so I see the genuine scholar as the preserver of truth. Whether his mind assembles a few facts or a multitude, he remains

This essay appeared in *Saturday Review of Literature*, XV (January 23, 1937), 3–5. Allen Tate read it, in a slightly different form, for the ailing Glasgow at a meeting of the Modern Language Association in Richmond, December 31, 1936.

for me the true scholar so long as he strives with unswerving fidelity for a permanent good. And because the dead cannot strive, scholarship must have its own capacity for germination, for growth, for change and development. It must be as sensitive to the promise of tomorrow as to the fulfillment that has been dead and buried and safely turned to dust for a thousand years. The relation it bears to the creative impulse is that of the elder to the younger brother. Throughout the ages, from the first grey dawn of human history, down from the "Mahabharata"[1] or the "Iliad," we find these two vital forces working steadily together and fighting side by side in the long conflict of enlightenment with the powers of darkness. The will that creates has combined with the will that defends, restrains, selects, eliminates, safeguards, and keeps alive for the future. Even when they are ranged in opposing movements, as in the classical and the romantic traditions, they are still united in the fundamental service of life.

It is an arresting thought that, if the ancient treasures of literature belong to us now, we owe them less to art which has been generous than to scholarship which has been prudent. During the Dark Ages in Europe, when the creative impulse had turned from art to the auto-da-fe, it was the patient learning of the East that protected these treasures, not embalmed as mummies for burial, but alive in the mind and heart. Yet we speak of the dead tongues and memorable shades of the past. We have ceased to remember that the great shades who so eloquently people the world of scholarship were more than shades when they left their immortal impressions. They did not live in the past; they lived instead, and very vitally, in their own immediate present. They marched with the years. They are the contemporaries of time.

It would seem, perhaps, that I have taken too leisurely a way when I approach contemporary letters from the vanishing-point of the perspective. But what I wish to do is simply to acknowledge that intimate relation which exists today, and has always existed, between the impulse to create and the will to preserve. Although I am not in any sense a scholar, I am, in every sense of that abused word, a reader. And by "every sense" I mean you to understand

1. The great epic poem of India, reputed to be the work of the sage Vyasa

that I read not with the eyes alone, but with the imagination, the heart, the nerves, and the blood-stream. Since all experience must come to life for me in the imagination or remain inanimate, there is only one mental image I do not welcome, and that is the visitation of a dead idea. If it enters, it must come attached by indestructible ties to the living. Not necessarily the new—for many old ideas are more vital than new ones—if there is, indeed, any such thing as a new idea—but it must have at least a connection with what (because we know so little about it) we are fond of calling Reality. An idea may be decrepit, but finished it must not be. So Goethe felt, no doubt, when he explained: "I thank God I am not young in so thoroughly finished a world!"[2]

Our quarrel, then, is not with the old; it is with the finished. For good or ill, we must have a hand in the making. The present, in spite of its failures, which are numerous, has for us an immeasurable advantage over the Age of Pericles or the Age of Elizabeth—it is our own. We may not like it, but we belong in it. Future centuries will judge us not by what we thought of the Elizabethans, but by what we made of ourselves—of our own vastly inferior opportunities.

In one of his perennially delightful essays, Walter Bagehot makes a few pungent comments on a literary ancestor worship that is too exclusive. He quotes, with gentle malice, a familiar passage from Macaulay:[3]

> Plato is never sullen. Cervantes is never petulant. Demosthenes never comes unseasonably. Dante never stays too long. No difference of political opinion can alienate Cicero. No heresy can excite the horror of Bossuet.

And Bagehot laments:

> But Bossuet is dead; and Cicero was a Roman; and Plato wrote in Greek. Years and manners separate us from the great. After dinner, Demosthenes may come unseasonably; Dante might stay too long. We are alienated from the politician and have a horror of the theologian. Dreadful idea, having Demosthenes for an intimate friend. He had pebbles in his mouth; he was always urging action; he spoke such good Greek; we cannot dwell on it—it is too much. . . . But what gives to

2. The quotation unfortunately does not appear in the standard collections of Goethe's maxims.

3. From Bagehot's "Thomas Babington Macaulay" in *Estimations in Criticism* (1908–9). Walter Bagehot (1826–77) quotes from Macaulay's essay "Lord Bacon."

the speeches of Demosthenes the interest they have? The intense glowing interest of the speaker in all that he is speaking about. Philip is not a "person whom posterity will censure," but "the man whom I hate."

And so, Bagehot concludes, "a writer must have a life of *some* place and *some* time before he can have one for all space and all time." Posterity, "that expected authority, is most ungrateful; those who think of it most, it thinks of least. The way to secure its favor is to give vivid, essential pictures of the life before you, to leave a fresh glowing delineation of the scene to which you were born."

In my own limited experience I have observed with wonder so many intellectual and literary fashions that I have come at last to rely positively upon one conviction alone. No idea is so antiquated that it was not once modern. No idea is so modern that it will not some day be antiquated. The intellect will outlive the assault on intellectualism. The Revolution will outlive revolutionaries. To seize the flying thought before it escapes us is our only touch with reality. The one thing needful, it would seem, is not to be consistent. For one may accept, as I do, Hume's theory of mind, and yet believe that mind regarded as a series of perceptions is not less real or significant than mind regarded as an entity.[4] One may even call oneself a skeptic, as I do also, and yet prefer the Enneads of Plotinus[5] to a symphony orchestra. Only a single aspect of intelligence is fatal to a living culture, and that is the closed comprehension, the finished process.

If I may glance, for a moment, over my personal history, I might illustrate more forcibly what I mean by the value of inconsistency as an outlook on life. More than thirty years ago I began my literary work as a rebel against conventions. I am still a rebel, but the conventions are different. Although I have not lost the heart of a revolutionary, I like now to be firmly convinced that I am standing on the right—by which I mean the humane—barricade. No longer would I

4. According to *The Encyclopedia of Philosophy*, the major propositions of David Hume's (1711–76) *An Abstract of a Treatise of Human Nature* (1740) are: "All our ideas are derived from impressions of sense or inner feeling"; and "a matter of fact can never be proved by reasoning *a priori*. It must be discovered in, or inferred from, experience." The mind creates general terms or ideas by *associating* ideas "whose impressions are alike or contiguous in space or time."
5. Roman philosopher, who elaborated the concept of the Chain of Being

make a revolution for the melancholy privilege of calling things by their worst names. Nevertheless, the mood of my earliest work was the rebel mood of today. In the stern school of neglect and misrepresentation I was taught that being the only rebel in one's world is very nearly as futile, and quite as tragic, as being the only Christian. At that age, I was fond of saying: Nothing but the inevitable is worth fighting. Now, after an ineffectual revolt, I have come to realize that the inevitable is a poor adversary—that it does not obey the rules of civilized warfare and has no true sporting instinct. Yet I still believe that the mood, if not the manner, of revolution is the most fertile soil of ideas.

We are, in fact, living nowadays in a period of insurgent interests. The worse the world becomes, the more exciting we shall find it as material for fiction and criticism. Ours may be, indeed, as Bradley has observed, the best of all possible worlds and everything in it a necessary evil.[6] Well, no matter. In our universal comedy of errors increasing knowledge may be trusted to bring its own recompense. Just here, curiously enough, a voice complains, "But the less we know, the better novelists we shall make"—which sounds strangely like Omar, the Caliph, but is merely one of our contemporaries industriously digging wells in his subconscious mind.[7] Now, I have nothing whatever against the digging of wells, either within or without. Indeed, the dark labyrinth of human psychology is among my favorite backgrounds in fiction. There is, however, always the danger that we may drown in the muddy shallows before the clear water has risen. Such primitive soundings have validity only in the mind that has lived and remembered, that has learned already to feel and measure the depths.

That has learned to feel and measure the depths! This knowledge, it is safe to assert, is the supreme endowment we need in the writing of both fiction and criticism—especially in the writing of criticism. In an undisciplined age, blind yet active, eager yet aimless, rushing vehemently nowhere, we need, above all other benefits, courageous discrimination in the criticism of life. We need the strong,

6. F. H. Bradley (1846–1924), English philosopher, in *Appearance and Reality* (1893), argues that "the Absolute is Good, and it manifests itself throughout in various degrees of goodness and badness."

7. Omar Khayyám, Persian poet and astronomer of the twelfth century, whose *Rubáiyát* was freely translated by Edward FitzGerald in 1857–59

clear note of authority in the midst of the incessant exaltation of the inferior, in the midst of the endless tumult over the cheap, the immature, the rowdy, even the obviously defective. We need insight; we need a standard of excellence; we need integrity and audacity; we need really to live in the modern world we inhabit.

For not the least noticeable feature in much recent writing is what I may call, perhaps, the strong emphasis on nullity. In spite of all this downward boring into profundity, too many well-thought-of modern novels sound as if they had issued from mere windy emptiness. Although prose of this variety has lost the stale odor of genteel tradition, it has failed, unfortunately, to capture and hold an original flavor. It lacks seasoning that is characteristic. If it has any scent, it is the smell of nothing.

But these remarks apply, of course, only to a single literary aspect. If I have touched upon it at all, it is because I think that in our nervousness lest we overlook authentic genius, we spend ourselves too lavishly encouraging the minor talent. The danger is that we may lose, if we have not already lost, that sharp sense of values which distinguishes closely between budding promise and mediocrity. For there is promise around us. There is a fresh feeling in the air, and it may be, in truth, that tomorrow will become another day in our letters. Side by side with dullness and decay we may perceive, here and there, the new greenness of confident growth. And confident growth is the very essence of both national and regional literature.

It is well that the creative writer should be original, should be experimental, should be revolutionary and even extreme. These tendencies are all signs of vitality, and they have their part in man's progress and in a universe where change appears to be the only permanent law. I believe in the new, but I believe in the old also, and, most of all, I believe in that living fusion of the past with the present. There is room for both—there is room for all in so variable a world.

To the scholar and the critic, I would say simply: Keep an open mind, but hold fast to the standard of excellence—for an open mind without standards may become little more than a rubbish heap. For example, the Cambridge professor who teaches—or so I have heard —that Mr. T. S. Eliot has "dislodged" Milton, whatever that may mean, and that there is greater reality (or is the fashionable word "validity?" or is it even "content"?) in Sweeney than in Lycidas may keep a wide-open mind, though he has scarcely upheld the standard of excellence.[8]

Courage alone can do that. For in an epoch of general disintegration, when the lowest common denominator is the popular hero, it takes finer courage to commend excellence than to applaud mediocrity. And it takes more than courage—it takes irresistible daring—to cherish and defend that benign, if discredited virtue, good taste. Yet I have always liked Goethe's saying, "The assassination of Julius Caesar was not in good taste." One may imagine that even lynchings and automobile killings might be abolished by a people that possessed good taste in such matters.

If this is so, if the pursuit of the good and the true is the chief end of scholarship, then it would seem that the standard of excellence must remain securely in the grasp of the scholar, the student, the teacher of youth. With that standard, we must move forward or backward. One fact alone is certain, we cannot grow into the ground. Our direction we may choose, but scarcely more, and since it is impossible to escape the future, it is wiser to embrace it, however reluctantly, before it destroys us. In our own minds at least we may cultivate an aversion from the inferior and a preference for what is vital and reasonably enduring.

Already, while we are still undecided, we are on our way. Whether we fight or yield, the final victory will always belong to time. The most that we can do is to cling fast to some perception of truth or beauty, to some principle in art or criticism, to some special enjoyment even, or to some unbroken attitude in philosophy. For it is necessary to assure ourselves that only by changing as the world changes shall we be able to protect our rich inheritances and our vested intellectual interests in any future.

In one of the last letters of Pascal there are a few wise sentences which we may still take to heart.

---

8. Milton's *Lycidas* first appeared in 1638 as "A Monody." Eliot's "Sweeney Erect," "Mr. Eliot's Sunday Morning Service" (which includes Sweeney), and "Sweeney Among the Nightingales" appeared in *Poems* (1920); *Sweeney Agonistes* appeared in 1932. Sweeney is Eliot's representative vulgar and brutal modern man. The Cambridge professor was F. R. Leavis (1895–1978) in "Milton's Verse," *Revaluation: Tradition and Development in English Poetry* (1936).

"The Jesuits," he wrote, "have obtained a Papal decree condemning Galileo's doctrine about the motion of the earth. It is all in vain. If the earth is really turning around, all mankind together will not be able to keep it from turning, or themselves from turning with it."[9]

9.   Blaise Pascal (1623–62), French mathematician and philosopher, in *The Provincial Letters*, Letter XVII, To the Reverend Father Annat, S.J., March 24, 1657. Galileo (1564–1642), in his 1613 *Letters on Sunspots*, had openly supported the Copernican theory, in contradiction to the Bible, by asserting the motion of the earth and stability of the sun. The controversy thus initiated simmered until 1632, when Galileo was summoned to Rome to face the Inquisition; his 1632 work *Dialogue Concerning the Two Chief World Systems* was condemned, and he was sentenced to life imprisonment but managed to spend his last years under house arrest at his own villa near Florence.

An Inadequate Comment on "Primary Literature and Coterie-Literature" by Van Wyck Brooks

In reading Mr. Brooks's brilliant and scholarly paper, one's first thought may be: "The hour has struck; and the counter-reformation was long overdue." Just as there is the one perfect time for revolt, so it follows, inevitably, that there is the one perfect time to revolt from a revolt.[1] For these reasons, among others, Mr. Brooks's stirring challenge to the present is the most significant utterance in the recent history of American criticism. I read this definition of primary literature with that rare intellectual excitement which is one of the few permanent rewards of the critical faculty.

In a confused and disordered period, Mr. Brooks has not relinquished his inspiring faith in humankind and its place in the scheme of things. Although, unhappily for me, my less confident spirit is

Brooks's paper was delivered at the Second Annual Conference on Science, Philosophy and Religion, Columbia University, September 10, 1941, and included in Brooks's *The Opinions of Oliver Allston* (New York: E. P. Dutton, 1941). Those attacked by Brooks as coterie writers included Eliot, Joyce, Proust, Paul Valéry, and Gertrude Stein. Glasgow's comments were read by Hoxie N. Fairchild of Hunter College, along with written comments by Thomas Mann and Dorothy Canfield Fisher; none of the commentators was present.

1.   Although Brooks's early criticism in such works as *America's Coming-of-Age* (1915) had argued that the Puritan tradition crushed American culture, his later books, including *The Opinions of Oliver Allston*, revealed his antipathy to many twentieth-century literary movements.

unable to share, in its fullness, his larger vision of humanity, I believe, with him, that the survival of our culture and the existence of our democracy will depend upon a vital sense of human dignity and the greatness of human achievement. In a crisis, if anywhere, ideals are an indispensable element.

I agree also, even more heartily, with Mr. Brooks's judgment of the arrogance, the aimlessness, and the general futility of coterie-literature, in a world where one must either march with the living or sleep with the dead, but must not ever exist, consentingly, through a twilight stage of spiritual maladjustment. Even if we are hastening nowhere, it is safer, as well as merrier, to go gallantly. Whether the battle is won or lost, it is better to fight on the side of the angels; and what angels are left to our unbelief, except the pragmatic virtues of truth, justice, loyalty, courage, compassion?

In the first decade of the twentieth century—how far away and long ago that seems!—I was, so far as I am aware, the only Southern novelist who rebelled against what I then called the evasive idealism of the American mind. After forty years, in which I have watched various literary fashions and innumerable schools of writing flourish and fall, I still accept that earlier break with a tradition which appeared, oddly enough, to have died of perfection. Poetry, having reached the heights, was obliged either to turn backward or to plunge over; and what other instinctive choice remained to the novel?

"It is a possible contention," wrote Virginia Woolf, "that after those two perfect novels, *Pride and Prejudice* and *The Small House at Allington*, English fiction had to escape from the dominion of that perfection, as English poetry had to escape from the perfection of Tennyson. . . . If fiction had remained what it was to Jane Austen and Trollope, fiction would by this time be dead."[2]

But it is easier, one imagines, to escape from perfection than it is to break out of the vast modern laboratory of scientific civilization, which, as Dr. Alexis Carrel admits, "has destroyed the life of the soul." Regretfully, this foremost apostle of science concludes:

2. Quoted from "The Novels of George Meredith" in Woolf's *The Common Reader: Second Series* (1932). *Pride and Prejudice* was published in 1813, *The Small House at Allington* in 1864; the latter is the fifth of the six Barsetshire novels by Trollope.

"Despite all the marvels of scientific civilization, human personality tends to dissolve."[3]

In every generation, as Mr. Brooks reminds us, we have had our coteries of little thinkers. They are avid for detail, for they possess an articulate sense of an hour, not of an age. In their day, these little thinkers are often conspicuous; but at best they are period pieces, and in a far reflective vision we fail to distinguish them. When we search the vanishing point in the distance, we find that the larger figures alone remain visible. Nevertheless, we should ask ourselves: How much of the stale post-mortem smell in contemporary criticism is the outward sign of a period so greedy for decay that it will snigger at the human degradation in *Tobacco Road,*[4] while it enjoys picking bare the disinterred skeletons of the great? Does the moral tone of a period determine the nature of its criticism, if not of its imaginative literature? Are even the greatest critics of life and letters able to change the ingrained pattern of experience, or to alter the immediate tendency of an epoch? Is it only in the long perspective of history that we are able clearly to define the Age of Aristotle or the Age of Goethe?

That we should pause to ask these questions is a tribute to Mr. Brooks's creative criticism. He has held an undistorting mirror before our moment in time; and the reflection has shown us an urgent need, not only to replenish the failing "life-drive" in our literature, but to restore, possibly to disinter, those lost and half-forgotten symbols in which our race expressed its nobler endeavours. If language is a vehicle of communication, it is, nonetheless, a symbol of character. To measure the disintegration of our spiritual values, we have only to trace "the private history," not of Mr. John Crowe Ransom's lively "detail item," but of such fallen epithets as honour, virtue, wisdom, dignity, greatness, and, above all, nobility.[5] All these now discredited terms, avoided by those well-thought-of modern authors who have

3. French surgeon and biologist (1873–1944), Alexis Carrel argues against a scientific civilization in *Man the Unknown* (1935); see especially his chapter "Mental Activities."

4. The popular and sensational novel (1932) by Georgia-born Erskine Caldwell

5. Tennessee-born poet, cultural critic, and prominent New Critic, Ransom was in 1941 a professor of English at Kenyon College and editor of the *Kenyon Review*. In his critical essays he stressed the importance of physical details as opposed to abstractions.

fought for and won the right to speak bawdy words—all these discredited terms possessed, formerly, a spirit as well as a body. With the world literature that recognized them, they made, or helped to make, the social contract we call civilization; and the new order, if it endures, must, inevitably, summon them back into service. Once again, to repeat Mr. Brooks's apposite quotation from Sainte-Beuve,[6] they must become "important *for us*."

Just here, as I had finished, I am drawn back to this particular passage in Mr. Brooks's discussion. "It is important," he has written with deep insight, "for us to possess an American memory. . . . The sense of the past behind them is the tap-root of American writers, the sense of the achievements of their group; and, behind this, they must have a sense of the life and achievement of all mankind, a sense of the collective effort of the human race. . . . Such is tradition, the great sustainer of primary literature, the sum of the literary wisdom which the race has kept, the embodiment of those traits which humanity needs for its survival and protection."

6. Charles Augustin Sainte-Beuve (1804–69), French critic and author. Sainte-Beuve's quotation gives the essence of Brooks's concern in *Oliver Allston*, especially in the chapters on primary literature and coterie-literature; it does not appear in the published version of the essay.

IV Pleasures and Favors

The Soul of Harlem

It is unfortunate that a southern reviewer must approach Mr. Van Vechten's fine novel[1] by that literary valley of humiliation which lies between the inaccessible peaks of Uncle Remus and Uncle Tom.[2] For in a country where the burlesque still holds the balance of power, the caricature of Uncle Tom, as its shade slants over the southern scene, has plunged in the gloom of pathos even the historic figure of Uncle Remus. Only by dismissing these ancient influences are we able to approach the throbbing heart of a book that is devoid alike of burlesque and condescension.

It is true that these tormented inhabitants of Harlem are far removed from those cheerful yet fatalistic images that peopled the romantic fields of our childhood. It is true that the dialect is too difficult for a Virginian without the convenient glossary at the end of the book. Yet this strangeness is the result of a barbaric simplicity, of a barbaric color and life. Unlike the other novels by Mr. Van Vechten, "Nigger Heaven" borrows little from that flattering gloss of dilettantism so dear to the innocent and envious pursuers of "Sophistication."[3] For the roots of this book cling below the shallow surface of sophistication in some rich primitive soil of humanity.

The drama of Byron and Mary is one of those human comedies which are more terrible because more sardonic than tragedy.[4] It is a triumph for Mr. Van Vechten's art that he should have been able to

This brief essay, a review of Carl Van Vechten's *Nigger Heaven*, appeared in *Bookman* (New York), LXIV (December, 1926), 509–10.

1. Iowa-born Carl Van Vechten (1880–1964) was a former music and drama critic turned novelist. *Nigger Heaven* (1926) has been called "a sympathetic realistic treatment of Harlem life, which did much to stimulate the sophisticated interest in Negro culture." Van Vechten and his wife were Glasgow's close friends after 1925.

2. Here Glasgow seeks to free her mind of the powerful stereotypes of submission and avuncular wisdom created by Harriet Beecher Stowe in *Uncle Tom's Cabin* (1851–52) and by Joel Chandler Harris in his various Uncle Remus books (1881–1908) so that she can respond to Van Vechten's more realistic presentation.

3. Van Vechten's *Firecrackers* (1925), *Spider Boy* (1928), and *Parties* (1930) had dealt with social life in New York and Hollywood.

4. In *Nigger Heaven*, Mary Love falls in love with Byron Kasson, a penniless writer, but obstacles arising from their race lead to a tragic end.

reveal the souls of these pathetic hybrids as completely as he has revealed the physical convulsions that passed for the souls of Campaspe Lorillard and Ella Nattatorrini.[5] That the book attempts to prove nothing, that it does not masquerade as ethnology in the fancy dress of a novel, that it points no moral and preaches no doctrine of equality—this absence of prophetic gesture makes "Nigger Heaven" only the more impressive as a sincere interpretation of life.

A thrilling, a remarkable book. There is a fire at the heart of it.

5. Campaspe Lorillard is a character in Van Vechten's *The Blind Bow-Boy* (1923). Ella Nattatorrini is the title character in his *The Tattooed Countess* (1924). Both reappear in his *Firecrackers* (1925).

Modern in Tempo and American in Spirit

"Never Ask the End" is written in the modern tempo and is essentially American in spirit.[1] The scene is foreign; but the rootless psychology of a new country in its newest region is implicit in an adventure of the mind which unfolds as life unfolds in modern fiction without the happily discarded form of a superimposed plot. Books as well as human beings have their own inner lives. The inner life of this novel is sad and gay, brave and elusive.

Ten years after the World War, three Americans, a man and two women, who have known one another in the past meet again in Paris, "where one should have everything or want nothing." All are still young, or at least young enough, though with reflective eyes just turned toward the moment when youth passes. All had grown up in the Middle West in a period when there was no fixed social code on the last edge of the prairies. All have secret loyalties to the past, and a certain integrity, or fineness of nature, which does not include respect for the artificial conventions. Intensely realized as they are, these three persons bear no resemblance whatever to the crowd of gin-soaked, sex-intoxicated sensation hunters that whirled through the pages of Franco-American fiction immediately

This essay, a review of Isabel Paterson's *Never Ask the End*, appeared in New York *Herald-Tribune Books*, January 8, 1933, p. 3.

1. In addition to writing novels, Isabel (Bowler) Paterson wrote the "Turns with a Bookworm" column for New York *Herald-Tribune Books* (1922–49). She had reviewed Glasgow's *They Stooped to Folly* (1929) and *The Sheltered Life* (1932).

after the war. Rootless but not shallow, these wandering Americans are capable of great joy and great sorrow, and have known both in the past. Indeed, joy and sorrow have burned in so deeply that the memory is still alive and still aching. More wistful than hungry for delight, they meet and separate and come together again. "And all the meetings leading up to this chance conjuncture of the three of them, which meant nothing whatever, would lead to nothing. And they were glad of it, preferred it should be so; therein lay its special value." For "a breath might dissolve the bubble. Out of their weariness, their disenchantment, their defeat, they had together created this fragile happiness, by asking no more. That was the condition of it, as the magicians stipulated drawing a circle, saying only certain words, not looking over your shoulder."

Of the three, there is Pauline, with the kind of loveliness that Nattier had painted over and over:[2] "the delicate long nose and clove-pink mouth, that lifted upper lip, and the unbroken line of her cheek and chin, drawn with one stroke." There is Russ, still troubled by an old faithfulness, who "was through. The doctor didn't need to tell him that. If he could hold out two years—though it didn't matter." And there is Marta, a singularly living creature, who makes the book warm and human.

She has had bad years, and remembers them; for she has grown up in poverty and isolation on the border of the vanishing wilderness.[3] Yet she feels that it is absurd to call Americans materialists. "They won't even bother about food. What is it we want? Something—something *more*. Beyond anything that has ever been. To fly, to resolve into a finer essence, pure spirit, above the law. It's why we are unhappy in love, except at moments, when even passion is outdone, forgotten." Now, in Paris, when she has learned not to expect more than the shadow of ecstasy, she is aware of three selves. "There was now; there was the girl who had been herself; and there was the child she had been. She could see the child with objective distinctness. She had left the child behind when she left home. She could see the girl, though the point of discontinuity

2. Most likely Jean-Marc Nattier (1685–1766), French painter of historical subjects and portraits

3. Paterson was born on Manitoulin Island, Lake Huron, Canada, and lived in Calgary, Vancouver, and Spokane before coming to New York (*ca.* 1920).

was not so definite. But the girl existed only in that forsaken prairie town; the woman who went away from there was her present self."

She had started her life in a prairie schooner and covered the last lap by aeroplane. And she knew that to experience all the stages of civilization in one lifetime, from the nomad to the machine age, demands the utmost. . . .

She was seven the year the family moved West, part of the last great wave of emigration. They had been drifting westward ever since she was born. She could not think of her father without terror. Not physical fear, but "the dark night of the soul." Her mother had said: "I don't think I believe in marriage. But I don't know what else people can do." A worn little old woman whose face for many years had held the strange, sad, peaceful expression of the dead. . . .

As a child, as a girl, Marta had worked. She had cooked, scrubbed, waited, studied at night. At eighteen, "a shy, bold, moon-faced minx," she was a waitress in a hotel in the Middle West. "Her black uniform was as simple and severe as a calyx, and the continuous line gave meaning to her least gesture, bringing her whole body into complicity. Leaning backward and sidewise, with her skirt swirling about her ankles, she swam down the room with her chin lifted, swaying on the slender stem of her waist to balance the heavy tray." Here it was that she had loved disastrously, that she had married the wrong man, that she had known the failure of happiness and the sudden courage which springs back from despair. "Out of a million men, I set my heart on one; and nobody else would do. So did Pauline. And Russ—I suppose it was his wife until he got her, and then she was the obstacle."

After the failure of joy and sorrow, she had come to New York, and then the World War had begun. She had been sick and sad and alone and penniless; she had given up her youthful hope of happiness, and was starting over again, with new work, on pure courage, and then Liège fell. . . . "It wasn't any use. Folly. In spite of reason, the pinnacled city crumbled in her soul, the towers bowed and fell. Because it had answered to her own infinitesimal griefs, came precisely then, when she perceived her girlhood was over, spent for nothing." . . .

And now, at last, after the war, after ten years, she is in Europe, and happiness, the shadow of ecstasy is beginning again. This, she thought, is the moment. Today. You couldn't have more. . . .

Happiness, as fleet as the moment, unfolds and folds again and is over. She tells herself bravely that it couldn't last. Nothing lasts. Or is there something? There must be, she adds, or what should the three of us, so tired and spent, have to offer? What does one ask of life? To be always young, and light-footed, and in love. But they were none of those things, yet they had valued each other.

And, then, in one last lovely passage:

> In the long grass of the garden, fragments of medieval sculpture reposed tranquilly. Their granite features were blunted, all but effaced. It gave them a ghostly aspect, an infinite calm. It is the material substance that is ghostly, she thought. It wears thin, dissolves with time. Something more powerful and enduring wears it out. . . . The soul, having stooped to embrace mortality, is caught in the net of time. It strives to break through by the keen devices of the intellect, the intensity of passion, the persuasion of tenderness, even the violence of anger; and falls back on silence at the last. But at parting it cries out, wait; one moment more and I could have told you. . . . oh, wait! What we desire is communication—perhaps, some other where, we achieve it, by a persistence to which even granite must yield.

The whole modern approach to life, with its eagerness, its lightness, its disenchantment, its feeling for the moment as it passes and because it passes, its joy but not too much joy, its pain, but not too much pain, its courage in the face of time, its secret loyalties of the heart, and yet, somehow, somewhere, its lack of the state or quality of mind Spinoza called "blessedness,"—all this is woven here into a pattern that seems as real as the hour in which we are living. "Never Ask the End" is a book of delicacy, charm, truth, interfused with the something different that is personality.

Portrait of a Famous and Much Loved Dog

In this life, so slender in outline yet so rich and witty in substance, Mrs. Woolf has written a masterpiece.[1] Even to me who does

This essay, a review of Virginia Woolf's *Flush: A Biography*, appeared in New York *Herald-Tribune Books*, October 8, 1933, pp. 3, 21.
1. By 1933, the major works published by Virginia Woolf included *Mrs.*

not share the popular belief in the infallible judgment of posterity, it seems probable that "Flush" will be read and loved long after all the American literature that is made in France and all the British literature that is made in America have had their bright and windy day and are gathering dust in museums.[2] For this biography has the vital core that keeps writing alive. It stands alone in its field. Unhappily the field is not large, and it is so thickly strewn with natural pitfalls that only the consummate artist may venture there with discretion.

It is impossible in this review of a book essentially different from her novels to analyze minutely the elastic medium of Mrs. Woolf's art. In spite of her wide reading and carefully studied technique, her manner remains as individual as the texture of her mind. So deeply rooted, indeed, is her style in personality that it withers whenever an attempt is made to transplant it. Although she has her own high distinction, vulgarity appears to lie in wait for even the best of her imitators. Yet this distinction, which is innate and therefore inimitable, gives her work the timeless quality that is often outside but never behind its own epoch. Of all living writers, if we except, perhaps, Santayana, she is the least sentimental and the most civilized.[3]

In "Flush," Mrs. Woolf has avoided the complete immersion of her novels, and has employed the method of liberal interpretation which she used so unerringly in "The Common Reader,"[4] particularly in those chapters of "The Common Reader" that deal with the lives of the obscure. As she herself has said in an essay on the new biography, "it is a method of writing about people as though they were at once real and imaginary . . . making the best of both worlds. It is not fiction because it has the substance, the reality of truth. It is not biography because it has the freedom, the artistry, of fiction." And a little

---

Dalloway (1925), *To the Lighthouse* (1927), *Orlando, a Biography* (1928), and *The Waves* (1931).

2. Part of Glasgow's continuing criticism of Hemingway and other expatriates. Her social interaction with Gertrude Stein (1874–1946) did not begin until 1935. The most important British author in America had been D. H. Lawrence, who, between summer, 1922, and September, 1925, spent much of his time in Taos, New Mexico, and in Mexico, where he began *The Plumed Serpent* (published in 1926) and wrote a travel book titled *Mornings in Mexico* (1927).

3. Glasgow's library included thirty-six volumes by the Spanish-born Harvard philosopher George Santayana, including the five volumes of *The Life of Reason, or the Phases of Human Progress* (1932).

4. Two collections of Woolf's reviews and critical essays, 1925 and 1932; the latter is titled *The Second Common Reader*. Glasgow obviously means the first.

later, she speaks of "that queer amalgamation of dream and reality, that perpetual marriage of granite with rainbow."[5]

With this definition clearly in mind, we may pass on, then, to a vivid portrayal of the world of intuition which borders upon and mingles with the more complex, though not more real, universe of the reflective mind. There is in this book none of the metaphysical adventure that keeps "The Waves" exciting and baffling. There is scarcely a glimmer of the elusive radiance that makes "To the Lighthouse" the most beautiful and satisfying novel written in our time. No long lovely sentences, wreathing clause within clause, are poured upward by a fountain of energy and scattered like a luminous spray in the mind. In "To the Lighthouse" the world and time itself appear as frail, fugitive and exquisite as a breaking wave, and there are no fixed stars in a firmament composed of pure spirit.

But in "Flush" the approach to experience is brief, simple, direct. Radiance is here, though it is no longer elusive, and the shower of light has settled into a steady incandescence. The illusion we call reality in art has become closer and more intimate. With her firm, swift strokes, Mrs. Woolf has stripped away all the thinking and the talking about life, and has dealt with the sight, sound, touch, taste and smell of life itself. By this intuitive method, so different from the mere literary technique of impressionism, she has crossed the imaginary boundaries of psychology, and has portrayed a sensitive and emotional but inarticulate being against a background of closely woven and singularly living detail. Vagueness is suddenly crystallized into a pattern. Yet the vision of the world is still the vision of poetry.

To one who has observed canine psychology from earliest childhood, who has studied the responses of animals not in a laboratory, where fear paralyzes the mind and distorts the personality, but in a long association so free and natural that it has been possible, in some instances, to establish a means of communication woven partly of sounds or signs and partly of intuitions—to such an ob-

5. Both quotations come from the essay "The New Biography," a review of Harold Nicolson's *Some People*. This review was published in the New York *Herald-Tribune*, October 30, 1927, and was reprinted (posthumously) in *Granite and Rainbow* (1958). Glasgow misquotes Woolf slightly.

server Mrs. Woolf's narrative will appear remarkable for its fidelity.[6] It is possible that she herself does not completely realize the accuracy and precision of her understanding.

Such is the theme of "Flush," such is the nearness to life. But entirely apart from its engaging subject, the animated human figures and the flawless perspective would win an honorable place for this memoir among recent biographies. To match the background alone we must search among the many unforgettable scenes in English literature. We see Three Mile Cross as plainly as if we had lived there. We see the working man's cottage near Reading, where Kerenhappock was the only servant; the chair covers were made by Miss Mitford[7] herself of the cheapest material; the most important article of furniture was a large table; the most important room a large greenhouse. We watch Miss Mitford playing cribbage with her father (an Apollo until gluttony and intemperance changed Apollo into Bacchus), and writing interminable pages at the table in the greenhouse in the attempt to pay their bills and settle their debts. We are thrilled with anticipation when at last she thrusts her papers aside, claps a hat on her head, takes an umbrella, and sets off for a walk with the dogs. Spaniels are by nature sympathetic, Mrs. Woolf remarks, and Flush, as his story proves, had an even excessive appreciation of human emotions. As his mistress strode through the long grass (the words are Mrs. Woolf's), so he leapt hither and thither, parting its green curtain.

> The cool globes of dew or rain broke in showers of iridescent spray about his nose. . . . Then what a variety of smells interwoven in subtlest combination thrilled his nostrils; strong smells of earth; sweet smells of flowers; nameless smells of leaf and bramble; sour smells as they crossed the road; pungent smells as they entered a beanfield. But suddenly down the wind came tearing a smell sharper, stronger, more lacerating

6. This review provided Glasgow the occasion to express her thoughts on two significant subjects, Virginia Woolf, whose writing she genuinely admired, and canines, for whom she had long felt a deep compassion.

7. "Miss Mitford" is Mary Russell Mitford (1787–1855), a successful writer of tragedies and of stories of country life (*Our Village*), who befriended Elizabeth Barrett (1806–61) in 1836. Woolf says of Dr. Mitford, Miss Mitford's father: "[H]e was utterly selfish, recklessly extravagant, worldly, insincere and addicted to gambling. He wasted his own fortune, his wife's fortune, and his daughter's earnings." Kerenhappock was the Mitfords' cook. Three Mile Cross is the village where the Mitfords lived; it is situated near Reading.

than any—a smell that ripped across his brain stirring a thousand instincts, releasing a million memories—the smell of hare, the smell of fox. Off he flashed like a fish drawn in a rush through water further and further. He forgot his mistress; he forgot all humankind. He heard dark men cry "Span! Span!" He heard whips crack. He raced. He rushed.

The scene shifts. Miss Mitford was at her wits' end, scarcely knew indeed, Mrs. Woolf reminds us, what tragedy to spin, what annual to edit, and was reduced to the repulsive expedient of asking her friends for help. But to sell Flush was unthinkable. He was one of the rare order of objects that cannot be associated with money. Was he not of the still rarer kind, ask Mrs. Woolf and Miss Mitford, that because they typify what is spiritual, what is beyond price, become a fitting token of disinterested friendship; may be offered in that spirit to a friend who lies secluded all through the summer months in Wimpole Street, to a friend who is no other than England's foremost poetess, the brilliant, the doomed, the adored Elizabeth Barrett herself?[8] Yes; Flush was worthy of Miss Barrett, Miss Mitford decided; Miss Barrett was worthy of Flush. . . . Thus, one day, probably in the early summer of 1842, Mrs. Woolf continues, a remarkable couple might have been seen taking their way down Wimpole Street—a very short, stout, shabby, elderly lady, with a bright red face and bright white hair, who led by the chain a very spirited, very inquisitive, very well-bred golden cocker spaniel puppy.

When every sentence falls with the rhythm of inevitability, the temptation to quote becomes irresistible.

> Miss Barrett's bedroom—for such it was—must from all accounts have been dark. The light, normally obscured by a curtain of damask, was in summer further dimmed by the ivy, the scarlet runners, the convolvuluses and the nasturtiums which grew in the window-box. . . . Nothing in the room was itself; everything was something else. Even the window-blind was not a simple muslin blind; it was a painted fabric with a design of castles and gateways, and there were several peasants taking a walk. . . . But again it was the smell of the room that overpowered him. Only a scholar who has descended step by step into a mausoleum and

8. In 1821, Elizabeth Barrett contracted the first of a long series of illnesses that kept her an invalid much of her life. During this first illness, her physician, Dr. Coker, prescribed opium, to which she remained addicted the rest of her life. The exact nature and cause of the disease is unclear. It may have been caused by an injury sustained while riding a horse. It affected her lungs and nervous system.

there finds himself in a crypt, crusted with fungus, slimy with mould, exuding sour smells of decay and antiquity, while half-obliterated marble busts gleam in mid-air and all is dimly seen by the light of a small swinging lamp which he holds, and dips and turns, glancing now here, now there—only the sensations of such an explorer into the buried vaults of a ruined city can compare with the riot of emotions that flooded Flush's nerves as he stood for the first time in an invalid's bedroom in Wimpole Street, and smelt eau de cologne.

Then, at last, while he was still advancing and retreating, he heard a door shut. Miss Mitford was slowly, was heavily, was reluctantly descending the stairs.

And as she went, as he heard her footsteps fade, panic seized upon him. Door after door shut in his face as Miss Mitford went downstairs; they shut on freedom; on fields; on hares; on grass; on all he had known of happiness and love and human goodness. The door slammed. He was alone. She had deserted him. . . . A voice said "Flush." He did not hear it. "Flush," it repeated a second time. He started. He had thought himself alone. He turned. Was there something alive in the room with him? Was there something on the sofa? . . . "Oh, Flush," said Miss Barrett. For the first time she looked him in the face. For the first time Flush looked at the lady lying on the sofa.

Each was surprised. Heavy curls hung down on either side of Miss Barrett's face; large bright eyes shone out; a

large mouth smiled. Heavy ears hung down on either side of Flush's face; his eyes, too, were large and bright; his mouth was wide. There was a likeness between them. As they gazed at each other each felt: Here am I—and then each felt: but how different! Then, with one bound, Flush sprang onto the sofa and laid himself where he was to lie for ever after—on the rug at Miss Barrett's feet.

Through the days, weeks, months, years, he still lay at her feet. To resign, to control, to suppress the most violent instincts of his nature—this was the prime lesson of the bedroom school, and it was one of such portentous difficulty, says Mrs. Woolf, that many scholars have learned Greek with less—many battles have been won that cost their generals not half the pain. And so in time he became indispensable to a poet. He inspired poetry. Once even, in a moment of mystic vision, he was mistaken for Pan.

The scene shifts again. In the year 1846 Flush was stolen. He was snatched up from Miss Barrett's heels as she entered her carriage, tumbled into a dog-stealer's bag, and tumbled out amid the vice and misery of Whitechapel—for behind Miss Barrett's bedroom was one of the worst slums in London.[9] Mixed up with that respectability was this filth. We must go back to Defoe or to Dickens, or, perhaps, only to Mr. Thomas Beames to find a more heart-breaking description of the Rookeries, for so they were called.[10]

> . . . where human beings swarmed on top of each other as rooks swarm and blacken tree-tops. Only the buildings were not trees; they were hardly buildings any longer. They were cells of brick, intersected by lanes which ran with filth. All day the lanes buzzed with half-dressed human beings; at night there poured back again into the stream the thieves, beggars and prostitutes who had been plying their trade in the 'west end.'

Mr. Beames had trouble in telling politely of a bedroom in which two or three families lived above a cow-shed, when the cow-shed had no ventilation, when the cows were milked and killed and eaten under the bedroom.

"But the faces of the men!" Miss Barrett exclaimed. She had but glanced at the faces of those men, as she drove down into Shoreditch on her mission of rescue, yet she remembered them all her life.[11] They were branded on her eyeballs. They stimulated her imagination, observes Mrs. Woolf, "as the divine marble presences," the busts on the bookcase, had never stimulated her. They were to come before her again years later in Italy and inspire the most vivid passages in "Aurora Leigh."[12] Yet Flush had lain at their

9. Whitechapel is an area just east of London. It is about three miles east-south-east of Wimpole Street, which is near Regents Park, in Westminster. Glasgow seems to have misunderstood Woolf. Woolf explains that wealthy areas and slums were intermingled in mid-nineteenth-century London, and mentions, by way of an example, that behind E.B.'s bedroom was one of the worst slums in London. But this slum is clearly *not* Whitechapel.

10. Thomas Beames (1814 or 1815–64) was the author of *The Rookeries of London* (1850), a study of the poor in London.

11. Shoreditch is an area about a mile north of London. It is about three miles east-northeast of Wimpole Street. Flush was actually stolen three times, though Woolf compresses these into one incident. On the occasion Woolf describes, Flush was stolen by a Mr. Taylor of Manning Street, Shoreditch. Mr. Taylor was a gang leader who made his living (two to three thousand pounds a year, according to Woolf) by stealing dogs belonging to the wealthy and ransoming them. This was a common practice in London at the time.

12. *Aurora Leigh* (1857) is a novel in blank verse by Elizabeth Barrett Browning.

mercy in their midst for five whole days. Now as he lay on cushions once more, cold water was the only thing that seemed to have any substance, any reality.

The scene has shifted once more. Flush was in Florence, where the light was dazzling, the shadows were deepened to violet, the floors were of reddish tiles; where old women were knitting in the market beside brown jars of red and yellow flowers; where flies buzzed on great pink melons that had been sliced open; where the smells in the street were ancient yet forever young, and all dogs that he met were his brothers. Even Mrs. Browning was different from Miss Barrett. She had discarded her Indian shawls, wore a cap of thin bright silk that her husband liked, and sat on a balcony, watching the people in the street. For there were people about her in Italy, not merely marble busts of dead poets.

In Florence Flush lived happily to a good old age, died, happily also, one hopes, and was buried in the vaults of Casa Guidi.[13] This bare statement is the only reference, and the date and manner of his death are unknown.

"Mrs. Browning was buried in the English Cemetery at Florence, Robert Browning in Westminster Abbey. Flush still lies, therefore, beneath the house in which, once upon a time, the Brownings lived."

One might continue to pick out favorite passages in this book, and still feel that the poetry and the subtle charm of the humor cannot be distilled. In an epoch when the sophisticated are striving to be barbarian, Mrs. Woolf has written a biography that is untouched by sophistication and completely civilized.

13. From 1847 until her death in 1861, the Brownings lived, on and off, in Florence, in the Casa Guidi, a palace on the Via Maggio near the Pitti Palace.

George Santayana Writes a "Novel"

In his preface to "Character and Opinion in the United States"[1] Mr. Santayana reminds us of Spinoza's saying that other

This essay, a review of George Santayana's *The Last Puritan*, appeared in New York *Herald-Tribune Books*, February 2, 1936, pp. 1–2.
1. Santayana's essays (1920) exploring the conflict between materialism and idealism in the American character. Santayana, a Spanish-born, Boston-reared Harvard philosopher, had since 1914 made his home in Europe, especially in Italy.

people's ideas of a man are apt to be a better expression of their nature than of his. And if this wise observation applies to a man, certainly it would seem to apply quite as appropriately to a book—especially to such a book as "The Last Puritan."

To know what a reader thinks of this remarkable memoir in the form of a novel would give me a finer understanding of his mental or moral susceptibilities than I could gather from a casual acquaintance of many years. For one either enjoys or does not enjoy this book according to one's natural bias of mind. Like a feeling for rhythm or a sense of humor, the perceptive faculty is there or it is not there. As a philosophical narrative, "The Last Puritan" possesses every merit, if I except the breath of the body or the pulse of the heart; yet, for this very reason no doubt, I should hesitate to recommend it to the confirmed reader of fiction.[2] I should hesitate, in particular, to offer it to an adherent of any one of the flourishing cults in recent American letters—to the sentimental conservative, the new barbarian, or the earnest believer in social regeneration through literary violence. On the contrary, I should heartily recommend it to all those who prefer to think while they read, who relish a deep inward irony, who are interested more in the drama of ideas than in the play of conditioned or unconditioned reflexes.

For we have here, at the rare, right moment, an analysis of our civilization by the only modern philosopher (as all true lovers of "The Life of Reason"[3] will maintain) who has been able to make philosophy into an art. "I am an ignorant man, almost a poet," Mr. Santayana confesses blandly; and he is also, though he does not confess it, the greatest contemporary master of English prose. It does not matter whether one accepts or rejects, or accepts only in part, Mr. Santayana's system. It scarcely matters whether or not one is able to distinguish lucidly between essences and platonic ideas. For this novel is what philosophy so often is not, and that is litera-

2. *The Last Puritan* (1935) embodies Santayana's argumentative philosophy in two contrasting characters, a Puritan (Oliver Alden) and a hedonist (Mario Van de Weyer).

3. Santayana's major early work (5 vols., 1905) is a study of reason that finds matter to be the only reality. Aristotelian in conception, it argues that religion is a useful myth and science an effective hypothesis, that both are merely imaginative, and that art "makes the world a more congenial stimulus to the soul."

ture. As literature, therefore, and as literature alone, we may scrutinize its theme and its structure.

We watch, then, in a slightly frigid yet golden air, the conflict of intelligence with a universe that remains indifferent or actually hostile. Inevitably, I suppose, this book will be compared with "Marius the Epicurean."[4] It will be compared, not because the two books are alike, but because each, in its separate and lonely field, is unlike any other work in prose fiction. Both are novels not so much of life as of dialectic, although in "The Last Puritan" one may miss, perhaps, the antique harmony of "Marius," that luminous curve of reason which transcended, when it could not redeem the Age of the Antonines.[5] Still, if the form of Mr. Santayana's novel appears less symmetrical, the substance is spiced with wit or tinctured with irony, and the clear and tranquil prose is eloquent with its own rhythms.

Unlike any other work in prose fiction, I have said; yet this, of course, is only a partial truth. Since, unhappily, comparison leads to comparison, I may admit that, in my first absorbed reading of "The Last Puritan," I tried to trace a subtle family resemblance to the treasured features of "The Way of All Flesh."[6] We may recognize, I told myself, the same flickering sardonic smile which casts a sudden light in the mind. Ernest and Oliver may be distant cousins in satire;[7] but in the treatment of poor Ernest both his career and destiny are more savage; and the malicious insight of Samuel Butler is subdued to the cutting edge of truth by Mr. Santayana's urbane manner.

Surely this is well. Surely it is well to be urbane, to be impartial, to be scrupulously exact. Nevertheless, I find myself asking: Is it that malicious insight or that savage temper which made the characters in "The Way of All Flesh" so dangerously human? For the many

4. Historical novel (1885) by Walter Pater (1839–94), a tutor of classics at Oxford. *The Oxford Companion* calls this book "a philosophical romance." Pater traces the reactions of Marius to various spiritual influences, including philosophers (Heraclitus, Aristippus of Cyrene, Marcus Aurelius), Roman religion, drama, and Christianity.

5. The period of Antoninus Pius (86–161), who was Roman emperor from 138 to 161, and of Marcus Aurelius Antoninus (121–80), who succeeded his uncle, father-in-law, and adopted father, from 161 to 180

6. Novel by Samuel Butler (1835–1902), published in 1903

7. Ernest Pontifex from *The Way of All Flesh* and Oliver Alden from *The Last Puritan*

persons in "The Last Puritan" act as human beings act, and yet are never quite human. They will appeal most strongly to those reflective readers who are satisfied to enjoy abstractions in art, without demanding that the symbol shall be made flesh or the incorruptible put on corruption. These symbols are not what we call "real" characters; yet, in some miraculous way, they live and move in the brilliant air of the mind. They live and move with that singular vividness which is the best, if not the only, substitute for reality. The illumination is so intense that it appears to deepen the intellectual twilight in our novels.

To many of us nowadays, the contemporary novel seems to have wandered into a blind labyrinth, where it must either break down the decaying barriers we know as "naturalism" or else destroy itself in an endless maze of futility. And so we may still regard the creation of living character as the chief glory of the novel, and yet welcome with enthusiasm a re-examination of ideas.[8] Whether we look for understanding of life or for emotional and intellectual excitement, we are content to let the novelist select his own material and pattern. All we require of him, indeed, is that he shall conform, as thinker and artist, to his inner vision, that he shall obey the laws of his own universe. To banish soliloquy and speculation from the vast area of fiction appears to us as unreasonable as to decree that only humanity in the roots or consciousness at the source offers a fair transcript of life. The world of "The Last Puritan" is a complicated and highly organized world, and the author has dissected its nature with unerring integrity.

In an earlier work, written immediately before the war, Mr. Santayana has diagnosed those diseases of culture which have afflicted not only our novels, but our whole civilization and even ourselves.

> "Trustful faith in evolution," he wrote in his essay on the Intellectual Temper of the Age, "and a longing for intense life are characteristic of contemporary sentiment; but they do not appear to be consistent with that contempt for the intellect which is no less characteristic of it. Human intelligence is certainly a product, and a late and highly organized product, of evolution; it ought apparently to be as much admired as the eyes of molluscs or the antennae of ants. And if life is bet-

8. Glasgow's 1935 novel *Vein of Iron* centered on the philosopher John Fincastle, whose stoical idealism embodies an austerity similar to Oliver Alden's.

ter the more intense and concentrated it is, intelligence would seem to be the best form of life. But the degree of intelligence which this age possesses makes it so very uncomfortable that, in this instance, it asks for something less vital, and sighs for what evolution has left behind. Finding their intelligence enslaved, our contemporaries suppose that intelligence is essentially servile; instead of freeing it, they try to elude it. . . . Having no stomach for the ultimate, they burrow downwards towards the primitive. But the longing to be primitive is a disease of culture; it is archaism in morals. To be so preoccupied with vitality is a symptom of anaemia."⁹

I have quoted this passage because it describes the age and the moral climate in which Oliver Alden, the last puritan, suffered defeat. Seldom in fiction, or even in biography, has a life been so completely recorded, or a character so scrupulously examined. In spite of Mr. Santayana's incurable antipathy to puritanism, he has held the balance fairly between an idea and a universe.

"I am afraid" [the narrator remarks in the Prologue to "The Last Puritan"] "I am afraid that there will always be puritans in this mad world. Puritanism is a natural reaction against nature.

"But in Oliver puritanism worked itself out to its logical end. He convinced himself, on puritan grounds, that it was wrong to be a puritan.

"And he remained a puritan notwithstanding.

"That was the tragedy of it. . . . He kept himself for what was best. That's why he was a true Puritan."

"His puritanism had never been mere timidity or fanaticism or calculated hardness; it was a deep and speculative thing: hatred of all shams, scorn of all mummeries, a bitter merciless pleasure in the hard facts. . . . I don't prefer austerity for myself as against abundance, against intelligence, against the irony of ultimate truth. But I see that in itself, as a statuesque object, austerity is more beautiful, and I like it in others."

For there are, we must remember, two logical attitudes towards experience. We may seize it as an essence, this perfume of the moment, this "transcript of the immediate," or we may reject the life of nature, and refuse, like the true puritan, to "accept anything cheaper or cruder than our own conscience." It is "a petrified conscience, a moral cramp," protested Oliver's father, Peter Alden, who had escaped from puritanism after committing murder with

---

9. "The Intellectual Temper of the Age" is the first essay in Santayana's *Winds of Doctrine* (1913).

the college Bible.[10] But to Oliver the whole of life is "either the truth or nothing," and, as Mr. Santayana has remarked elsewhere, to covet truth is a very distinguished passion.

In this disintegrating world, then, in this age, in this dry New England atmosphere, Oliver Alden was born of adequate, if not irreproachable, ancestry. We are first introduced to him in prenatal darkness, at the crucial instant when "his little organism, long before birth, had put aside the soft and drowsy temptation to be a female. It would have been so simple for the last pair of chromosomes to have doubled up like the rest, and turned out every cell in the future body complete, well-balanced, serene and feminine." But no. Instinctively and inevitably, before he was formed, Oliver made his first unconscious and characteristic choice. "One intrepid particle decided to live alone, unmated, unsatisfied, restless and masculine." And some years after that great refusal, when Mario, his cousin from Europe, a joyful hedonist, inquired: " 'I say, Oliver, were you brought up on the bottle or did you have a wet nurse?' Oliver laughed at the idea of a wet nurse. Fancy Miss Tirkettle in that capacity! Nobody had a wet nurse in America. Of course, he was brought up on the bottle. 'I thought so!' Mario exclaimed triumphantly, 'You don't know what a woman is.' "

Our popular fiction, ably assisted by Freudian psychology, has accustomed us to dark views of our ancestors. We are used to seeing the old Puritan portrayed as a hypocritical rogue hiding our sinister inheritances beneath a sanctimonious exterior. It is, therefore, surprising, it is even startling, to find that Oliver's sincerity was his sole point of offense. Unlike so many other puritans in modern American novels, Oliver met disaster, not because he was a hypocrite, but because he was not one. He suffered the terrible fate of being consumed by his virtue.

While he continues to exist and agonize (somewhere, I think, Mr. Santayana has called Calvinism "an expression of the agonized conscience"),[11] we know him thoroughly. We know him, not perhaps as a fellow being, but as we know the works of a clock that we have

10. Peter Alden, a wealthy New Englander addicted to drugs, travels about the world seeking to replace the puritanical dogma of his family with a better vision.
11. In "The Genteel Tradition in American Philosophy," delivered at the University of California, August 25, 1911, and included in *Winds of Doctrine* (1913)

taken apart and put together again. We share in his infancy, his childhood, his predispositions and antipathies, his frustrated loves and his more vital friendships. "Women were rather a difficulty to him. He thought he liked them and they thought they liked him; but there was always something wanting. He regarded all women as ladies, more or less beautiful, kind, privileged and troublesome. He never discovered that all ladies are women."

The book is crowded with characters, and each character has some significant relation to the whole; each character means something more than itself. Not only a life but an era unrolls before us. Although the greater part of the scene is placed in New England, my difficulties arise when I try to think of "The Last Puritan" as an American novel. In spite of the publishers' label, this for me is an impossible act of thought; and I recall Mr. Santayana's avowal that only an American can speak for the heart of America, that he has tried to understand it as a family friend may who has a different temperament. Understand us, I think he does, so far at least as we are composed of mind and conscience; but the quality I feel in him —it may be, as he implies, the mellow tone of Catholic tradition— has no place in that "long Arctic night" of the Nordics. He might be, indeed, some brilliant and dispassionate observer from another, and a more civilized, planet.

Nevertheless, we must admit that the figures in this novel are to be found, without too wide or diligent a search, in America. Some few may have wandered from an older society; but beyond their upright outlines even when they are in Europe, we seem to see the spiritual horizon of New England. All are here, and all are recognizable—the conscript mind, the rebel mind, the old Puritan, the new Epicurean, the casual Christian, the sincere sensualist and the myth of woman, ancient and modern, with "something wanting." For the rest, what and where is the true, the "real," America? What American has understood more of it than the fact or fiction of his own particular time and place?

In the end we receive the indelible impression of a way of life called Oliver Alden, of a way of life which was defeated and yet vaguely triumphant. Nothing, we think, could be more bitterly ironic than Oliver's death. "We have dedicated ourselves to the truth," he reflects, "to living in the presence of the noblest things we can conceive." So he goes into the war, impelled by duty, "to fight the Germans whom I like, on the side of the French whom I don't like." And with one last satirical twist of unreason for the reasonable, he is denied even the right death because he dies at the wrong moment.

"Whatever the Germans may be guilty of," Mario said, "they didn't kill Oliver, and in a literal sense there was no question of blood in his case. It was several days after the armistice. All firing had ceased, but the troops were advancing rapidly; and somebody on a motor-bicycle, who thought all danger was over, came round a curve without warning on the wrong side of the road. Oliver, in trying to avoid a collision, ran into a milestone. His car turned turtle; he was caught under it and his neck was broken. There were no external injuries, hardly a bruise. . . . It was possible to take a photograph. I have one here."

"You were always taking his photograph," Rose interposed coldly, as she continued to pour out the tea. Oliver had loved her; he had wanted to marry her; he had left her a legacy.[12] But Rose continued to pour out the tea.

Thus appropriately, it appears, Oliver, who had always made the right choice, died because somebody else was on the wrong side of the road. Beneath this catastrophe to good intentions, to virtue out of touch with its age, there may be, or there may not be, a symbolical irony. But, strangely enough, there is, in literature as in life, a deeper irony than the creator's, and that is the futile and unconscious irony of the creature. For when we have turned the last page of this extraordinary novel, when we pause and look back over the animated scenes to the vanishing point in the long perspective, we discover that, not only as a statuesque object, but even as a state of mind, austerity may be more beautiful than prodigality. Among all the human beings, wise or foolish, that people this hard-hearted yet soft-minded world, poor Oliver, the tenderly despised puritan, is the only one who proved himself to be capable of a genuine passion for reality, of a bitter merciless pleasure in the hard facts.

12. Rose Darnley, however, loves Oliver's good friend Mario Van de Weyer, who fails to recognize her preference for him.

But even so: "When life is over, and the world has gone up in smoke, what realities might the spirit in us still call its own without illusion save the form of those very illusions which have made up our story."[13]

13. The closing sentence of *The Last Puritan*

V   The Notorious Mr. Cabell

Mr. Cabell as a Moralist

t is the peculiar merit or demerit of Mr. James Branch Cabell that he should have chosen to write not for the moment but for immortality. Disregarding the obvious truth that only those who answer the questions of the hour can be sure of their audience, he has, with characteristic gallantry, rejected the easy vices which are popular in literature for the unprofitable virtues which should be permanent. From the general democratization of letters, he remains serenely apart and the muddy stream of the vernacular has left his prose undefiled.[1] Because he has refused to compromise with our national preference for the second best he has become the solace of that diminishing minority to whom neither the voice of the people nor the verdict of the producer constitutes the ultimate authority in matters of art.

To be ignored by one's own generation is a disheartening if indubitable compliment to a writer, and though Mr. Cabell has come recently into belated recognition the long neglect of twenty years or more condemned him to the solitude which genius requires.[2] Only since the appearance of that elaborate legend in which Jurgen delicately pursues the unholy grail[3] has one of the sternest moralists of

---

This essay, a review of James Branch Cabell's *Straws and Prayer-Books*, appeared in New York *Herald-Tribune Books*, November 2, 1924, pp. 1–2. It played a part in creating the deep friendship that flourished between the two Richmond authors during the next two decades.

1.   Glasgow has noticeably singled out values she felt she and Cabell shared. Her deafness since young womanhood left her insensitive to the advantages of vernacular styles, which in the fiction of Gertrude Stein, Ring Lardner, Sherwood Anderson, James Joyce, Ernest Hemingway, and William Faulkner evolved, in power and lyrical flexibility, well beyond the phonetic dialect writing of Thomas Nelson Page and Joel Chandler Harris she had known before the mid-1890s, when her hearing failed. (The copy of *Adventures of Huckleberry Finn* in her library was a 1915 edition.) In her early novels she had used awkward phonetic spellings to suggest class and racial differences.

2.   Cabell's first novel, *The Eagle's Shadow*, appeared in 1904, seven years after Glasgow's first, *The Descendant*. He had published fifteen books by the time the prosecution of *Jurgen* (1919), for violating New York's pornography law, made him an international figure.

3.   In *Jurgen*, Cabell uses the various symbols of chivalry in an obviously Freudian manner.

his time achieved the inglorious popularity that consists in being read by people who do not understand what he writes.

Whimsically, he calls himself a romancer, but unlike other romancers of his age (who are content to fly their kites without strings), he attaches his iridescent fancies to a philosophic idea. If he rises above his contemporaries it is because he has realized that in order to be impressive, or even interesting to a mature intelligence, an extravaganza must have substance as well as sparkle. Though moonshine may prettily adorn a reasonable philosophy of life it is not sufficient alone to fill even the slenderest volume of prose.

In "Straws and Prayer-Books" Mr. Cabell, who is nothing if not versatile, reveals himself again as a moralist and a merrymaker.[4] Not since Voltaire[5] has pessimism worn so gay and gallant a smile. If occasionally Mr. Cabell indulges in the kind of comedy that is the very special privilege of improper little boys and Mr. George Moore,[6] he provides also in abundance the Attic salt which is the surest preservative of either sentiment or philosophy. Concession to prejudice is not his weakness, and when he compromises it is only with beauty. Though, as someone, I think, has pointed out, beauty is truth for him rather than truth beauty, he has never confused the fleeting actuality with the essential verity which the artist has discovered.

Beneath the lightness and gayety of his surface the burden of his philosophy is as depressingly moral as the wisdom of "Ecclesiastes." Vanity of vanities. Dust and ashes. This he repeats, in spite of all the preachers and the poets, is the end of every man's desire. Only the

4. In the "Introduction" to *Straws and Prayer-Books* in the Storisende Edition of his works, Cabell explains that this book serves as an epilogue to the series of books that constitute the "Biography of the Life of Manuel" and an explanation of why these books were written. The book mixes criticism with more fanciful material.

5. Voltaire, French writer (1694–1778), the author of *Lettres philosophiques* (1734), *Candide* (1759), *Dictionnaire philosophique* (1764), and many other stories, poems, plays, and historical and philosophical writings

6. George Moore was an Irish novelist, playwright, and short-story writer. His most notable books are *Esther Waters* (1894), a novel, and his autobiographical trilogy, *Hail and Farewell* (*Ave*, 1911; *Salve*, 1912; *Vale*, 1914), which includes (somewhat unreliable) accounts of his famous acquaintances, such as William Butler Yeats, George William Russell (1867–1935), and Lady Gregory. Glasgow seems to be referring to Moore's sensational reporting of his sexual life in his autobiographical works: *Confessions of a Young Man* (1888), *Memoirs of My Dead Life* (1906), and *Hail and Farewell*. Cabell discusses Moore's works in "A Theme with Variations," an essay in the book under review.

unattainable is the eternally desired. Helen is Helen and immortal only until she is touched. The virtue of austerity prolongs the vision of delight, creates the beauty of the beloved and imparts the incomparable ecstasy to adventure. So it is that man,

> always nearing and always conscious of approaching death with its unpredictable sequel, and yet bored beyond sufferance by the routine of his daily living, must in this predicament have playthings to divert him from bringing pitiless reason to bear upon his dilemma; and he must have, too, the false values which he ascribes to these playthings.

What plaything can be more amusing, he demands, than "a satisfying evasion of that daily workaday life which is to every man abhorrent"? Since there is no such thing as Truth, but only innumerable truths, why waste our time in pursuing the shadowy archetype among the multitude of imperfect copies? Sufficient it is for the artist, who accepts everything and believes nothing, to play ceaselessly with "beautiful happenings," with "the intrepid men and flawless women and other monsters who were born cleanly of the imagination . . . in whom, rather frequently without knowing why, the artist perceives a satisfying large symbolism." All this is written for those who understand in "Straws and Prayer-Books," which may be described as one man's pilgrimage among charming monsters to the high place of intellectual enchantment.

This endless quest is for the artist who is also a scholar. It is for the poet whose philosophy is compounded not of voluptuous enjoyments but of fastidious discriminations and aesthetic restraints. The gray dust of use and wont lies over all experience, and only the artist who has lived austerely and dreamed beautifully is able to escape into the "enchantment of the disenchanted." In this imaginary world love is less an end to desire than a series of magical episodes, and the perfect lover is the dreamer who is disillusioned most completely of the reality of passion. Above all, it is a world where beauty is superior to logic and where even the devil, when he moves, walks delicately. From our unlovely Freudian psychology, which has reduced all vices to the familiar virtue of self-control,[7] it is a relief to pass into the legendary woods of Elfhame and find that

---

7. Glasgow here indulges herself in the popular view that Freud wished to liberate the instincts from all restraint by the superego.

there are "no longer two sides to everything and a man need look for no reverses."[8]

A strange and beautiful volume. For those who are venturesome to the point of preferring their literature unlabeled "Straws and Prayer-Books" will be a perpetual delight. The book has wit, charm, intellectual audacity and that subtle magic which is the transmuted essence of personality.

8. *Straws and Prayer-Books* contains a story called "The Thin Queen of Elfhame," set in the enchanted Wood of Elfhame.

Van Doren on Cabell

For the artist who is also a scholar there can be no more sympathetic interpreter than the scholar who is also an artist. Mr. Van Doren brings to his subject a flawless understanding, an appreciation tinged with enthusiasm, and that rare gift of luminous discernment which elevates the profession of criticism from a pedestrian pursuit into one of the nobly adventurous arts.[1] For those who have been prevented by fear of reproach from an excursion into the formal and flowery country of Poictesme,[2] he will make a wise and witty conductor. There is, I believe, no study of Mr. Cabell's elaborate biography that can compare with this significant volume.

Happily or unhappily, we live in an age which is afflicted with an incurable suspicion of superiority. Difference we tolerate and even welcome, provided it is the artless difference of mediocrity, and does not, like Mr. Cabell's insane fish from which we are descended, aspire to live in some thinner medium than the complacent mind of the mass. But so mistrustful are we lest any departure from the normal should conceal an erratic regard for distinction in letters that we have invented a special epithet of opprobrium for

This essay, a review of Carl Van Doren's *James Branch Cabell*, appeared in New York *Herald-Tribune Books*, April 5, 1925, pp. 3–4.

1. Carl Van Doren (1885–1950), a professor at Columbia University since 1911, had been the literary editor of the *Nation* (1919–22) and *Century* (1922–25) and had published *Contemporary American Novelists, 1900–1920* in 1922. He was also the managing editor of the *Cambridge History of American Literature* (1917–20).

2. The mythical medieval country in which Cabell set the romances of Dom Manuel, beginning with *The Soul of Melicent* (1913) and including *Jurgen* (1919).

those intrepid spirits who cherish a preference for the English language over the vernacular and who do not incline to the theory that the knowledge or even the practice of grammar constitutes a pedantic impediment to veracity.

To those who have rallied with this diminishing minority to the forlorn hope of literary tradition, Mr. Van Doren and Mr. Cabell are inspiriting companions. For, in spite of the formidable cult of commonness, which has reduced our fiction, as it has reduced our politics, to the depressing level of the lower average, genius still escapes from the multitudes in our valley of decision to dwell alone upon the remote and solitary peaks of consciousness. With the serene fidelity of the predestined artist Mr. Cabell has rejected the favor of the crowd as urbanely as he has ignored the fashions of the moment. "Like another Adam," Mr. Van Doren observes, "he has found his Eden, has dressed and tended it, has populated and civilized it, and has made it the home of valor and beauty and wit." So faithful has he been in letter and in spirit to his iridescent illusion, that we can imagine him, were too long a taste of the forbidden fruit to drive him from his dreamer's paradise, still patiently pursuing loveliness beneath any curse that did not impose the tilling of actual ground. For from the red clay and the white sand of Virginia he has remained completely detached. It is his peculiar distinction that he stands not only apart from the crowd, but above all compromise with the dissolving views of the age. More exclusively than any other writer of our day, he has dedicated his powers to a single flaming vision of beauty.

Mr. Van Doren has divided his brilliant analysis into three parts: I, Cabell Minor; II, Cabell Major; III, Scholia.

Cabell Minor is the immature Cabell of "The Eagle's Shadow" and the earlier short stories, which appeared when American fiction was revolving in the more or less historical costumes of a national masquerade.[3] It was a period when no author was so poor as to do reverence to realism, and when even Mrs. Mary E. Wilkins Freeman was beguiled into fancy dress in the midst of scenery which was

---

3. *The Eagle's Shadow* (1904) is a romance of modern money-worship. *The Line of Love* (1905) consists of short stories set in the Middle Ages.

prevented from being Balkan by the simple device of being early Virginian instead.[4]

That Poictesme should have survived the ruins of these innumerable kingdoms is due to that ironic wit which, though it is seldom practiced by the sentimental, is the only antiseptic of sentiment. It is true that the country of Janicot[5] differs from other promised lands in American romance (as Mr. Cabell differs from the usual literary Moses) in as much as it rests not upon moonshine, but upon the solid substance of an intellectual idea. Though the magic of Poictesme is above Nature, it remains subservient to the unalterable laws of logic; and if Mr. Cabell has inherited the evasive idealism of the American point of view,[6] he has halted consistently on the verge of reality, which he pursues and yet turns to question in the very act of pursuit.

For his flight is not so much from reason as from the unreasoned actuality; and his dynamic illusions, for all the mental dynamo that inhabits them, are not unrelated to the metaphysical shadow-world of the religious dreamers. Signs are not wanting, indeed, that in an earlier and more generally benighted period of the world's history his essentially monastic mind might have dreamed less of embodied romance and more of disembodied mysticism. From this final refuge of disillusionment he has been saved, notwithstanding the neat felicity with which he labels himself "Episcopalian," by an intellect which, like the Emperor Septimius Severus,[7] has "been everything, and found all things of little value."

Genius, which Mr. Van Doren reveals as nothing if not perverse, has evolved Cabell Major from the vanilla-flavored tradition of Southern literature; and Southern literature, resisting his valiant wit, still languishes, as it has always languished, for lack of the tonic ingredients of blood and irony.[8] Irony, to be sure, he has provided in

---

4. Massachusetts-born Freeman did her best work as a local-colorist in *A New England Nun* (1891), but *The Heart's Highway* (1900) is a historical romance set in seventeenth-century Virginia and *Edgewater People* (1918) a collection of stories of the supernatural.

5. Janicot appears in *The High Place* (1923), by Cabell.

6. Contrast Glasgow's 1916 interview by Joyce Kilmer, in this collection.

7. Lucius Septimius Severus (146–211), Roman emperor from 193 to 211

8. A slogan Glasgow enjoyed applying to her own ironic realism

generous measure, but it is a harmless, distilled irony; and his allegorical heresies, like his pictorial infidelities, are so etherealized that only the barest residuum of blasphemy or impropriety is left.

> With conscience and immortality and blasphemy (Mr. Van Doren writes in a subtle and beautiful passage), Mr. Cabell's wit plays as intrepidly as with less formidable prejudices. It has no fears. It stares open-eyed at the blazing sun and good-humouredly strokes the beard of Jehovah. . . . Mr. Cabell is thus as free to admire loveliness wherever he finds it as to discover the possibilities of mirth in whatever theme. He finds beauty glittering in the midst of ugly sins, and snares it in his tolerant net. He builds fresh beauty about ominous symbols, inventing or elaborating them if need be. He does not, like Hawthorne, feel the obligation to check the wings of his vision by comparing it with reality. Mr. Cabell, by questioning the reality of reality, has been naturalized in the world of dreams till he moves about there without the scruples lasting over from another allegiance.

It is a world of dreams, and since it is a world of dreams, it embraces only a "bright emptiness" in the shape of humanity. The inhabitants of Poictesme are clothed in the fugitive enchantment of the sunrise, and the women, whom Mr. Van Doren praises for this glimmering quality, are less women than changeful, delicately-tinted aspects of "the face that launch'd a thousand ships."[9] The world of chivalry, real or imaginary, is one where women have always presented an extravagant appearance, but where, or the tale does not tell, they have never expressed an authentic opinion. In common with all male descendents of that first recorded figure of gallantry, probably Arboreal, the romantic dreamer is content to regard woman in allegory as merely the highest and ripest fruit on the tree.[10]

Fortunate in the rich conclusion of his biography, Mr. Cabell is doubly fortunate in the selection of his interpreter. There could be no better approach to a distinguished philosophy of escape and to a reality that is not real than this book by a scholar who is a literary artist.

---

9. Glasgow is suggesting that Cabell's female characters are variations on the Helen archetype as it exists in Cabell's (or man's) imagination. See *Doctor Faustus* (v, i) by Christopher Marlowe (1564–93).

10. In other words, gallants have evolved from the ape who proved hardest to satisfy.

"The Biography of Manuel"

With one of those sardonic jests that sprinkle the paths of life, as well as the pages of literature, Mr. James Branch Cabell has chosen to write of beautiful happenings in the midst of what is probably the ugliest civilization ever invented by man. The sauvity of his art alone protects him from the concrete monotony of an industrialized South. Beauty, if it survives at all, must flower from within. So he has created a planetary sphere which is entire, balanced, symmetrical, and subject only to the laws that govern dynamic illusion. As far as it is possible for one of the inhabitants of earth, he has withdrawn not only from the world as victorious mediocrity has made it, but from an example of "divine handiwork" that is "not good; or, at any rate, not good enough." Yet even here, in this virgin territory of the mind, he has failed to win release from the processes of decay. Fragments of earth still cling to the allegorical virtues. Like Jurgen's quest of the unholy grail, the exploits of Dom Manuel's progeny reflect the whole tragic story of mortal combat with Fate.[1] It is true that shapes of land and sky and sea, with all the brilliant fauna and flora of this magic kingdom, could exist only in a country that has never known the blight of reality. And it is this external world, not the bloodless but convincingly animated symbols, that makes the sense of escape a part of the bright lustre of Poictesme.

At this point, before turning to the long Biography of romantic man, it may be well to pause and examine more closely the elusive mind and temper of its creator. In the year 1879, midway of the appropriate month of April, James Branch Cabell entered the right "unliterary" circle of Richmond, a charming city, where in a less tender age children had gathered to mock the alien Poe when he

---

This essay, a review of the *Storisende Edition of the Novels of James Branch Cabell*, appeared in *Saturday Review of Literature*, VI (June 7, 1930), 1108–1109.

1. After *Jurgen* made Cabell famous, he revised many of his earlier books to bring them together in eighteen volumes, called the Biography of Manuel, published from 1927 to 1930. Dom Manuel is a pessimistic individualist who strives for an unattainable ideal; like Jurgen, one of his descendants, he inhabits the mythical medieval country of Poictesme.

passed in the streets.[2] More fortunate than Poe, however, the author of the Biography was born into a family that could be properly accounted for in the annals of gossip. Not only did he arrive at a safe distance from the generally unsound "people who write," but he could rely upon progenitors who were as invulnerable to liberal ideas as other well-established Virginians.[3] Though impoverished by the War between the States, the social order was one in which the art of living was still practiced at a sacrifice of the less honorable arts of pen and brush. Reduced in circumstances but not in spirit, the right circles in Richmond, and indeed all over Virginia, had not forgotten how to enjoy themselves. There was, of course, the necessity to earn one's bread as best one could in a period when all Southerners in good standing were hungry together; but appetites were neither so large nor so fastidious as they have become in a modern plutocracy. It was all, no doubt, charming enough, in spite of frugal diversions.

Yet a society in which one is never alone, however favorable it may be to the soldier or the statesman (who necessarily moves in a crowd and depends upon a correct posture), is seldom hospitable to the philosopher and the creative artist. The grace of privacy, so dear to the strange mind of the thinker, was regarded quite simply and naturally in Virginian circles of the 'seventies and 'eighties as a kind of superior social affront. Never was it visited upon any well-born Southerner except as the last humiliation in a code of poetic justice. In this transitional period, it is true, the old culture was dying, and the new industrialism was only beginning to prepare the ground for its ultimate triumph. Much was lost of the past, but the little that was left contrived to be picturesque; and in Richmond, where the charm of a village still lingered, the little James, peculiar only in his

2. Edgar Allan Poe was adopted by the Allans in 1811 and lived in Richmond with them from 1811 to 1815 and again, after five years in England, from 1820 to 1826 (when he entered the University of Virginia). Poe returned to Richmond several times during the remainder of his life. In these later years, Poe was usually exceedingly poor and had acquired some degree of notoriety through his writings and his drinking.
3. Cabell's great-grandfather William H. Cabell was governor of Virginia; his grandfather Robert Gamble Cabell was Robert E. Lee's personal physician; Cabell's father, Robert Gamble Cabell II, was also a physician. The Branches were a distinguished family as well.

occasional spells of silence, encountered the usual perils of infancy. As he grew up, the world was changing without violence. In his youth, the familiar welcome still awaited one in country houses. The gardens on James River, though untended and fast running to seed, were enchanting places in which to play games or make love. Even in Richmond, where assembled law-makers were already dismantling the scene for democracy, the established social order had not surrendered unconditionally to its Chamber of Commerce.

For the rest, the author of the Biography was not alone among Southern writers when he made his choice between the friendliness of legend and the indifference of a commonwealth in which books were once respected less than conversation and are now respected less than steam whistles. For conversation, which triumphed not only over every other form of art, but even over every vicissitude, has been muffled, if not extinguished, by the roar and clash and whistle of the victorious machine. For ten, perhaps for twenty years, the celebrated tongues of the South have been running down into silence. Even ladies in bombasine,[4] even colonels in Confederate gray, have found their audiences melting to air. Only the bluster of religious or political creeds is able to rise above the noise, the numbers, the bigness of material success. For the democratic South, which has produced by accident, one must believe, the Kingdom of Poictesme, has always been, and is even today, blown about by every wind of doctrine that is loud enough to make sound without sense. Yesterday, we were demolishing evolution in the mask of the devil. Tomorrow, we shall probably be embracing Fundamentalism, in cap and gown, calling itself Humanism, and brandishing a diploma instead of a Bible. And this Humanism, I hasten to explain, will bear as little resemblance to the favorite doctrine of Professor Irving Babbitt[5] as the demon of monkey descent bears to the Dar-

---

4. A silk fabric in twill weave dyed black, or a twilled fabric with a silk warp and worsted filling, with a suggestion here of ladies in mourning

5. Irving Babbitt (1865–1933) was at this time a professor of French at Harvard, a leader of the New Humanist movement, and a critic of romanticism, especially of Rousseau. The New Humanism that flourished in the 1920s stressed the human ethical element of experience as distinguished from supernatural or natural dimensions. In their revolt against romanticism, New Humanists turned to what they considered the Hellenic doctrine of reason and stressed subjection to inner law.

winian hypothesis. For the combined learning of Mr. Babbitt and Mr. Foerster[6] is powerless to hold back the most dignified word from the scrap-heap after it has once started down the interminable slope of popularity.

* * *

But if this is the scene of action from which Mr. Cabell escaped, it is evident that his revolt is not confined to any particular place. "Art," he tells us, "is a criticism of life only in the sense that prison-breaking is a criticism of the penitentiary."[7] He has, indeed, no kinship with those superficial thinkers who imagine that an age or country, and not the intrinsic scheme of life, is at fault. If he is detached, it is from modern Virginia only as a part of the "divine handiwork" which he has judged as an artist, and as an artist has pronounced "not good enough." An immeasurable distance lies between him and those elegiac Southerners who are sighing, beneath the very wheels of the machine, for the lost freedom of slavery.[8] No, as he would be the first to admit, freedom for the artist, as for the moralist, has never existed; every age has been ready to kill or die in defense of its own favorite evils; and a telegraph pole in the landscape may be a fair exchange for a gibbet. For the flaw lies not in any personal predicament, but is bound up with the lot of man and his deepening sense of universal futility. He does not find, indeed,

> the comedy ever to be much altered in essentials. The first act is the imagining of the place where contentment exists and may be come to; and the second act reveals the striving toward, and the third act the falling short of, that shining goal, or else (the difference being negligible) the attaining of it to discover that happiness, after all, abides a thought farther down the bogged, rocky, clogged, befogged, heartbreaking road, if anywhere. That is the comedy which, to my finding, as well as

6. Norman Foerster (1887–1972) was a leader of the New Humanism and professor of American literature at the University of North Carolina (1914–30). In 1929, he published *The American Scholar*. From 1930 to 1944 he directed the School of Letters, University of Iowa. Contrary to what Glasgow says here, southern Fundamentalism in the twentieth century has remained virulently anti-Humanist.

7. This is the basic position argued in *Beyond Life* (1919) and a stance that underlies Cabell's general aesthetic of the romance: art gives us our power to imagine things "as they ought to be."

8. In 1930, Glasgow had not yet begun her friendships with Stark Young and Allen Tate, two of the twelve contributors to the 1930 collection *I'll Take My Stand: The South and the Agrarian Tradition*, which Glasgow as a spokesman for the New South may have viewed as excessively elegiac.

to the finding of Felix Kennaston,[9] the life of Manuel has enacted over
and over again on every stage between Poictesme and Lichfield.[10]

It is interesting but vain to speculate if the bittersweet fruit of Mr.
Cabell's philosophy could have sprung from a soil more congenial to
art. At fifty he refuses to break either his head or his heart against injustice that is adamantine and may be eternal. But it must not be forgotten that he began life, as his youthful books bear witness, very
much of a sentimental romantic. As I remember him in boyhood, he
appeared shy, reserved, over-sensitive, with a face of tempered melancholy, and the manners of the Victorian age. It is possible that his
detachment may spring from an inherent disdain of popularity. On
the contrary, all his later remoteness from democracy may prove
merely that, like Gibbon[11] in the midst of the French Revolution, he
had arrived at the early conclusion that he is "the sort of person a
populace kills."[12] For, as Bagehot remarks so pointedly in this connection, whenever the populace kills a man or a book it is for the sin
of being superior.[13]

And from any point of view, it must be acknowledged that the Biography sins in being superior. Here, at last, in true chronological
order, and in a stout array of distinguished volumes, we have the
Life of Dom Manuel the Redeemer, which is also the Life of Man the
Romantic, "that alone of animals," asserts Mr. Cabell, in a general-

9. In *Cream of the Jest* (1917), the author Felix Kennaston grows tired of his marriage and escapes into a dream world of the past to rediscover his lost love, Ettarre.
10. The modern setting of Cabell's novels including *The Cords of Vanity* (1909)
and *Something About Eve* (1927), as explained in *The Lineage of Lichfield* (1922)
11. Edward Gibbon (1737–94), English historian, author of *The History of the
Decline and Fall of the Roman Empire*
12. Glasgow and Cabell grew up within a few blocks of each other in Richmond.
As a child, when Glasgow would call on Cabell's grandmother, Cabell and his
brothers would stare indifferently at her, then disappear. Glasgow knew Cabell again
during his senior year at the College of William and Mary, when he became the victim of popular gossip because a friend of his, a college librarian, was accused of being
homosexual. Although Cabell was cleared of wrongdoing, he did not forgive
Glasgow for including the incident in her autobiography published nine years after
her death in 1945 and four years before his own death in 1958. His comments about
Glasgow's work in *As I Remember It* (1955) reflect his hurt.
13. Walter Bagehot, English economist and journalist, author of *Physics and
Politics* (1873). In *Estimations in Criticism* (Vol. II, 1909), Bagehot speaks of victims
of the French Revolution whose "calm superior condescension" the mob could not
endure, and, in discussing Gibbon's (May 20, 1792) letter to Lord Sheffield, writes
that Gibbon "had arrived at the conclusion that he was the sort of person a populace
kills."

ization from which I am inclined to dissent, "plays the ape to his dreams." Beginning with the prologue "Beyond Life," the Biography sweeps down from "Figures of Earth" and "The Silver Stallion" to "Domnei: A Comedy of Woman Worship" and "Chivalry: Dizain Des Reines." Rising again with "Jurgen: A Comedy of Justice," and "The High Place," it descends anew, through several centuries, to "The Rivet in Grandfather's Neck" and the town of Lichfield, Virginia.[14] If the design of the work is tremendous, the texture is as close and the detail as intricate as if the scene were woven in tapestry.

Meanwhile the Biography has become a completed and individual book—a fairly longish book, in twenty parts, and a book which deals with the life of Manuel as that life has been perpetuated through some twenty-three generations. For that life always is my protagonist. Time, as I have said, has altered this protagonist unceasingly and subtly, but only as time alters any other life. Fundamentally my protagonist does not change in any one of my eighteen volumes; but remains, instead, under all temporal garbs and all surface stainings, very much the same blundering male ape, reft of his tail and grown rusty at climbing, forever aspiring and yet forever cautious, forever hungering for companionship and for comprehension and for sympathy, and yet, none the less, retaining forever inviolate that frigid, and pale, and hard, small core of selfishness which, as you may recall, Queen Freydis[15] very long ago discovered—at the cost of heartbreak—to be the heart of Manuel. . . . Yes; I am afraid that, at bottom, under every permissible human grace and large human gesture, and under each of my three human attitudes,[16] that obscure slight heart-trouble has been perpetuated

14. The works Glasgow mentions were originally published as follows: *Beyond Life* in 1919; *Figures of Earth* in 1921; *The Silver Stallion* in 1926; *Domnei*, as *The Soul of Melicent*, in 1913; *Chivalry* in 1909; *Jurgen* in 1919; *The High Place* in 1923; and *The Rivet in Grandfather's Neck* in 1915. She omits *The Music Behind the Moon* (1926), *The Line of Love* (1905), *Gallantry* (1907), *Something About Eve* (1927), *The Certain Hour* (1916), *The Cords of Vanity* (1909), *From the Hidden Way* (1916), *The Jewel Merchants* (1921), *The Eagle's Shadow* (1904), and *The Cream of the Jest* (1917).

15. In *The Figures of Earth* (1921), Queen Freydis vivifies Manuel's spiritual descendants after he molds them from earth.

16. The passage is quoted from the "Author's Note" to the Storisende Edition of *Straws and Prayer-Books*, which serves as the Epilogue to the Biography of Manuel. In the paragraph preceding this passage, Cabell refers to "the three main types" that appear in these books; they are exemplified by the "dauntless poet Madoc," the "chivalrous Dom Manuel," and the "gallant copious sweep of Jurgen's adventuring."

in every one of the descendants of Manuel as ineradicably as it yet endures in all the race of Adam.

Meanwhile the Biography has become a completed and individual book. Its major theme I take to be the theme and the truly democratic doctrine of our own world's Author, that the average of one human life should not, or at least does not, differ appreciably from the average of any other human life. . . .

This, in its final summing up, is the purpose of the "Biography of Manuel." Yet the author tells us that not until he was well into the stories in "The Line of Love" did he receive an apocalyptic vision of the eternal recurrence.[17] In this everlasting cycle, as Horvendile watches it through twenty-three generations, only the fashion of dress and the cut of hair and beard alter with the changing epochs of history. The characters and the events repeat themselves with a changeless rhythm and pause. If the underlying pattern is there, it appears only as the logical result of irresistible laws working together. More in the character of the God of evolution than the God of Genesis, the creator of Poictesme has, apparently, started his design on its way and left it to prove what it would.

And yet the wonder remains that so courageous an interpretation of life should contain so frugal a measure of human passion. It may be that I have over-estimated the importance of the esthetic sense in Mr. Cabell's cosmogony; and certainly romantic love is scarcely more at home in Poictesme than it is in our own moral Republic. In both countries, the beauty and the desire that "offend against the notions of thy neighbor" are equally frowned upon. There is reason, indeed, to believe that in Poictesme, as in Lichfield, the Goddess of decorum, though continually defied, is still generally worshiped. But there is no spot in the Biography where we can find, even after the most painstaking search, either the passion of revolt or the more familiar passion of love. Fidelity, when it is the unprof-

17. *The Line of Love* (1905), a group of short stories set in medieval times, was Cabell's second book but his first romance of historical themes. Horvendile, Lord of the Marches of Antan, appears in the various volumes of Manuel's biography. Eternal recurrence is the doctrine that contends that every event in the universe, along with all its details and cosmic context, will recur an infinite number of times in exactly the same way; it was held by pre-Socratics, Stoics, Plotinus, opposed by Judaism and Christianity, and revived by Nietzsche in *Thus Spake Zarathustra* and *The Will to Power*.

itable, and often inconvenient, fidelity of women, is treated simply as another marsh-fire of romance; and the spectator of the endless conflict appears to be as indifferent to the pangs of thwarted desire as he is to the major cruelties which have failed so conspicuously to justify the ways of God to man. All the natural injustice which has made the universe a torture chamber to the few artists who are completely sensitive to the world's pain provokes from him merely the comment that his "admiration for the laws of nature has always been remarkably temperate" and that "for the laws of society" he has "never had any patience whatever." If cruelty resides at the heart of being, then the sensible man, as artist or citizen, will discreetly turn away his eyes from the heart to the head. For the truth is that his interest in emotion is even more temperate than his admiration for what we have agreed to call the solid substance of matter. He is, in all essentials, a citizen not of the actuality, but of the clearer world of ideas. And who is able to prove that a fact is more real than an idea? Is a clod of earth or even a spasm of heart-break more real than the image of it we form in our mind? Here, as elsewhere, it would seem that one philosopher's guess is as good as another.

Since the "Biography of Manuel" does not, as the author explicitly asserts, attempt to deal fairly, except perhaps in a Jurgenian sense, with the nature of woman, the protagonist of the drama remains always that first Puritan, a blundering male ape, reft of his tail and embarrassed because he has not yet adjusted his fig-leaf. For romantic man, even so far back as our arboreal propositus,[18] was more of a Puritan at heart than a lover. If he has revolted, through the better part of twenty-three generations and on innumerable reams of paper, from the severe Goddess of Decorum, it is because he still worships her under strange names and in strange fashions of heresy. Man, even romantic man, does not spend his time or waste his paper defying a divinity in which he has ceased to believe. No honest atheist ever found a thrill in mocking either Jupiter or Jehovah. Even the most impudent small boy feels little interest in thrusting out his tongue when there is nobody to shock. It is doubtful, indeed, if any novelist since Henry James[19] has surpassed Mr.

18. That is, the male ape just mentioned
19. American novelist Henry James was noted for his studies of refined moral discernment.

Cabell's emphatic if unwilling homage to the moral sense of mankind. After the casual habit of historians, we are disposed to confine the Puritan conscience within geographical boundaries, and to ignore the fact that, abetted by Scotch-Irish Calvinism, the Puritan influence has conquered, almost without resistance, the once Cavalier South.[20] But, conforming to the truth of experience, as well as to most of the books written by men, Mr. Cabell has endowed each and all of his male characters, even the gayest rakes among them, with an indestructible capacity to be shocked by the loss of prudery in women. Clasping in his arms the beloved of his youth, Dorothy la Désirée, Jurgen discovers that she has mislaid the domestic virtues somewhere in the garden between dawn and sunrise, and he earnestly advises her to adopt a proper frame of mind toward her husband.[21] "Jurgen drew away from her," writes Mr. Cabell, in a passage which contains even more than the average wholesome moral tone of American novelists, "with a shiver of loathing, and he closed his eyes to shut away that sensual face."

It is true that Jurgen speaks, though reluctantly, of his "one real passion," but it would seem that the distinction between romantic passion and romantic appetite is that romantic passion cannot be annihilated by the act of fulfillment. And it is this insistence upon appetite in place of passion that lends an air of unreality to all these fragile shapes of women, as if they were outlines seen dimly through a luminous rain. Lovely as they are, they remain always inventions of desire rather than creatures of time. There is not sufficient weight in their combined bodies and emotions to hold them to earth. Even Helen is Helen and immortal only until she is touched.[22] In "Domnei," it is true, woman-worship is the unfalter-

---

20. Between 1717 and 1775, two hundred thousand or more Scotch-Irish migrated from northeastern Ireland to America, most of them settling in the (until then) largely English South. The Presbyterian church was the chief institution of the Ulstermen from northern Ireland. The conflict between the Scotch-Irish and Cavalier southerners provided a major tension of Glasgow's life and fiction; it is present in many of her novels, including *The Miller of Old Church*, *The Romantic Comedians*, and *They Stooped to Folly*.
21. In *Jurgen* (1919), Jurgen, a middle-aged pawnbroker, goes in search of his miraculously vanished wife, but early in his quest he encounters Dorothy la Désirée, the sweetheart of his youth. Seemingly tongue-in-cheek, Glasgow here reinforces the moralistic pretense of Cabell's good-humored erotic story.
22. Jurgen's erotic adventures include an encounter with Queen Helen.

ing theme of the tale, which is woven of the texture of phantasy.[23] Love is triumphant, but the lovers melt into spirals of iridescent illusion. Perion the lover has none of the solid substance of Manuel the Redeemer or of Jurgen the pawnbroker. One surmises that Perion, for all his hazardous service of love, is merely worshiping the unattainable under the name of Melicent, and that long desire in romantic man leads inevitably to the embraces of Melior. For Melior is the symbol of use and wont, and she was designed by Koshchei the Deathless, who made things as they are.[24]

Just here is the place, I think, where one will pause either to assent or deny, in obedience to one's confirmed habit of mind. It may be true that mortal life is so futile; but we are moved occasionally to question if love is really so frail? Is the power that has combatted death and robbed the grave of its victim nothing more than a physical hunger? One must be logical, insists Mr. Cabell, and answers according to reason. Yet some fragile thread of hope, he assures us, is not denied the believer. Anything, he admits, even immortality, may be possible for the descendants of that "insane fish, who somehow evolved the idea that it was his duty to live on land, and eventually succeeded in doing it. So, now that his earth-treading progeny manifest the same illogical aspiration toward heaven, their bankruptcy in common-sense may, even by material standards, have much the same incredible result." Meanwhile, as fugitive desire creates and destroys, both fish and man, to borrow Nietzsche's aphorism, shall be surpassed.[25] Or, as Mr. Cabell regards the tragic predicament, "man as he now exists can hardly be the finished product of any Creator whom one would very heartily revere. We are being made into something quite unpredictable, I imagine; and we are sustained, through the purging and the smelting, by an instinctive knowledge that we are being made into something bet-

23. *Domnei* (1920) is the revised version of the first published of Cabell's romances of Dom Manuel set in Poictesme, *The Soul of Melicent* (1913). It recounts the various loves of Manuel's eldest daughter, Melicent, including her interest in Perion de la Forêt.

24. In *The High Place* (1923), Young Florian, smitten by the dream that contains music, becomes a follower of Princess Melior and is doomed to the life of a romantic; she becomes his wife, the attained unattainable. In *Jurgen* (1919), when Jurgen is let into Heaven, he discovers Heaven has been built by Koshchei, who made things as they are, including God.

25. Friedrich Wilhelm Nietzsche, German philosopher, prophet of the Superman

ter.'' And in the making, though love and the finer sentiment of pity are both absent from that "hard small core of selfishness" which is the heart of Manuel, there are moments in the Biography when even the vulgar little soul of Jurgen, son of Coth, is stirred by a ripple of tenderness. For Jurgen "avoided that part of Heaven wherein were his grandmother's illusions; and this was counted for righteousness in Jurgen. That part of Heaven smelt of mignonette, and a starling was singing there.''

Though speculations concerning the work of a living writer are usually extravagant, there is little hazard in the repeated assertion that Mr. Cabell is already a classic. Barring an invasion by a reincarnated Caliph Omar[26] or a roving band of Christian converts, his books will probably survive many changing fashions in literature. In periods like the one we are evidently approaching, when the distinction between good and bad writing is safely obliterated, his fame will suffer, no doubt, a partial eclipse. But this also will pass.[27] Styles in philosophy and letters will change again, in spite of the faculty criticism possesses for believing in the immortal rightness of its own futile pronouncements. The rhythm of his prose which clothes so perfectly the rhythm of his theme will become with age an infallible preservative from the taint of decay. Even amid this speeding modern world, in which the life of a book appears scarcely less ephemeral than the life of a May-fly, it would seem that the "Biography of Manuel" is composed of the nature of things that time does not kill. For Mr. Cabell has achieved the detachment of those courageous thinkers who refuse to flatter and dare to examine our destiny. In this act of courage which, like a clean wind, purges the mind of intolerance and superstition, there is always a beneficent spirit; and this is especially true when the beneficence is disguised in the brightness of an irony which, of all civilized attributes, men find it hardest to understand and forgive. A world that has been governed by fear since it was capable of being governed at all dreads nothing else so much as to be-

---

26. Omar Khayyám, a twelfth-century Persian mathematician, astronomer, and teacher; author of numerous rhymed quatrains collected as *Rubáiyát* and published in a popular and free English translation by Edward FitzGerald (1859)

27. In the 1970s, when many young Americans showed a renewed interest in fantasy literature, several of Cabell's books appeared in inexpensive editions, but the revival seems not to have continued.

hold that awful power dissolve beneath the searching light of ridicule. Yet in this refusal to acknowledge the supremacy of fear, the creator of Manuel has reached the peak of his philosophy. Almost alone among American writers he has dared to look into the encompassing void and to laugh because it is bottomless.

Branch Cabell Still Clings to His Unbelief

Regarded from the historical point of view, Mr. Cabell stands out bravely as one of the few fortunate American artists in words.[1] His place may have diminished in size and in prominence, but that it is still firm underneath is well shown in his latest romance. Although the lighter fringes of his public have turned to fresher and rawer fashions, he has gained in leisure and in contemplation what he may have lost to younger novelists in noise and numbers and popularity. Serenely he awaits that slow revival of esthetic values which will conceivably slacken the pace we have agreed to call "realism" in fiction while it produces a beneficent infant mortality in the arts.

In the midst of a world that rocks, Mr. Cabell has shown yet again in "Smith" the constancy to cling to his unbelief and the courage to place his hopeless hope in disillusionment.[2] A sound, almost a predestinarian, faith supports Mr. Cabell. When other comforts fail, he has shown unfalteringly that disenchantment may wear the mask and become the able understudy of fortitude; and whether or not this confers what we in our bird's-eye view may regard as immortality, it brings at least the securer blessing of invulnerability. As long as the menagerie triumphantly invades the ivory tower, it appears that the land beyond commonsense is the only province in which the artist may still make a peace about him and call it solitude.

Meanwhile, the little popular effigies on the college campus

This essay, a review of Branch Cabell's *Smith: A Sylvan Interlude*, appeared in New York *Herald-Tribune Books*, October 6, 1935, p. 7.

1. Following the 1927–30 publication of the Storisende Edition of *The Works of James Branch Cabell*, Cabell published for a time under the shorter name Branch Cabell.

2. *Smith* (1935) is the second volume in a trilogy that also includes *Smirt* (1934) and *Smire* (1937).

change and dwindle. All the strutting minor Cabells of a few years ago are followed by the minor Hemingways or Faulkners into the hospitable heaven of redeemed sophomores.[3] But romance, Mr. Cabell repeats, is immortal.

"Smith: A Sylvan Interlude" is, in my opinion, the most beautiful book that Branch Cabell (to distinguish him from his more famous self) has yet written. The work begins as virtually pure romance, shifts toward irony in the third book, the fourth being all irony, and the fifth book turning, I suspect, perilously near burlesque. But in the end we work back by degrees to the entirely romantic tone of the beginning.

Part One: The Book of Branlon (which I would have longer) is tender and lovely and a little wistful, as true romance must be wherever we find it. The prose is Mr. Cabell's own, which defies imitation. In the hands of another writer this style becomes mere glittering smartness, affected and vulgar. But for his own use Mr. Cabell has created a medium of expression that is firm, silken and mellow.

The tale leads us at outset deep into the enchanted forest of Branlon, and it tells how a peddler stood there upon a primitive road and barred the Emperor Charlemagne's armed advance with a wooden staff.

> Then said the peddler: "Let the young poets come to Branlon. Let the gray poets whose hearts yet keep their comfort. So will Branlon delude all these into contentment; for the magic of Branlon is compassionate and above reason. For absurd loyalties this forest has made a haven; this forest feeds magnanimity; this forest revives the hurt daydreams of youth."

And so the romantic who is a poet and the youth who is a romantic and the poet who is all things that keep fresh the heart of youth —together these set out again upon that ancient quest which leads always in a circle and never straight, since it must follow perpetually the way of eternal recurrence.

For, in the strange allegorical way of dreams, this peddler turns

3. Ernest Hemingway's works of the period included *A Farewell to Arms* (1929), *Death in the Afternoon* (1932), *Winner Take Nothing* (1933), and *Green Hills of Africa* (1935). Since *Sanctuary* (1931), William Faulkner had published *Light in August* (1932), *Pylon* (1935), and three collections of short stories, *These 13* (1931), *A Green Bough* (1933), and *Doctor Martino and Other Stories* (1934).

out to be that Smirt who, in an earlier book by Mr. Cabell, dreamed himself to be a supreme god;[4] but whose place has now so diminished in size and in prominence that he has awakened to find himself a mere local deity known—in the most prosaic terms conceivable—as Mr. Smith. And the young poets who come by and by to the magic haunted forest of Branlon are the children of his own great vanished dream, all seeking, as their no longer divine father had done before them, for the magnanimity and the half-remembered beauty of their youthfulness. How the divergent desires of Volmar and Elair and Clitandre and Little Smirt—and in the end of Mr. Smith also—are gratified by "the compassionate magic of Branlon" makes up a story which demonstrates that the magical powers of Mr. Smith are still firm underneath.

All is beautifully told. We learn once more, yet with a morning freshness of words, that dreams outwear actualities even while the actuality triumphs; that love may be a high adventure, but affection is a permanent shelter; that all questing in the land of common-sense must end either in defeat or in a compromise with contentment. Now and then a mere mortal may pause to take issue with the logic of fable. To some of us, for example, youth may not appear, even to the reflective vision, as a period of bright dreams and high hearts and impossibly fine notions. To some of us that too-brief period of time may contain an abundance of tragedy and heartbreak, and the ignoble desire of a moth, not for a star, but for a firefly. But I suspect the youth of which Mr. Smith dreams so fondly is that rose-and-white youth of magic, and that the dreaming serves him more completely than it ever served the "boy's fancy that creates more nobly than God creates."

For it is true that I have never known any mortal boy who created in this super-divine fashion, nor have I ever known any youthful visions that could compare in beauty or wisdom with the "dynamic illusions" of Mr. Cabell's wholly resigned middle age.

4. *Smirt* (1934)

VI A Reasonable Doubt

What I Believe

To begin with my start in life, since all of us who are not converts for an advantage bring a measure of our belief into the world with us, I was born with a nonconformist mind at a time when being a rebel, even an intellectual one, was less exciting and more uncomfortable than it is nowadays. By temperament I was on the side of the disinherited, a position which is neither commendable nor the reverse, but simply a matter of the thickness of the skin over one's nerves. The world I lived in as a child was, in part at least, the world of Dickens, and he, as Santayana has said, "was a waif himself, and utterly disinherited." Even now, I cannot tell whether I loved Dickens because he had compassion for "the deformed, the half-witted, the abandoned, or those impeded or misunderstood by virtue of some singular inner consecration," or whether the early influence of Dickens made me pity these unhappy creatures.[1]

Although I was different from other children whom I knew, I excelled only in imaginary adventures, and I could never, no matter how hard I tried, learn to do sums. But a thin skin and oversensitive nerves made my childhood unhappy. I saw painful sights that did not distress other infants or even the adult minds that surrounded me. For I had come into the world hating cruelty as Voltaire hated superstition (though, of course, Voltaire[2] hated, too, the cruelty in superstition), yet I saw the needless suffering of human beings and especially of animals wherever I looked. I was a delicate child, and, perhaps for this reason, the tragedy of life and the pathos which is worse than the tragedy worked their way into my nerves

This essay appeared in *Nation*, CXXXVI (April 12, 1933), 404–406. It was reprinted in several anthologies.
   1.   Glasgow here wants to establish the position that one's sensibility and values largely determine the ideas one is likely to find attractive or even plausible. She was reading Dickens in her home before she ever attended a school. For the most part, her education came from her family and in response to her own curiosity. The quotation comes from Santayana's essay "Dickens," in *Soliloquies in England, 1914–1918* (1922).
   2.   Voltaire was noted for his skepticism.

and through my nerves into my beliefs.[3] Yet, even at this tender age, my sense of humor was an adequate defense against the more destructive winds of doctrine.

In the first of my books I was moved to speak for the despised and rejected;[4] but the raveled sleeve had not become a fashion in literature, and the disinherited was less welcome in that year of grace than he finds himself in an epoch that prefers the style of illiteracy to the language of romance. "The Descendant," an honest, defiant and very immature book, bearing as its motto Haeckel's phrase, "Man is not above Nature, but in Nature,"[5] and softened here and there to satisfy the reluctant publishers' demands for "a moral or at least a pleasant tone," records, in words that are hot and crude and as formless as the revolt of youth, many of the things I believed passionately as a girl and believe reasonably as a woman.

For it does not alarm me to hear that an economic system must be revised or discarded. I had heard this as a schoolgirl—though in a republic which was still watching the Rockefeller fortune with admiration and envy, it was not at school that I heard such opinions. My own special interests were in the direction of history and literature; but it was my privilege to study economics (it was all political economy when I was sixteen, and Mill had not ceased to be a major prophet) under the guidance of a brilliant and fearless mind. A profound thinker and student, at least thirty years ahead of his time, my friend died at the age of twenty-six, crushed by physical pain, and crowded out of a world which required not brilliance, and certainly not fearlessness, but conformity.[6] Yet wherever I look today I see

3. In her autobiography, Glasgow writes that she was so small and frail that for her first three weeks she was carried on a pillow. In her early years she was ill again and again; in one year, for example, she was thought to be dying of diphtheria and scarlet fever.

4. *The Descendant* (1897) tells the story of Michael Akershem, the illegitimate son of a "poor-white" southern woman; Akershem, in his twenties, edits *The Iconoclast*, a freethinking New York newspaper in whose pages he attacks the major institutions of society.

5. Essentially a paraphrase of Charles Darwin's thesis in *The Descent of Man* (1871) that the distinctions between man and lower animals are differences not of kind but of degree. Ernst Heinrich Haeckel (1834–1919) was a German biologist and philosopher and originator of the familiar evolutionary principle that ontogeny recapitulates phylogeny.

6. George Walter McCormack of Charleston, South Carolina, whom Glasgow met in 1890 when he was twenty-two. During the four years before his death in a New York hotel (an apparent suicide), McCormack guided her through the major

his prophecies coming true. Though he did not predict the World War, he did predict other wars and a period of social evolution which would either overthrow our economic structure or result in a more equitable distribution of wealth under the present system.[7] He said to me the first time I heard of Karl Marx, "The economists of the future will have to reckon with that force."[8] There were other predictions, though he was never a convert to any theory; but, after all, I was asked to write an article on what I believe, not on how I came to believe.

To return, then, to my creed, I believe that the quality of belief is more important than the quantity, that the world could do very well with fewer and better beliefs, and that a reasonable doubt is the safety-valve of civilization. So I believe what I believe with an open mind. I am, I hope, ready to reject anything or to accept anything that does not embrace the old infamy, cruelty. I am not frightened by systems. I am not frightened even by names, since I have been called by almost every name, except the right one, as far back as I can remember. When I was one and twenty, it was all very exciting, for one and twenty is the proper age for revolt. One is still young enough then to have faith in some miraculous system which will abolish cruelty and greed, and change the primary instincts that have made civilization so uncivilized. One has not learned that systems are made by human nature, not human nature by systems, and that the ancient evils may still function through any social order. Nevertheless, if I firmly believe anything in later years, these are the things I believe:

Since I have no superstition concerning an economic structure, I

---

works of John Stuart Mill, Henry George, Charles Darwin, and Ernst Haeckel, plus an assortment of other scientists, economists, and cultural theorists.

7. In 1892, McCormack, now Glasgow's brother-in-law, ran for the House of Representatives on the Reform ticket, modeled on the radical Ocala Platform, by which Populists swore. He was defeated.

8. Glasgow is writing in the heart of the Depression and during the heyday of American literary Marxism. Glasgow's most recent novel, *The Sheltered Life* (1932), had been dismissed as irrelevant by Clifton Fadiman in the *New Republic* because the novel dealt with the southern upper-middle class rather than the laboring class. Her next novel *Vein of Iron* (1935) would provide a powerful empathic picture of victims of the economic system in the Depression. Glasgow here is understandably eager to establish her credentials as a spokesman for the disinherited even in a world of changing literary fashions, but the credo that follows seems to transcend all political orthodoxies.

believe that our system should be revised by economists with an eye for facts, not by prophets with the gift of visions. As a general theory, leaving the ways and means to specialists, I believe that the private ownership of wealth should be curbed; that our natural resources should not be exploited for individual advantage; that every man should be assured of an opportunity to earn a living and a fair return for his labor; that our means of distribution should be readjusted to our increasing needs and the hollow cry of "overproduction" banished from a world in which millions are starving; that the two useless extremes of society, the thriftless rich and the thriftless poor, should be mercifully eliminated by education or eugenics; that human progress cannot be weighed in noise and measured by many inventions; that the greatest discovery of the mind was neither fire nor electricity but the power to share in another's pain; that self-pity, the favorite vice of a generation too "hard-boiled" for compassion, is the softest and most primitive form of sentimentality; that art is older, as well as younger, than propaganda, and less subject, therefore, to the processes of change and decay; that freedom in literature should mean freedom not for the bawdy word alone but for the honest word also, freedom not only to be the "tough guy" in letters, but freedom even to wear, without rebuke, the white flower of a blameless speech; that civilization may include a chicken in the pot for every peasant but it includes something more; that if man were really civilized, any system ever invented might usher in the millennium; that fear of the end is an ignoble delusion; and that, to return to Santayana, writing now of the Homeric Age, "nothing can be meaner than the anxiety to live on, to live on anyhow and in any shape."[9]

Furthermore, I believe that a change is approaching; whether for better or for worse, who would dare prophesy? Chance [change?] is not necessarily progress; evolution does not imply evolving upward. I should like to think that a fairer social order might be attained in an orderly way, through some third party with high principles; but is it probable, I ask myself, that the selfishness and greed

9. Akin to positions taken by Santayana in *Reason in Religion*, Vol. II of *The Life of Reason* (5 vols., 1905). The quotation itself appears in "The Intellectual Temper of the Age," *Winds of Doctrine: Studies in Contemporary Opinion* (1913); he goes on to say that those (the Homeric Age) "were the truly vital and instinctive days of the human spirit."

of political parties can be overthrown by high principles and an appeal to right reason? It would be pleasant to imagine that the American people may experience, within the next hundred years, a great social and moral awakening, and begin ardently but intelligently to make over the world, that the citizens of this Republic may sweep away the cobwebs, old wasps' nests, and dead issues of politics, and reaffirm a noble faith in democracy. It would be pleasant, but is it not also incredible? Incredible, it seems, so long as the mass of human beings everywhere can find an escape from social injustice and cruelty, not in resisting, but rather in the thrill of inflicting, however vicariously, injustice and cruelty upon others. Thus I believe that the approach to a perfect state lies not without but within, and that the one and only way to a civilized order is by and through the civilization of man. "Blessedness," Spinoza has said, "is not the reward of virtue, but virtue itself."[10] And, surely, the greatest menace in an epoch so noticeably deficient in "blessedness," is the menace of material power which has outstripped philosophy, and placed the dangerous machinery of life and death in the grasp of an impatient and irresponsible child, with a child's instinctive worship of savagery and a child's contempt for the sober merits and counsel of adult wisdom.

Economists, believing naturally that economics can make or mar a world, tell us in many books that we are speeding to disaster, and I, for one, am inclined to believe that the prediction is true. Yet I believe also that, before we have reached the last turn on the way to disaster, we shall apply the brakes just in time to avoid the full force of the shock. Or, even if we fall, we are obliged to fall somewhere; and both history and anthropology assure us that we can never fall so low that the discredited will-to-live[11] cannot pick us up, shake us well, and start us off again on our uncertain road between two eternities.

Still other observers insist, with a share of truth also, for truth is many-sided, that the crisis we are enduring is one of character, not of economics at all, and that men will not be saved until they have found a new religion. These prophets forget that men do not find a

10. Proposition XLII in Spinoza, *Ethics*, Part V: "Of the Power of the Intellect; or of Human Freedom." Baruch *or* Benedict Spinoza (1632–77) was a Dutch philosopher.

11. Glasgow's next novel, *Vein of Iron* (1935), would focus on this major impulse, which also figured importantly in *Barren Ground* (1925) and earlier novels.

religion, but a religion finds men. It may or may not be true that the nearest approach to a vital religious impulse is embraced in the Russian experiment.[12] Yet, granting this and much more, can anyone alive today imagine the American mind in a posture of adoration before an idol of government? The more Asiatic Russian temperament may not miss the luxury of a public criticism it has never possessed. To the American, however, the liberty to scoff is an inalienable right, protected by the law and the Constitution; and is it possible to picture the farmers of the South and West and the industrial workers of the North and East uniting in the worship of any powers assembled at Washington? The very force that would prevent our making a religion of any social system is, I think, the same imponderable agent that would defeat a violent revolution—that red hope of the left wing in politics. For the strongest power in our United States is, in my opinion, the relentless pressure of mass, not class, consciousness. The social divisions are too shallow; the classes feel and look too much alike either for reverence or for hostility.

Those zealous converts who are enriching our language with long foreign words will have trouble, I predict, not in persuading the American workingman that he is oppressed, but in convincing him that he is a "proletarian."[13] For it is more agreeable to assign than to accept classification, and the restless proletarian may inquire in his turn, "But what are you?" Since we have lost, happily or unhappily, even the semblance of an aristocracy, there remains only an enormous public composed of self-centered individuals, each living for himself but all thinking in mass-consciousness. The scattered groups that we still call, more from habit than politeness, "the best people" are continually replenished by the upper levels of the order we are learning boldly but not without embarrassment to speak of as "the proletariat." It is this essentially fluid nature of our social divisions that makes a violent class struggle appear to be less a disaster than an absurdity.

12. The Bolshevik movement that came to power in November, 1917, and passed from Lenin's leadership to Stalin's after 1924.

13. Joseph Freeman, Max Eastman, and other writers associated with the *Masses*, the *Liberator*, and the *New Republic* were urging American writers to adopt the Marxist class outlook in treating problems of the Depression.

Let an American workingman of active intelligence change places with an American banker, also of active intelligence, and in a few weeks neither the workingman nor the banker could be sure of the class in which he belonged. The gulf between an unwashed peasant and a perfumed aristocrat may have been too wide for a touch of nature to bridge; but even the most earnest revolutionist would hesitate, one imagines, to display on a pike a head that so nearly resembled his own. Yet, even so, and however mild the reversal, it would seem that, in a time of unrest, of intellectual defeat, of spiritual destitution, it is safer to examine our structure and make the necessary repairs. It would seem, too, wiser to profit by the past than to ignore or deny it; and the most superficial glance back into history will prove that more social disorders have been prevented by common sense with bread than have ever been put down by desperation with bayonets.

At this point we may stop long enough to ponder the changing fashions of intellectual revolt. Twenty-five years ago, when I remarked that it made no difference whether or not a man had stepped out of the gutter if only he had stepped out, I was taken to task by several of the deep young men of the period.[14] For the deep young men of that day were not investigating the gutter. Instead, they were straining their muscles in the effort to write of the American plutocracy or the English aristocracy after the best manner of Henry James or Oscar Wilde.[15] It is amusing, nevertheless, to remember that the word "gutter" offended the sensibilities of an earlier decade quite as severely as the phrase "well bred" shocks our hardened nerves nowadays. Yet it seems not only embarrassing but absurd to be obliged to explain to adult persons one of the first lessons every Southern child is supposed to learn at his mother's knee, or, failing a mother's knee, when he passes through kindergarten, and this is that the term "well bred" does not mean either well

14. Her *The Romance of a Plain Man* (1909), which treats this subject, was reviewed by H. L. Mencken in a piece titled "Novels and Other Books—Chiefly Bad" in the *Smart Set*.

15. American-born James had treated the British aristocracy with respect and cerebral detachment in, for example, *The Portrait of a Lady* (1881). Irish-born Wilde handled them with less respect but greater comic detachment in his plays *Lady Windermere's Fan* (1892) and *The Importance of Being Earnest* (1894–95).

dressed or wealthy. It has, in fact, as little to do with gentility or re-spectability as writing a book has, and all of us know, I assume, how very little that is.

Many ill-bred persons have been the children of royalty; many others have been, no doubt, sons or daughters of bishops. For good breeding may go in rags and often has gone in rags; it may step into the gutter; but it does not belong in the gutter and usually contrives to step out again. The first time I heard the words, I remember, they were used by mother to describe an old colored man who came to clean out our hen-house and do other work befitting his years. "Uncle Will is so well bred," she told me, "I like you to be with him." He was not servile. Only a person who considered Epictetus[16] servile could have charged Uncle Will with servility. What he had learned was the old Greek acceptance of fate, or better still, superiority to adverse fortune; all the qualities that lend needed dignity to human nature and appear on the surface of life as fine breeding—courtesy, restraint, forbearance, consideration for others. This is what Ortega y Gasset means when he speaks of "the nobly disciplined mind," and he adds discreetly, "It is not rare to find today amongst workingmen nobly disciplined minds."[17]

And so, believing in, as well as sympathizing with, the nobly disciplined mind wherever it is stranded in an age that scorns discipline, it follows naturally that I prefer the spirit of fortitude to the sense of futility. It follows, too, I suppose, that I prefer, among other things, civilization to savagery (though, if we must return to the wilderness, I should choose the noble savage of Rousseau[18] as my neighbor rather than the "sophisticated barbarian" or sentimental sadist of Franco-American fiction);[19] that I prefer good manners

16. The teachings of the first-century Greek Stoic philosopher had been a mainstay of Glasgow's world view since 1894 and would figure in her forthcoming novel of the Depression, *Vein of Iron* (1935). Epictetus, like Uncle Will, was born a slave.

17. José Ortega y Gasset (1883–1955), Spanish philosopher and statesman, so writes in "The Coming of the Masses," the opening chapter of *The Revolt of the Masses* (trans. 1932).

18. Swiss-born Jean-Jacques Rousseau (1712–78) conjectured that man in his natural state, free of corrupting institutions, would be a noble savage.

19. One of Glasgow's many jabs at Ernest Hemingway, whom she knew largely through his story collection, *Men Without Women* (1927), and to whose "school of sophisticated barbarians" she referred in a 1933 letter to Irita Van Doren, an editor of

to rudeness, especially toward the weak, the defenseless, and all those who are placed in what we call inferior positions; that I prefer, not new and popular alignments of the persecutors and the persecuted, but a social order in which nobody may be persecuted for his opinions.

Other things also I believe, and these other things are bound up with what I feel to be permanent issues. I believe in the evolution of life on this planet, and though I think that evolution does not imply evolving upward, I do believe that humanity has groped its way out of primeval darkness. I believe, as well, that on this long journey upward from lower forms man has collected a few sublime virtues, or, more accurately perhaps, a few ideas of sublime virtues, which he has called truth, justice, courage, loyalty, compassion.[20] These ideas, and these ideas alone, seem to me to justify that bloodstained pilgrimage from the first cannibal feast, past the auto-da-fé of too much believing, to the moral and industrial crisis of the twentieth century.

Because the church has evaded these issues and imprisoned its faith in arbitrary doctrines, I think it has failed to satisfy the intellectual and spiritual needs of the modern world, in which primitive consecrations and barbaric symbols have lost, for many of us, their earlier significance. Yet I think, too, that the mass of men will not be content to live entirely without religion or philosophy as a guide.

And, finally, beyond this, I can see only the vanishing-point in the perspective, where all beliefs disappear and the deepest certainties, if they exist, cannot be comprehended by the inquiring mind alone, but must be apprehended by that inmost reason which we may call the heart.[21]

New York *Herald-Tribune Books*. Here Glasgow is restating the primacy, in her world view, of concern for others.

20. Glasgow dramatizes such values in a number of characters, including Marmaduke Littlepage (1929), General Archbald (1932), John Fincastle (1935), and Asa Timberlake (1941 and 1966).

21. Glasgow is doubtless echoing Blaise Pascal's famous comment that the heart has its reasons that reason does not know. In her autobiography, Glasgow reports that during her late twenties she had sought an absolute "known of the reason as well" that would allow her to "live with certitude and with serenity, with reason in the ascendant, but still in sympathy with all animate nature."

I Believe

Few of us, I imagine, would regard our unimportant theories of life and death as a philosophy; and concerning my own private opinions I cherish no such delusion. Nevertheless, even those of us who think in symbols as concrete as facts, and scarcely more flexible, continue to be governed by rules of custom and doctrine which embody in essence the highly concentrated philosophy of the ages. Whenever and wherever we may speculate upon the mysteries of nature or upon the mortality of man, we are, in our humble degree, invoking some august metaphysical system. Although it is true that speculation represents only a single branch of philosophy, still it contains within itself the whole substance of root and flower. So long as one lives at all, one must, of necessity, hold by some fixed principle, if it is merely the common assumption that it is safer to be good than bad, or that the sun will rise again after it has gone down, or that, in any event, there is always tomorrow. But even these few certainties must have arisen in response to some elementary conjectures.

As a very small child, I was a believing animal. I believed in fairies; I believed in witches; I believed in white and gray and black magic; I believed in Santa Claus and in Original Sin; I believed in souls—not only in the souls of men and women and children and animals, but in the souls, too, of trees and plants, and of winds and clouds. I believed that, by some miraculous performance, all this countless multitude of souls would be taken care of, through a Sabbath day without ending, in an infinite Heaven. But in one thing, I cannot recall that I ever believed; and that was in the kind of God who had once savored the smoke of burnt offerings, and to whose ghost, in churches everywhere, good people were still chanting hymns of immelodious praise. From the paternal stock, I had inherited the single-minded Scottish creed of generations. On the distaff side, I derived my free and easy faith from the gentler piety of the Episcopal Church. Yet I have no recollection that I ever truly believed either in the God of the Shorter Catechism or in the God of

This essay appeared in *I Believe: The Personal Philosophies of Certain Eminent Men and Women of Our Time*, ed. Clifton Fadiman (New York, 1938).

the Thirty-nine Articles.[1] I could not trust an Everlasting Mercy, whether stern or mild, which was omnipotent, but permitted pain to exist, and the Prince of Darkness to roam the earth in search of whom he might devour.[2]

Had my parents been alike in mental and physical characteristics it is possible that I should have continued a united family tradition. The longer I observe experience, the greater emphasis I place upon determinism both in our beliefs and in our bodies.[3] Regarding the freedom of the will, and regarding that doctrine alone, I suppose I may call myself more or less of a pragmatist. Indefensible in theory, no doubt, that exalted error—if it be an error—appears necessary to the order of civilized man, and seems to justify, on higher grounds, its long record of service as a moral utility.[4] But certainly every consequence, whether material or immaterial, must follow a cause; and so, it then seemed to me that I had inherited not only my inquiring mind and sensitive nerves, but, less directly perhaps, some tragic conflict of types. My father, a man of sterling integrity and unshakable fortitude, accepted literally the most barbaric texts in the Scriptures, and was equally sound on doctrine, from the fall of Adam to infant damnation. My mother, magnanimous to a fault, would have divided her last hope of Heaven with any spiritual beggar. Defying modern theories of heredity, I was always, in sympathy at least, a mother's child, endowed, I liked to imagine, with some generous prenatal influence.[5] When I think of her, after forty years of absence, I see her eternally poised in an attitude of giving or blessing,

1. The Catechism consists of an introduction and 107 questions and answers used by English-speaking Presbyterians and others to instruct children in the doctrines and duties of Christians; written during the English Civil War, it was approved by Parliament in 1647 but suspended with the restoration of the monarchy in 1660. The Thirty-Nine Articles, enacted by Parliament in 1571, clarified the Anglican church's position on the significance of communion, justification by faith, and other controversies of the Reformation.

2. As in her "What I Believe" essay, Glasgow here establishes the primacy of ethical considerations in abstract speculations.

3. Although her larger subject here is religion, the immediate context indicates she has scientific determinism (genetic and environmental factors) in mind, rather than Providential determinism.

4. That is, belief in freedom of the will. Her argument here echoes that of William James in *Pragmatism* (1907). In *Barren Ground*, Dorinda Oakley strives, like many Glasgow heroines, toward such freedom.

5. In contrast, her autobiography claimed she inherited nothing from her father "except the color of my eyes and a share in a trust fund." Her mother's character in part inspired the portrait of Virginia Pendleton (1913).

as if time, or the past, or merely an illusion of memory, had crystallized around her lovely and beneficent image.

It is because of her that, in looking back, I seem never to have
been too young to side with the helpless. And it is still because of
her that I have fought against cruelty and intolerance as my arch-
antagonists. For I was barely more than a child—or so it seems to
me now—when I found myself first confronting the knowledge of
good and evil in the things my elders believed. By this time, I had
seen not only the joys and sorrows of human life, but the joys and
sorrows of that vast and imperfectly understood animal world; and,
for me, the fate of animals in a hostile universe had demolished all
the airy towers of theological dogma. I worried, too, at that early
age, for I was a child who dreamed dreams and saw visions, over
the unhappy end of the heathen. Suppose, I would ask myself when
I awoke in the night, that, after all, damnation should turn out to be
true at the Last Judgment? So many things were true that I could not
believe in! I was only ten, I remember, when I told myself, with a
kind of cheerful desperation, "If I am damned, I am damned, and
there is nothing to be done about it." Whatever happened to the
larger unredeemed part of creation, I would stand, with my mother,
on the side of the heathen, and on the side too, of our lesser breth-
ren, the animals; for none of these disinherited tribes, I was assured,
could expect so much as a crust or crumb of divine grace in the exclusive plan of salvation.[6] Then gradually, as I grew up, these questions dissolved and evaporated, and at last ceased to disturb me.
While I groped my way toward an unattainable meaning in life, I
found that orthodox Christianity, in company with orthodox Judaism, retreated to a position among yet older mythologies, beside
other impressive but inadequate symbols of man's communion
with that Unknown Power he has called God. As time flows on, and
creeds soften, the immaterial, if not the material, rights of the
heathen are coming slowly to be recognized; and as time moves still
nearer its end and softened creeds disappear, our elastic sense of
justice may extend even into the animal kingdom.[7]

6. In "To My Dog," one of her poems collected in 1902, she seems to reject
heaven because her pet would be excluded.
7. A position consistent with her long-standing, basically Darwinian notion that
true morality arises from extending the sense of kinship, the so-called social instincts, to include groups beyond the immediate family, tribe, nation, and species

But if I could not worship my father's God, I could, and did with all my mind and heart, adore my mother's goodness of soul. This faith I have never lost, since it is rooted, not in the mind alone, but in the deepest sources of personality. As the image of a revealed Deity faded beyond the vanishing point in the perspective, my vague religious instinct leaned toward a distant trust in some spirit, or divine essence, which many poets and a few philosophers have called the Good. Although the Good was only a part of the whole (was there not proof of this all around us?), it was nevertheless the most pure and the highest part.[8] In a universe such as ours, the existence of an all-powerful Providence, concerned with the intimate hopes and the special fate of mankind alone, was, for me at least, then and always incredible. Yet was it not even more unreasonable to assume that there existed no consciousness superior to ours in an infinity of universes? To this question, I could find no answer; but I knew, or thought I knew, that wherever we looked in nature or in civilization, we could not fail to perceive the signs, explicit or implicit, of an actual presence we had named goodness. We might observe also, if we persevered with an open mind, that during our life on this planet, the Good, though always struggling and refusing to surrender, was seldom wholly triumphant outside the pictorial fantasies of the saints.

Like Mr. Santayana, whose work I came to know only in later years, I had been repelled in youth by that "moral equivocation" which seemed to pervade the best-thought-of philosophers. This was "the survival of a sort of forced optimism and pulpit unction, by which a cruel and nasty world, painted by them in the most lurid colors, was nevertheless set up as the model and standard of what ought to be. The duty of an honest moralist would have been rather to distinguish, in this bad or mixed reality, the part, however small, that could be loved and chosen from the remainder, however large, which was to be rejected and renounced. Certainly the universe was in flux and dynamically single; but this fatal flux could very well take care of itself; and it was not so fluid that no islands of a relative permanence and beauty might not be formed in it."[9]

8. Perhaps an echo of Plato's position in *The Republic*
9. George Santayana, Spanish-born American poet and philosopher, author of *Winds of Doctrine: Studies in Contemporary Opinion* (1913). Such moral discrimi-

In this pronouncement I might have found comfort had I stumbled upon it at the exact right moment in youth. Unlike Mr. Santayana, however, since I am no philosopher, I was repelled also by his early idol, Spinoza, whose system appeared to my youthful mind as a pure anatomy of the intellect.[10] Compared with Schopenhauer, indeed, who seemed to me essentially human, I felt that Spinoza's philosophy needed a covering of flesh and blood over its bare structure.[11] Yet, even then, I was beginning slowly to understand that a man's religion or philosophy is as natural an expression of his identity as the color of his eyes or the tones of his voice. When he has not accepted an inherited and traditional way of living and thinking, he obeys the special compulsion of his education and of his environment.

But to return. Was this Good, I then asked myself, a spirit or an immanence, indwelling and all-pervading, though not all-powerful? Or was it merely one of those inevitable results of biological expediency which have accompanied the slow processes of evolution? Certainly I could not believe that goodness was rewarded either in the present world or in some problematical Heaven. In a state of nature, goodness had too often gone down before the cannibal necessities; nor had it appeared constantly victorious among the utilitarian morals of civilization. Yet, in spite of these weaknesses—for I was compelled to recognize the limitations of the Good, just as I recognized the more obvious limitations of the True—I continued to revere this power as the one and only principle deserving of worship. Not, I thought, because the Good is omnipotent, but because, though lacking in omnipotence, it has endured and survived in the struggle with evil, whether or not that evil is inseparable from the nature of life on the earth.

So far I have dealt only with my early search for a faith—or at

nations are a recurring concern of Oliver Alden in *The Last Puritan* (1935). But the passage appears in "Brief History of My Opinions," an essay Santayana contributed to *Contemporary American Philosophy: Personal Statements*, ed. George P. Adams and William Pepperell Montague (2 vols.; London, 1920), II, 246–47; Santayana is referring to Josiah Royce, Hegel, Browning, and Nietzsche.

10. Spinoza, a Dutch philosopher born of a Portuguese Jewish family, used mathematical demonstration to arrive at God and perfect goodness; his pantheism leads to mystical surrender to the "intellectual love of God." Glasgow explored a Spinoza-like position in her 1906 novel, the autobiographical *The Wheel of Life*.

11. Arthur Schopenhauer, German philosopher, noted for his pessimism and for his concept of the Will, the life-force that makes the struggle for existence, as described in *World as Will and Idea* (1819)

least for a stable conviction. In this youthful pursuit feeling was naturally more active than reason; for religion is, after all, an affair of the heart, and we have not forgotten that "the heart has its reasons which reason does not comprehend."[12] We worship a personal God, not a First Principle. We worship him the more passionately because we know nothing about him, not even that we know nothing. We have created our idea of him in our own image, and he embodies the wish fulfillment of an ego we believe immortal.[13] Twenty-five centuries ago Xenophanes[14] first remarked: "Men have always made their gods in their own images—the Greeks like the Greeks, the Ethiopians like the Ethiopians." And so it has continued down to our distracted epoch. The god of astronomers is an astronomer, the god of mathematicians is a mathematician, the god of geologists is a geologist, the god of poets is a poet, the god of dictators is a dictator, the god of democrats is a democrat, and, incredible as it may appear, the god of politicians is, no doubt, a politician. This practice has never varied, notwithstanding the commandment, "God is a spirit; and they that worship him must worship him in spirit and in truth."[15]

Thus it was in the beginning that my heart more than my mind was left unsatisfied by theological dogma. Years afterwards, when I began a comparative study of religious beliefs, this yearning was still unappeased; but it was my intelligence now, not my emotions, that demanded a reason. Few religious figures, and fewer religious creeds, appealed to my individual blend of inherited and acquired characteristics. It is true that the ineffable dim figures of the Christ and the Buddha affected me deeply. Still, I could not deny that the last place to search for them, either in spirit or in truth, would be the imposing systems of theology which had borrowed their names and so frequently rejected their natures. My sense no less than my sensibilities revolted from the primitive myth, confirmed in blood-

12. Pascal's contention; see "What I Believe" in this collection
13. In other words, God is a projection of human potential originating in the human imagination.
14. Wandering Greek poet of the sixth century B.C., who noted the evolution of the earth, attacked the polytheism and anthropomorphism of Greek religion, and asserted the singleness and eternal nature of God. His philosophical poem on nature survives in a few fragments.
15. John 4:24, King James Version

guiltiness, of a murdered god, whose body must be partaken of, whether by consubstantiation or transubstantiation. Yet the image of St. Francis of Assisi,[16] who has been called the only Christian since Christ, almost persuaded me in one of "the dark nights of the soul." There was a summer many years ago when I followed the footsteps of the saint over Italy, and that journey moved me as poetry moves me—or the poetry in religion. Here indeed was the way of the heart as well as the way of the cross! Then, as I came down the hill from Assisi, I met one of the wretched "little brothers" of St. Francis, a small skeleton of a horse, staggering under a lash as it dragged several robust Franciscan friars up to the church. And I saw then, as I saw again and again throughout my Italian pilgrimage, that St. Francis was one alone, but the Franciscan friars are a multitude.

It was not long after this that I studied the Sacred Books of the East, and found inspiration, however fleeting, in the *Upanishads*, but more especially in the Buddhist *Sutras*.[17] The figure of the Compassionate One, whose mercy embraced all living things, regardless of race or tribe or species, seemed to fulfill that ancient Hindu invocation, which Schopenhauer considered the noblest of prayers, "May all that have life be delivered from suffering." Moreover, the appeal of Buddha was not to the heart alone. I agree with Mr. H. G. Wells[18] when he says: "The fundamental teaching of Gautama, as it is now being made plain to us by the study of original sources, is clear and simple, and in the closest harmony with modern ideas. It is beyond all dispute the achievement of one of the most penetrating intelligences the world has ever known."

But even more than the religion of Jesus, since Buddhism is many centuries older, the Eightfold Path[19] has been buried beneath the

16. Giovanni Francesco Bernardone (1182–1226), Italian friar, founder of the Franciscan order. Glasgow's autobiography elaborates on the 1908 visit to Assisi.

17. *The Upanishads*, composed in India between 600 and 300 B.C., are speculative treatises that form the basis of later Vedanta philosophy, the doctrine of salvation by knowledge. In general, Vedanta is an orthodox system of Hindu philosophy developing, in a qualified monism, speculations on ultimate reality and the liberation of the soul. The *Sutras* are the discourses of the Buddha, Siddharta Gautama, 563–483? B.C., "the Compassionate One."

18. H. G. Wells so writes in "The Rise and Spread of Buddhism," Chap. 26 of *The Outline of History, Being a Plain History of Life and Mankind* (1919–20).

19. One of the four great truths of Buddhism, the path directs us to destroy the desire that causes the sorrow that is life through right belief, resolve, speech, behavior, occupation, effort, contemplation, and concentration.

parasitic growths of human greed, stupidity, and ignorance. No, my mind could not rest there. My mind could not rest anywhere, since neither of the world's greatest religions held the right message for me. I was young; I was groping my way; and I was impeded by that serious obstacle to contentment, the certainty that one may grasp and hold, not only facts, but even truth itself, if one seeks it very earnestly.

There was a period, following grief and illness, when I turned to the philosophy of mysticism, and endeavored to reach, through intuition alone, that absolute truth which is denied to the intellect. For several years, I read widely in the writings of the mystics, both pagan and Christian; and I drew strength from Krishna in the *Bhagavad-Gita*,[20] from the Alone of Plotinus,[21] from Pascal's God known of the heart.[22] I remember an August afternoon high up in the Alps, when I persuaded myself that I had felt, if only for an infinitesimal point of time, that inward light which shone for Jakob Böhme when he looked through it into "the essences" of the waving grass and herbs on the hillside.[23] For an instant only this light shone; then it passed on with the wind in the grass; and I was never, in all the years that came afterwards, to know it again. The world and the time spirit together bore down on me. In the end, I recalled

20. The *Bhagavad-Gita* constitutes the moral vision of the 400,000-line Hindu epic *Mahabharata*, based on a tenth-century B.C. battle and written in the first century B.C. Krishna, a reincarnation of the god Vishnu, appears as the charioteer and moral instructor of the hero Arjuna. Glasgow's copy of the *Bhagavad-Gita* bears annotations dated 1903.

21. Egyptian-born Roman philosopher, the chief exponent of Neoplatonism, author of the *Enneads*. A man so spiritual that he "seemed ashamed to be in a body," Plotinus developed a concept of the universe as a hierarchy that rose from matter to soul to reason to God, an ultimate abstraction with no form or matter, pure existence. The phenomenal world has no real existence; reality is the spiritual realm encountered through reason.

22. Glasgow's essay "What I Believe" concludes with the same thought from Pascal.

23. Jakob Böhme, German mystic and theosophist (1575–1624), who held that nothing exists or is intelligible except through its opposite. Böhme argued that man exists in two worlds, the outward and the inward, that we have a separate self and a separate language for each of these worlds, and that, in general, we lie in a dungeon, captured by the spirit of the outward world. Matter, for Böhme, is a veil over nature through which at times he detects the half-revealed but overpowering meaning in nature, the inner symbolic essence of things. Glasgow, in her autobiography, speaks in more detail of an experience like, or the same as, that she describes here, and explains that it came at the end of her painful affair with the man she called "Gerald B." (in 1905).

that moment of vision merely as a lost endeavor to escape from physical boundaries.

So it was that I passed, briefly and safely, through a perilous metaphysical stage; and if my search taught me nothing else, at least it left me with a broader tolerance of the unseen and the unknown, and with a knowledge, drawn directly from experience, of the urgent needs of the spirit.[24] In the fresh enthusiasm with which I turned toward the material aspects of nature and the immediate testimony of science, I could still rejoice that I had once inhabited both the visible and the invisible worlds. After all, what I wanted from life was to live, to feel, and to know as completely as the circumscribed scope of my being allowed. It was inevitable, no doubt, that I should move on to another angle of vision; yet I have never lost a consuming interest in the origin of ideas, and in philosophy as an expression of man's relation to the mystery around him. For I believe matter to be only a single aspect or manifestation of that mystery, though I doubt whether we shall ever know, through our perceptions alone, a world far other than the world of matter—or the sensations we assume to be matter.[25] If life has a deeper meaning, it must forever elude us. Neither science nor philosophy can do more than illumine or enkindle the senses through which impressions or what we call knowledge must come. Yet it is of these vague impressions and of this uncertain knowledge that the scholar, as well as the creative artist, must assemble and build up the very substance, the feeling, sight, taste, touch, scents and sounds, of reality.

It is true, nevertheless, that even in my efforts and my failures, in my belief and my skepticism, I had arrived at the basis of what I may call a determining point of view, if not a philosophy. In my endless curiosity about life, I had fallen by a happy accident (how else could this occur in my special environment?) upon a strayed copy of *The Origin of Species*; and this single book had led me back, through biology, to the older philosophic theory of evolu-

---

24. Here Glasgow reinterprets her earlier search for an Absolute as a psychological rather than a metaphysical quest. This shift signals that she had crossed one of the significant boundaries between the nineteenth-century approach to truth in fiction and the modernist approach.
25. In short, from the world of matter we have access only to phenomena upon which to base our knowledge—*not* noumena or things in themselves.

tion.[26] The Darwinian hypothesis did not especially concern me, nor was I greatly interested in the scientific question of its survival.[27] In any case, it was well able, I felt, to take care of itself and fight its own battles. What did interest me, supremely, was the broader synthesis of implications and inferences.[28] On this foundation of probability, if not of certainty, I have found—or so it still seems to me—a permanent resting place; and in the many years that have come and gone, I have seen no reason, by and large, to reject this cornerstone of my creed.

All this, precipitate as it appears in print, was by no means within the nature of a revelation, though it is true that my discovery of the vast province of ideas was not without the startled wonder, and the eager awakening, of a religious conversion.[29] When I came upon them, in the beginning, all philosophies were new, exhilarating, and bathed in a mental climate that was like the freshness of dawn. It was as if my intelligence, eager and undisciplined, had escaped suddenly into some new republic of the mind. The charming social culture in which I had lived and moved regarded all abstract ideas as dangerously contagious; and in our incessant sprightly talk we had confined our topics to light gossip of persons or food or clothes, or occasionally to the blunted malice of anonymous scandal. I had known in my younger years only two persons with whom I had ever discussed books or intellectual ideas.[30] Such subjects were not only avoided, as they are nowadays in many circles both in New

26. An essentially evolutionary philosophy existed as early as the elemental theories of Anaximander and Heraclitus, and influenced Empedocles, Democritus, Epicurus, and, thereby, Lucretius' great poem, *De Rerum Natura* (*On the Nature of Things*). This early materialism was all but eclipsed by the popularity of Platonism.
27. In *The Origin of Species* (1859), Charles Darwin (1809–82) sought to explain the transformations of species through "natural selection," a process that comes about because variations among individuals of a species may be passed to offspring through heredity and because offspring with beneficial traits seem to be favored in the struggle for existence.
28. The application of Darwin's new biology to social, ethical, and psychological problems by theorists like Darwin himself, Herbert Spencer, William G. Sumner, Walter Bagehot, John Fiske, August Weismann, Leslie Stephen, G. J. Romanes, Thomas H. Huxley, Peter Kropotkin, William James, John Dewey, and Sigmund Freud
29. Biographical evidence indicates that young Ellen Glasgow used the new science as a counterforce to free her spirit from the restricting and threatening theology of her Presbyterian father.
30. Perhaps her older sister Cary and Cary's eventual husband, George Walter McCormack

York and London, but they were, in some strange fashion, classed as socially untouchable. When I look back upon this Southern ostracism of the abstract, it appears amusing. Yet only a year or two ago I was warned by a literary Frenchman that I must never speak of books if I wished to find a welcome in "the best circles" of London. My problem was simplified, however, because I wanted, above all things, to know the truth of life, and I cared nothing whatever for the best circles anywhere. In my eagerness to test experience, to be many-minded, as well as many-sided, I had often lost my ground and grasped vainly at shadows. Still, in that eagerness there was a vital impulse; there was energy; there was intensity of purpose. Almost every phase of thought, indeed, I seem to have shared, or at least recognized, except the state of vegetable calm which is usually mistaken for resignation.

It is far indeed from Plotinus to Locke or Hume[31] or Darwin; yet I traveled that journey through the ether to what I feel to be the solid ground under my feet. And all the while, though I had never suspected this, I was revolving in a circular course, which would lead me back to the nature of self in the end.[32] While I imagined that I traveled into space, I was, in fact, merely turning round and round within the area of my own consciousness. In seeking alike the known and the unknowable, I was trying to discover the laws of my own being, and to establish my own inner harmony. This, for a novelist of reality, remains, I think, the source of all indispensable knowledge; to order one's internal sphere, until the conflict of outward forms with the substance of personality may deepen the tone without impairing the design and proportion of a world the imagination reflects. If my growth had been slow, and my apprenticeship long, this was partly because life, the enemy of reflection, was con-

31. John Locke (1632–1704), English philosopher who in the *Essay Concerning Human Understanding* (1690) denied the existence of innate ideas and called the newborn mind a *tabula rasa*, a blank slate; and David Hume, Scottish philosopher and historian who in *An Enquiry Concerning the Principles of Morals* challenged the rationalism of the eighteenth century by arguing that the "ultimate end of human actions can never . . . be accounted for by *reason*" but only through such "sentiments and affections" as derive from pain and pleasure.
32. This suggests that, for Glasgow, psychology sets the outward boundary of philosophy and therefore of a novelist's special knowledge. What follows here indicates that even a "realistic" novelist must use the inner world to counterbalance the world of environmental forces; see her discussion of Jakob Böhme (above).

stantly—or so it then seemed to me—thrusting its more vital activities into the necessary mood of reverie or contemplation. There is mystery in the abstract, and mystery never loses its fascination for the inquiring mind, but there are possibilities and fulfillments to be found upon the shifting surface of experience. I had tried both, I told myself, however inaccurately, and I had won, if not wisdom, at least the quick and nimble exercise of intelligence. It is well, no doubt, that an artist should hold by a rational code; but it is even better, I believe, that he should have charted the obscure seas of his own consciousness, and that he should perceive clearly the distance that divides the subject within from the nearer objects, as well as from the far perspective, of the external world.

Side by side with the inquiring faculty, that other half of my mind, the creative faculty, had been perpetually at work spinning an imaginary universe of earth, sun, and moon. Sometimes these two factors of the intelligence would labor together in harmony. At other times, they seemed to break apart, and there would follow long intervals when one or the other of these powers would lie dormant for months or even a year. Because, both by temperament and outlook, I share the artist's prepossession with nuances rather than the scientist's preoccupation with analysis, everything that has ever happened to me, whether in the material or the immaterial sphere, has become in time the property of my imagination, and has passed on into my work as a novelist.

When I turn now and look back over the past, I can discern, however dimly, that, beneath the ambiguous maze of ideas, a protective barrier was forming between my identity as a human being and a scheme of things which would always appear hostile. Even when I was unaware of the impulse or especially when I was unaware of the impulse, this subconscious wall was slowly expanding. Pain I feared, but not truth; and even had I feared truth, something stronger than volition, that deep instinct for reality, would still have sought after it. The dual conscience within me, that union of the Calvinist with the Episcopal, was mortally stricken, but dying slowly.[33] Although it survived merely as a double-edged instinct, still it survived. There were moments when I suffered again from

33. The Calvinist from her father, the Episcopal from her mother; the union is moot, inasmuch as a good deal of her fiction reflects the conflict between the values

the feeling, so familiar in early youth, that a moral being has no right to seek happiness in a world where many fellow mortals are enduring on earth the extreme tortures of hell. Yet as I wandered farther away from the older horizon, I discovered a more steadfast serenity in fortitude than in any dubious faith. I could not put in any doctrine my entire trust. Nor would everlasting identity possess, for me, an allurement. But mortal existence, here, now, in the immediate present, would impose its own obligation.

In late years, while we were engaged in our most recent war to end war,[34] many fine words were scattered lavishly among throngs that demanded phrases with blood. Some of us liked then to speak of "the conscience of mankind," and of "breaking the heart of the world." Well, whatever delusions I may have picked up in that moment of exaltation or hysteria, I mislaid them some twenty years ago among a forgotten generation. Nowadays, in a state of what appears to be recovered sanity, I distrust not only rhetoric, but the heart of the world; and I believe, moreover, that a conscience may have evolved, by and through biological necessity, in some men and women, but not yet in mankind. I believe that the masses of men continue to live not by bread alone, but by bread and circuses; and that no circus can compare in thrills with a national conflict or a world crusade. I do not believe that nations are driven to war as patient beasts to the slaughter. On the contrary, I believe that there survives in the human race a deep destructive instinct;[35] and that this unconscious energy, whenever it is inflamed by hatred, and yet unassuaged by war, will find an outlet in vicarious cruelties, and in those racial and religious animosities which still exist below the surface of a state we have agreed to call peace. Nobody wants war, we hear everywhere. What we do not hear is that many people, the vast majority, in some place and time, will presently be in need of something that war, and war alone, can accomplish. And war, when it

---

based on compassion she shared with her mother and those based on authority she resented in her father.

34. World War I; the essay appeared in 1938.

35. In *Beyond the Pleasure Principle* (1920), reacting to the slaughter of World War I, Freud had argued for the primal nature of the death wish when he asserted that "the goal of all life is death." But Glasgow's naturalistic and Darwinian mentors in the late nineteenth century had often spoken of atavism and of reversions to animal-like violence.

comes at last, will seem again, as always, to be an inevitable choice between a greater and a lesser evil. But under the semblance of right or justice or liberty, psychologists assure us that the old Adam of our primary function will still discharge its repressed sadistic tendency in its natural outbreak of violence.[36] Having lived through one world war, I can remember that the worst of such hostilities was not the thought of death in battle; it was not even the thought of the young and the best who were sacrificed: but it was the pleasurable excitement with which so many men, and more especially so many women, responded to the shock and the hatred and even the horror. For I still think, as I thought then: the worst part of war is that so many people enjoy it.[37] In my childhood I was accustomed to hearing decorous Southern pillars of society declare that the happiest years of their lives were the four years in which they marched and fought and starved with the Army of Northern Virginia. Only yesterday, I recalled this when a mild-mannered woman confided to me that, though she hated war and worked in peace to avert it, the most interesting part in her life was the time that she had spent with the Red Cross in France. Certainly no impartial and unsentimental observer could have missed, in the attitude of the noncombatant nations, an involuntary recoil from enthusiasm to disappointment or even disgust, when the recent crisis in Europe postponed, for a breathing space, yet another world war to end war. So it would seem that the only effective way to end war forever would be to make all our ideas of war as unromantic and unheroic as is the average man's daily struggle for his drab-colored existence. Meanwhile, "If war were called mass murder," remarks an eminent psychiatrist, "the term mass murder would soon lose its horror and in time become even a designation of honor."[38] There remains, it is needless to point out, a minority that dissents; but this

36. Freud had demonstrated that the superego and the id could "collude" in acts of seemingly righteous violence. Having lived through the political and religious idealism that fueled World War I, Glasgow fully understood such self-deception.

37. A trait demonstrated by characters in Glasgow's *They Stooped to Folly* (1929), who, in Europe during World War I, are liberated from the moral strictures of America—often through the moral imperatives of service and sacrifice.

38. Quoted loosely from Fritz Wittels, *Freud and His Times* (1931), from the discussion of "destructive energy" by Wittels, at the time a practicing psychoanalyst, but formerly an instructor at the New York Psychoanalytic Institute and the New School for Social Research.

dissenting minority can expect only the painful fate of all civilized minorities wherever we find them. For it is true that the most tragic figure in our modern society is not the semi-barbarian; it is not even the sophisticated barbarian; it is the truly civilized man who has been thrust back upon the level of Neanderthal impulses.[39]

I believe in evolution, though I do not believe that evolution must, of necessity, mean progress.[40] All change is not growth; all movement is not forward. Yet I believe that life on this planet has groped its way up from primeval darkness; and I believe likewise that, in this bloodstained pilgrimage from a lower to a higher form, humanity has collected a few sublime virtues, or ideas of sublime virtue, which are called truth, justice, courage, loyalty, compassion. I believe, therefore, in a moral order; and I believe that this order was not imposed by a supernatural decree, but throughout the ages has been slowly evolving from the mind of man.[41]

I believe in the scientific spirit, but I dislike the scientific manner when it forsakes the ponderable for the imponderable values. Although noble in motive, no doubt, science too often appears Janus-faced in behavior. Confronting us, it wears the bland features of a ministering angel; but turn the mask, and we have the grim countenance of a war goddess preparing weapons of destruction to kill or maim her children. And I dislike, too, the fetish that science has made of natural law, as if all things natural were excellent. It is not that I deny the ordinances of Heaven; but I find it a negligible distinction whether humankind suffers under the reign of natural law or under the rule of universal anarchy. Nevertheless, it is more agreeable, I confess, to regard oneself, not as a biological accident, but either as a thought in the mind of God or as a unit with an appointed harmonious place in the vast rhythm of creation.

39. Compare the way the civilized General Archbald lies to protect his granddaughter, Jenny Blair, and his neighbor, Eva Birdsong, after the equally civilized Eva has shot her husband, George, in a fit of jealous rage (in *The Sheltered Life*, 1932).

40. Here Glasgow is distinguishing her evolutionary position from the passive determinism of Herbert Spencer (1820–1903) and the Social Darwinists. Like William James and Thomas Huxley, Glasgow usually insisted on the necessity of man using his mind, with its unique interests, sentiments, emotions, values, and language, as an essential force in the otherwise biological (and mindless) process of evolution.

41. Here Glasgow stands against Herbert Spencer and with theories of moral evolution put forth by Darwin, Leslie Stephen, Thomas Huxley (1825–95), and Peter Kropotkin (1842–1921).

I believe in social justice, as I believe in peace on earth, good will toward men, as an ideal to be pursued, though scarcely to be attained this side of Paradise. I believe, as I have said elsewhere, that the approach to a fairer order lies, not without, but within; and that the only way to make a civilized world is to begin and end with the civilizing of man. "Blessedness," Spinoza has said in one of my favorite passages, "is not the reward of virtue, but virtue itself."[42] Though I feel an active interest in social philosophies, I am wholly indifferent to the labels we inaccurately assign to social systems. All forms of government, miscall them as we will, have been invented, cherished, debased, and finally demolished by that erratic quantity we know as human nature. And one cannot fail to observe how frequently in the pages of history this same human nature, as Karl Marx might have warned us, "has sown dragons' teeth and reaped —fleas."[43] Yet we must have observed also that men are enslaved by names, and that they will fight for a word more readily than for an idea or a fact. Nowadays, as in the past, they will rally to defend a name among other names; they will battle for the term "democracy" more zealously than they will safeguard those living principles upon which all stable democracies must rest. Freedom is won, not by counting noses, but by keeping alight the inward watch fires of liberty; and true liberty of conscience is as remote from license as it is from moral surrender.

There are honest souls in our midst who warn us, with increasing vehemence, that the Western civilization we have known and admired is already westering toward an abrupt decline.[44] Yet it is only the valiant heart of the pessimist that would dare even to prophesy. For it is at least possible that, whenever the threatened decline and fall of our culture overtake us in fact, those who are alive at the time will not know of the catastrophe, and would not care if they did. It

---

42. The conclusion of "Of Human Freedom," Part V of *The Ethics* (written 1663–73, published 1677); and thus the final proposition (XLII) of Spinoza's chief work

43. Karl Marx (1818–83), German political philosopher and socialist. The context suggests the quotation might apply to Marx as truly as to other philosophers of politics.

44. The word choice suggests Glasgow has in mind followers of the German philosopher Oswald Spengler (1880–1936), author of *The Decline of the West* (1919), perhaps the cyclical school of history associated with Arnold Toynbee.

is more plausible, on the whole, to assume that they will have something they like better to put in its place, and that, following our example, they will continue to miscall this something "civilization."

I believe that there are two equal and enduring satisfactions in life: the association with one's fellow beings in friendship, in love, or in a community of interest, and the faithful pursuit of an art, a profession, or an esthetic enjoyment, not for outward advantage, but in obedience to a permanent and self-renewing inner compulsion. I believe, moreover, in the now discredited faculty of good taste, which means discrimination in all things; and I treasure the pregnant saying of Goethe: "The assassination of Julius Caesar was not in good taste." Even cruelty and intolerance, one imagines, might be banished, with ugliness, from a society which had cultivated good taste in such matters. I prefer, among other things, victory to defeat, fortitude to futility, and consideration to rudeness, especially toward the weak, the defenseless, and all those who are placed in positions we think of as inferior. I believe that there are many evils, but that the only sin is inhumanity; and I believe, too, that benign laughter is the best tonic for life. If life is sad, it is also a laughing matter, and it has its moments of rapture.

I believe that the greatest need of the modern world is not for a multitude of machines, but for a new and a higher conception of God. Yet I believe likewise that any god of the modern temper would necessarily manifest himself as a spiritual sans-culotte; and as such could not ever divide the light from the darkness or bring order into the new chaos. For it would seem that the road to God Eternal is strewn with the earth-gods man has made in His name; and although a purer knowledge of Divinity would be the greatest human achievement, it is true, nevertheless, that the Ages of Faith were the Dark Ages of the Inquisition and the auto-da-fé. Around us nowadays we hear prophetic whispers of a "spiritual awakening," but before we welcome it too earnestly we should examine not only the spirit but the immediate process of the awakening. It is not easy, on the surface, to distinguish between spiritual and emotional vehemence. There is danger in any too sudden conversion of the unthinking mind; and the mob that would die for a belief seldom hesitates to inflict death upon any opposing heretical group. I believe, therefore, that faith has its victories, but that skepticism remains the only permanent basis of tolerance.

These things I believe; and I believe not less firmly in that Good which has been seldom recognized, and never apprehended completely. I believe not in the Good alone, but in the good life which Spinoza has called blessedness. I believe in the challenging mind, in the unreconciled heart, and in the will toward perfection. When, in spite of all the miracles of science and religion, we seem, for the moment, to sink into deeper despair of humanity, we are reminded, it may be, that somewhere a saint has given his life for mankind, or a hero has given his life for strangers, or a lover has given his life for his friends; and then at last we comprehend that the true value of life can be measured only, as it borrows meaning, from the things that are valued above and beyond life.

Index

Index

Green Hat, The (Arlen), 43*n*16
Green Hills of Africa (Hemingway),
 217*n*3
Green Mirror, The (Walpole), 133,
 133*n*9
Greenwood, John, 114, 114*n*36
Gregory, Lady Augusta, 199*n*6
Griswold, Francis, 88, 88*n*20
Gulliver's Travels (Swift), 66*n*13, 159

Haeckel, Ernst Heinrich, 220, 220*n*5,
 221*n*6
Hail and Farewell (Moore), 199*n*6
Hals, Frans, 107, 107*n*14
Hanska, Mme, 148, 148*n*19
Hard-Boiled Virgin, The (Newman),
 80*n*23, 87*n*15, 140*n*13
Hardy, Thomas: women characters in,
 28, 29, 30*n*7; *Jude the Obscure*,
 30*n*7; Glasgow's meeting with,
 40*n*9; Glasgow's comments on, 120,
 120*n*9, 146; as influence on Glas-
 gow, 128*n*19; *Wessex Tales*, 146*n*16
Harlem Renaissance, 87*n*14
Harraden, Beatrice, 15, 15*n*3, 20, 20*n*3
Harris, Joel Chandler, 60*n*7, 73*n*7,
 134*n*15, 178*n*2, 198*n*1
Harrison, Henry Sydnor, 135,
 135–36*n*18
Hart, James D., 134*n*15
Hartley, C. Gasquoine, 32, 32*n*11
Hawkins, Anthony Hope, 134*n*13
Hawthorne, Nathaniel, 83, 120, 120*n*9
He Sent Forth a Raven (Roberts),
 163–64*n*4
Heart of Midlothian, The (Scott),
 154*n*9
Heart's Highway, The (Freeman),
 203*n*4
Heat (Glenn), 80*n*29
Heaven Trees (Young), 88, 88*n*21
Hegel, Georg Wilhelm Friedrich, 232*n*9
Hello Towns! (Anderson), 93*n*4
Hemingway, Ernest: women characters
 in, 44, 44*n*19; *The Sun Also Rises*,
 44*n*19; Glasgow's library and, 99*n*4;
 Death in the Afternoon, 99*n*4,
 217*n*3; *Winner Take Nothing*, 99*n*4,
 217*n*3; *Men Without Women*, 99*n*4,
 152*n*5, 226*n*19; Glasgow's criticism
 of, 183*n*2, 198*n*1, 226*n*19; *A
 Farewell to Arms*, 217*n*3; *Green
 Hills of Africa*, 217*n*3
Henderson, Archibald, 90*n*1

Henry, Patrick, 50, 65
Henry Esmond (Thackeray), 28*n*4
Henry Frederick, Prince of Wales, 109,
 109*n*21
Heraclitus, 191*n*4, 237*n*26
Herbert, Philip, 105*n*5
Hergesheimer, Joseph: comments on
 the *Reviewer*, 86; style of, 86*n*13,
 137; women characters in, 131;
 works of, 131*n*5, 134, 134*n*14;
 Cabell and, 135, 135*n*17
Heroines. *See* Women; names of spe-
 cific authors and titles of novels
Hesselius, Gustavus, 115*n*37
Hesselius, John, 114–15, 115*n*37
Heyward, DuBose, 79, 79*n*18, 87,
 87*n*14, 89, 89*n*23, 90*n*1, 92–93,
 93*n*3
High Place, The (Cabell), 203*n*5,
 214*n*24
Hildreth, Jonathan, 53
Hilliard, Lawrence, 106, 106*n*7
Hilliard, Nicholas, 106, 106*n*7
Hinduism, 234, 234*n*17, 235*n*20
Hitler, Adolf, 96*n*10
Hogarth, C. J., 139*n*7
Holbein, Hans, 106, 106*n*8
Homer, 141*n*2
Homeric Age, 222, 222*n*9
Hoover, Herbert, 61*n*8
Hope, Anthony, 134*n*13
Hoppner, John, 110
House of Lost Identity, The (Corley),
 81*n*34
Howland, Hewitt Hanson, xviii
Hughes, Rupert, 121
Humanism, 207, 207*n*5, 208*n*6
Humble Romance, A (Wilkins), 129*n*22
Hume, David, 170, 170*n*4, 238, 238*n*31
Huxley, Thomas, 237*n*28, 242*n*40,
 242*n*41

Idealism, evasive, 5*n*2, 72, 97, 122–29,
 124*n*6, 126*n*10, 147, 175
Iliad (Homer), 168
I'll Take My Stand, 89*n*21, 208*n*8
Importance of Being Earnest, The
 (Wilde), 225*n*15
In Abraham's Bosom (Green), 79*n*20
In the Land of Cotton (Scarborough),
 81*n*32
In the Tennessee Mountains (Crad-
 dock), 74*n*9
In Their Own Image (Basso), 164*n*4

Index

In This Our Life (Glasgow), xviii, xix, 6n3
Incident and Other Happenings, An (Elliot), 135, 135n16
Innocence Abroad (Clark), 83, 83n1, 90
Interpretations of Poetry and Religion (Santayana), 167n16

James, Henry: Glasgow's meeting with, 40n9; Glasgow's comments on, 146–47, 147n17; *The Ambassadors*, 147n17; *The Golden Bowl*, 147n17; description of novelist, 158n19; moral discernment of, 212–13, 212n19; themes of, 225, 225n15; *The Portrait of a Lady*, 225n15
James, William, 229n4, 237n28, 242n40
James Branch Cabell (Van Doren), 201–204
James I, 108n16, 109n21
Jamestown, 46–48, 46n2, 67n15, 109n19
Jasbo Brown and Selected Poems (Heyward), 93n3
Java Head (Hergesheimer), 134n14
Jefferson, Thomas, 49, 49n5, 53, 65, 70, 70n5
Jefferson Davis (Tate), 93n3
Jennie Gerhardt (Dreiser), 128n20
Jeremy (Walpole), 133, 133n9
Jerry (Elliot), 135n16
Jesus Christ, 234–35
Jewel Merchants, The (Cabell), 134n14
Jewett, Sarah Orne, 129, 129n23
Johnson, Eastman, 110, 110n23
Johnson, Gerald W., 85n5, 88, 88n20, 165, 165n10
Johnston, Mary, 16n6, 74, 74n12
Jones, Howard Mumford, 85, 85n6
Joseph Andrews (Fielding), 69n3
Joseph Hergesheimer (Cabell), 134n14, 135n17
Joyce, James, 141n2, 143–44, 143n7, 150n23, 164, 164n7, 198n1
Jude the Obscure (Hardy), 30n7
Judging of Jurgen, The (Cabell), 134n14
Jung, Carl, 75n15
Jurgen (Cabell): *double entendres* in, 37n3; women characters in, 38n4; dedication of, 79n21; importance of, 87; pornography charge against, 87n17, 198n2; sexuality in, 131n4; response to, 138n1, 205n1; setting of, 138n4, 201n2; Freudian tones in, 198n3; characters in, 205; plot of, 213, 213nn21–22; heaven in, 214n24, 215

Kay, Ellen, 32, 32n11
Kelley, Edith Summers, 79–80, 80n24
Kelly, Eleanor Mercein, 80, 80n31
Kelly, William W., 53
Kennaston, Felix, 209, 209n9
Kenney, Annie, 19n1
Kentucky Cardinal, A (Allen), 74n10, 163n3
Kentucky Warbler, The (Allen), 74n10
Kerseboom, J., 108–109, 109n17
Key, Ellen, 32n11
Kilmer, Joyce, 122
Kipling, Rudyard, 36n1
Kneller, Godfrey, 106, 106n9, 110, 112nn30–31, 113
Knights of the Horseshoe (Caruthers), 69, 69n2
Krishna, 235, 235n20
Kropotkin, Peter, 237n28, 242n41

Lady Chatterley's Lover (Lawrence), 44n17
Lady Windermere's Fan (Wilde), 225n15
Lafayette, Marquis de, 105, 105nn1–2
Lagrenée, Anthelme François, 105
Lamb, Charles, 89, 89n22
Land, The (Sackville-West), 139–40, 140n11
Lardner, Ring, 198n1
Last Puritan, The (Santayana), 156n14, 189–97, 190n2, 191n7, 232n9
Lawrence, D. H.: sexuality in, 43–44, 44n17, 156, 156n17; *Lady Chatterley's Lover*, 44n17; *The Rainbow*, 44n17, 123n3; *Sons and Lovers*, 44n17, 123n3, 144n8; *Women in Love*, 44n17, 144n8; complexity of, 144; autobiographical nature of works, 144n8; *Aaron's Rod*, 144n8, 156n17; *Mornings in Mexico*, 183n2; *The Plumed Serpent*, 183n2; visit to America, 183n2
Lawrence, Thomas, 110–11
Leavis, F. R., 173n8
Lee, Robert E., 49n6, 50, 53, 65, 164, 164n6
Lee, Thomas, 112n29
Lely, Peter, 106, 106n10, 110, 110n24, 112n30, 113